P9-AOC-396

Cryptocurrency Investing

A Wiley Brand

Cryptocurrency
Investing

2nd Edition

by Kiana Danial

Cryptocurrency Investing For Dummies®, 2nd Edition

Published by: **John Wiley & Sons, Inc.**, 111 River Street, Hoboken, NJ 07030-5774, www.wiley.com

Copyright © 2023 by John Wiley & Sons, Inc., Hoboken, New Jersey

Published simultaneously in Canada

No part of this publication may be reproduced, stored in a retrieval system or transmitted in any form or by any means, electronic, mechanical, photocopying, recording, scanning or otherwise, except as permitted under Sections 107 or 108 of the 1976 United States Copyright Act, without the prior written permission of the Publisher. Requests to the Publisher for permission should be addressed to the Permissions Department, John Wiley & Sons, Inc., 111 River Street, Hoboken, NJ 07030, (201) 748-6011, fax (201) 748-6008, or online at http://www.wiley.com/go/permissions.

Trademarks: Wiley, For Dummies, the Dummies Man logo, Dummies.com, Making Everything Easier, and related trade dress are trademarks or registered trademarks of John Wiley & Sons, Inc. and may not be used without written permission. All other trademarks are the property of their respective owners. John Wiley & Sons, Inc. is not associated with any product or vendor mentioned in this book.

LIMIT OF LIABILITY/DISCLAIMER OF WARRANTY: WHILE THE PUBLISHER AND AUTHORS HAVE USED THEIR BEST EFFORTS IN PREPARING THIS WORK, THEY MAKE NO REPRESENTATIONS OR WARRANTIES WITH RESPECT TO THE ACCURACY OR COMPLETENESS OF THE CONTENTS OF THIS WORK AND SPECIFICALLY DISCLAIM ALL WARRANTIES, INCLUDING WITHOUT LIMITATION ANY IMPLIED WARRANTIES OF MERCHANTABILITY OR FITNESS FOR A PARTICULAR PURPOSE. NO WARRANTY MAY BE CREATED OR EXTENDED BY SALES REPRESENTATIVES, WRITTEN SALES MATERIALS OR PROMOTIONAL STATEMENTS FOR THIS WORK. THE FACT THAT AN ORGANIZATION, WEBSITE, OR PRODUCT IS REFERRED TO IN THIS WORK AS A CITATION AND/OR POTENTIAL SOURCE OF FURTHER INFORMATION DOES NOT MEAN THAT THE PUBLISHER AND AUTHORS ENDORSE THE INFORMATION OR SERVICES THE ORGANIZATION, WEBSITE, OR PRODUCT MAY PROVIDE OR RECOMMENDATIONS IT MAY MAKE. THIS WORK IS SOLD WITH THE UNDERSTANDING THAT THE PUBLISHER IS NOT ENGAGED IN RENDERING PROFESSIONAL SERVICES. THE ADVICE AND STRATEGIES CONTAINED HEREIN MAY NOT BE SUITABLE FOR YOUR SITUATION. YOU SHOULD CONSULT WITH A SPECIALIST WHERE APPROPRIATE. FURTHER, READERS SHOULD BE AWARE THAT WEBSITES LISTED IN THIS WORK MAY HAVE CHANGED OR DISAPPEARED BETWEEN WHEN THIS WORK WAS WRITTEN AND WHEN IT IS READ. NEITHER THE PUBLISHER NOR AUTHORS SHALL BE LIABLE FOR ANY LOSS OF PROFIT OR ANY OTHER COMMERCIAL DAMAGES, INCLUDING BUT NOT LIMITED TO SPECIAL, INCIDENTAL, CONSEQUENTIAL, OR OTHER DAMAGES.

For general information on our other products and services, please contact our Customer Care Department within the U.S. at 877-762-2974, outside the U.S. at 317-572-3993, or fax 317-572-4002. For technical support, please visit https://hub.wiley.com/community/support/dummies.

Wiley publishes in a variety of print and electronic formats and by print-on-demand. Some material included with standard print versions of this book may not be included in e-books or in print-on-demand. If this book refers to media such as a CD or DVD that is not included in the version you purchased, you may download this material at http://booksupport.wiley.com. For more information about Wiley products, visit www.wiley.com.

Library of Congress Control Number: 2023931103

ISBN 978-1-119-98912-7 (pbk); ISBN 978-1-119-98913-4 (ebk); ISBN 978-1-119-98914-1 (ebk)

SKY10066413_020524

Contents at a Glance

Table of Contents

Introduction

More than 20,000 cryptocurrencies currently exist at the time of writing this second edition of *Cryptocurrency Investing For Dummies*, ten times more than the number of cryptocurrencies when I first wrote this book in 2018. It's likely that the number will continue growing in the coming years.

Cryptos gained their first round of mainstream hype in 2017, when Bitcoin's value increased by 1,318 percent. This surge was nothing compared to the gains of some other digital assets, such as Ripple, which went up (hold your breath) a whopping 36,018 percent. These returns are more than what a stock investor could normally make in a lifetime, and they generated enough interest to create a true frenzy.

However, the bubble burst at the beginning of 2018, leaving many late investors, who bought cryptocurrencies at a very high price, at a loss. That was enough for some newbie investors to label the whole industry a scam and either give up on investing altogether or go back to traditional financial assets like stocks. Regardless, the cryptocurrency market continued evolving, became more stable, and caught the attention and support of many major financial institutions globally and in the United States. As more people get their hands on cryptocurrencies, more sellers feel comfortable accepting them as a payment method, and that's how the whole industry can flourish.

For instance, after the 2018 crash, Bitcoin, along with other cryptocurrencies, continued their rollercoaster ride: Bitcoin gained another 1,903 percent from 2019 to 2021, and then crashed again to just above its highest price from back in 2017.

Investors who continued holding Bitcoin throughout the years, and continued dollar-cost-averaging without panic-selling, are likely still in a profitable position. But many more sold at a loss, turning against this new category of financial assets altogether and reverted back to their old methods of investment or not investing at all.

The foundation of cryptocurrencies such as Bitcoin lies in a new technology called the *blockchain*; it's the infrastructure that cryptocurrencies are built on. Blockchain is a disruptive technology that many argue is bigger than the advent of the Internet. The applications of blockchain don't end with cryptocurrencies, though, just like the applications of the Internet don't end with email.

The unique thing about cryptocurrency investing and trading is that a crypto is a cross between an asset (like stocks) and a currency (like the U.S. dollar.) Analyzing the fundamentals behind a cryptocurrency is typically very different from analyzing any other financial asset. The traditional ways of measuring value don't work in the crypto industry, mainly because in many cases the crypto data isn't stored in a central hub somewhere. In fact, most cryptocurrencies and their underlying blockchain are *decentralized*, which means no central authority is in charge. Instead, the power is distributed among the members of any given blockchain or crypto community.

About This Book

You may have heard of some of the famous cryptocurrencies, like Bitcoin, but the industry doesn't end there — far from it. And although the crypto market has a ton of volatility, it also has the potential for you to make real money by investing wisely and developing strategies that suit your personal risk tolerance. In this book, I tap into the risks involved in cryptocurrency investing and show you the different methods you can use to get involved.

The topic of cryptocurrencies and their underlying blockchain technology can be a bit confusing. That's why I try my best to keep this book easily accessible and relatable, and free of intimidating terminology. But it does contain some serious information about strategy development, risk management, and the whole industry in general.

As you dip into and out of this book, feel free to skip the sidebars (shaded boxes) and the paragraphs marked with the Technical Stuff icon. They contain interesting information but aren't essential to becoming a crypto investor.

This book contains a lot of web addresses to get you additional information about certain topics. Some of the web addresses are affiliate links, meaning that if you click them and start using a company's services through that specific web address, I may earn an affiliate payment for making the introduction. You also may note that some web addresses break across two lines of text. If you're reading this book in print and want to visit one of these web pages, simply key in the web address exactly as it's noted in the text, pretending as though the line break doesn't exist. If you're reading this work as an e-book, you've got it easy — just click the web address to be taken directly to the web page. Just like magic!

Foolish Assumptions

I've made some assumptions about you and your basic knowledge of investing and the cryptocurrency market:

>> You may have heard of or even own some cryptocurrencies, but you don't really know how they work.

>> Though you may have invested in other markets like the stock market before, you aren't necessarily familiar with the terminology and the technical aspects of trading and investing cryptocurrencies.

>> You know how to operate a computer and use the Internet. If you don't have high-speed access to the Internet now, be sure you have it before trying to get involved in the cryptocurrency market. You need high-speed access to be able to work with many of the valuable online tools I recommend in this book.

Icons Used in This Book

For Dummies books use little pictures, called icons, to mark certain chunks of text. Here's what they mean:

REMEMBER

If something is particularly important for you to take away from this book, I mark it with this icon.

TIP

Watch for these little flags to get ideas on how to improve your crypto investing skills or where to find other useful resources.

WARNING

The cryptocurrency market and investing in general have many risks. Some mistakes can cost you a ton of money, so I use this icon to point out particularly dangerous areas.

TECHNICAL STUFF

This icon designates some interesting facts and sometimes funny anecdotes that I feel you may enjoy reading but that aren't essential to your crypto investing journey.

Beyond the Book

In addition to the material you're reading right now, this product also comes with some access-anywhere goodies on the web. When you just want a quick reminder of basics like what you need before you invest and how to check crypto fundamentals, check out the free Cheat Sheet at www.dummies.com; just search for "Cryptocurrency Investing For Dummies Cheat Sheet."

Where to Go from Here

What you're holding in your hands isn't your typical book, where you start from the beginning and read through the end. Depending on your interest, knowledge on the matter, and investment goals, you can start anywhere you want. For example,

>> If you're already familiar with cryptocurrency basics and know how they work, where to buy them, and where to securely store them, you may want to start with Part 4 to explore different investment and trading tactics.

>> Chapter 24 gives you an overview of things to consider before you start your cryptocurrency journey and cross-references to other chapters if you need further information.

>> Chapter 3 is a great (and essential) place to explore methods of risk management before pulling the trigger and jumping on the crypto wagon.

>> If you're looking for alternative ways to get involved in the cryptocurrency market, check out Chapter 13 for crypto mining, Chapter 12 for initial coin offerings (ICOs), and Chapter 16 for crypto futures and options.

1
Getting Started with Cryptocurrency Investing

Know what you're getting into before buying, investing, or trading cryptocurrencies.

Understand the risks involved in the cryptocurrency market and how to manage them.

Discover how the underlying technology behind cryptocurrencies (the blockchain) makes them unique and revolutionary.

Familiarize yourself with how different types of cryptocurrencies operate.

IN THIS CHAPTER

» Looking at the what, why, and how of the advent of cryptocurrencies

» Getting an overview of your first steps before starting your crypto journey

Chapter 1

What Is a Cryptocurrency?

So you've picked up this book, and your first question is probably this: "What the heck is a cryptocurrency, anyway?" Simply stated, a *cryptocurrency* is a new form of digital money. You can transfer your traditional, non-cryptocurrency money like the U.S. dollar digitally, but that's not quite the same as how cryptocurrencies work. When some cryptocurrencies become mainstream, you may be able to use them to pay for stuff electronically, just like you do with traditional currencies.

However, what sets cryptocurrencies apart is the technology behind them. You may say, "Who cares about the technology behind my money? I only care about how much of it there is in my wallet!" The issue is that the world's current money systems have a bunch of problems. Here are some examples:

» Payment systems such as credit cards and wire transfers are outdated.

» In most cases, a bunch of intermediaries, such as banks and brokers, take a cut in the process, making transactions expensive and slow.

» Financial inequality is growing around the globe.

» The threat of confiscation of your assets.

» Around 3 billion unbanked or underbanked people can't access financial services. That's a big chunk of the planet's population!

Cryptocurrencies aim to solve some of these problems, if not more. This chapter introduces you to crypto fundamentals.

Beginning with the Basics of Cryptocurrencies

You know how your everyday, government-based currency is reserved in banks? And that you need an ATM or a connection to a bank to get more of it or transfer it to other people? Well, with cryptocurrencies, you may be able to get rid of banks and other centralized intermediaries altogether. That's because cryptocurrencies rely on a technology called *blockchain*, which is *decentralized* (meaning no single entity is in charge of it). Instead, every computer in the network confirms the transactions. Flip to Chapter 4 to find out more about the blockchain technology that enables cool things like cryptocurrencies.

In the following sections, I go over the basics of cryptocurrencies: their background, benefits, and more.

The definition of money

Before getting into the nitty-gritty of cryptocurrencies, you need to understand the definition of money itself. The philosophy behind money is a bit like the whole "which came first: the chicken or the egg?" thing. In order for money to be valuable, it must have a number of characteristics, such as the following:

>> Enough people must have it.

>> Merchants must accept it as a form of payment.

>> Society must trust that it's valuable and that it will remain valuable in the future.

Of course, in the old days, when you traded your chicken for shoes, the values of the exchanged materials were inherent to their nature. But when coins, cash, and credit cards came into play, the definition of money and, more importantly, the trust model of money changed.

Another key change in money has been its ease of transaction. The hassle of carrying a ton of gold bars from one country to another was one of the main reasons cash was invented. Then, when people got even lazier, credit cards were invented. But credit cards carry the money that your government controls. As the world becomes more interconnected and more concerned about authorities who may or may not have people's best interests in mind, cryptocurrencies may offer a valuable alternative.

Here's a fun fact: Your normal, government-backed currency, such as the U.S. dollar, must go by its fancy name, *fiat currency*, now that cryptocurrencies are around. Fiat is described as a legal tender like coins and banknotes that have value only because the government says so. Get the scoop on fiat currencies in Chapter 17.

Some cryptocurrency history

The first-ever cryptocurrency was (drumroll please) Bitcoin! You probably have heard of Bitcoin more than any other thing in the crypto industry. Bitcoin was the first product of the first blockchain developed by some anonymous entity who went by the name Satoshi Nakamoto. Satoshi released the idea of Bitcoin in 2008 and described it as a "purely peer-to-peer version" of electronic money.

TECHNICAL STUFF

Bitcoin was the first established cryptocurrency, but many attempts at creating digital currencies occurred years before Bitcoin was formally introduced.

Cryptocurrencies like Bitcoin are created through a process called *mining*. Very different than mining gold, mining cryptocurrencies involves powerful computers solving complicated problems. Flip to Chapter 13 for more on mining.

Bitcoin remained the only cryptocurrency until 2011. Then Bitcoin enthusiasts started noticing flaws in it, so they decided to create alternative coins, also known as *altcoins,* to improve Bitcoin's design for things like speed, security, anonymity, and more. Among the first altcoins was Litecoin, which aimed to become the silver to Bitcoin's gold. But as of the time of writing, over 20,000 cryptocurrencies are available, and the number is expected to increase in the future. That includes active, valuable, and non-active cryptocurrencies. Non-active cryptocurrencies are also reffered to as *dead cryptocurrencies,* which means they don't have any investors or people using them anymore. Check out Chapter 8 for just a sampling of cryptocurrencies available now.

Key crypto benefits

Still not convinced that cryptocurrencies (or any other sort of decentralized money) are a better solution than traditional government-based money? Here are a number of solutions that cryptocurrencies may be able to provide through their decentralized nature:

>> **Reducing corruption:** With great power comes great responsibility. But when you give a ton of power to only one person or entity, the chances of their

abusing that power increase. The 19th-century British politician Lord Acton said it best: "Power tends to corrupt, and absolute power corrupts absolutely." Cryptocurrencies aim to resolve the issue of absolute power by distributing power among many people or, better yet, among all the members of the network. During the crypto boom some people have been able to manipulate the market, but once things are truly decentralized corruption could go lower. That's the key idea behind blockchain technology (see Chapter 4) anyway.

>> **Eliminating extreme money printing:** Governments have central banks, and central banks have the ability to simply print money when they're faced with a serious economic problem. This process is also called *quantitative easing*. By printing more money, a government may be able to bail out debt or devalue its currency. However, this approach is like putting a bandage on a broken leg. Not only does it rarely solve the problem, but the negative side effects also can sometimes surpass the original issue.

For example, when a country like the Islamic regime in Iran or Venezuela printed too much money, the value of its currency dropped so much that inflation skyrockets and people couldn't even afford to buy everyday goods and services. Their cash became barely as valuable as rolls of toilet paper. Most cryptocurrencies have a limited, set amount of coins available. When all those coins are in circulation, a central entity or the company behind the blockchain has no easy way to simply create more coins or add on to its supply.

>> **Giving people charge of their own money:** With traditional cash, you're basically giving away all your control to central banks and the government. If you trust your government, that's great, but keep in mind that at any point, your government is able to simply freeze your bank account and deny your access to your funds.

For example, in the United States, if you don't have a legal will and own a business, the government has the right to all your assets if you pass away. Some governments can even simply abolish bank notes the way India did in 2016. With cryptocurrencies, you and only you can access your funds. (Unless someone steals them from you, that is. To find out how to secure your crypto assets, flip to Chapter 7.)

>> **Cutting out intermediaries:** With traditional money, every time you make a transfer, an intermediary such as your bank or a digital payment service takes a cut. With cryptocurrencies, all the network members in the blockchain are that intermediary; their compensation is formulated differently from that of fiat money intermediaries and therefore is minimal in comparison. Flip to Chapter 5 for more on how cryptocurrencies work.

>> **Serving the unbanked:** A vast portion of the world's citizens has no access or limited access to payment systems like banks. Cryptocurrencies aim to resolve this issue by spreading digital commerce around the globe so that anyone

with a mobile phone can start making payments. And yes, more people have access to mobile phones than to banks. In fact, more people have mobile phones than have toilets, but at this point the blockchain technology may not be able to resolve the latter issue! (Flip to Chapter 2 for more on the social good that can come from cryptocurrencies and blockchain technology.)

Common crypto and blockchain myths

During the 2017 Bitcoin hype, a lot of misconceptions about the whole industry started to circulate. These myths may have played a role in the cryptocurrency crash that followed the surge. The important thing to remember is that both the blockchain technology and its byproduct, the cryptocurrency market, are still in their infancy, and things are rapidly changing. Let me get some of the most common misunderstandings out of the way:

» **Cryptocurrencies are good only for criminals.** Some cryptocurrencies boast anonymity as one of their key features. That means your identity isn't revealed when you're making transactions. Other cryptocurrencies are based on a decentralized blockchain, meaning a central government isn't the sole power behind them. These features do make such cryptocurrencies attractive for criminals; however, law-abiding citizens in corrupt countries can also benefit from them. For example, if you don't trust your local bank or country because of corruption and political instability, the best way to store your money may be through the blockchain and cryptocurrency assets.

» **You can make anonymous transactions using all cryptocurrencies.** For some reason, many people equate Bitcoin with anonymity. But Bitcoin, along with many other cryptocurrencies, doesn't incorporate anonymity at all. All transactions made using such cryptocurrencies are made on public blockchain. Some cryptocurrencies, such as Monero, do prioritize privacy, meaning no outsider can find the source, amount, or destination of transactions. However, most other cryptocurrencies, including Bitcoin, don't operate that way.

» **The only application of blockchain is Bitcoin.** This idea couldn't be further from the truth. Bitcoin and other cryptocurrencies are a tiny byproduct of the blockchain revolution. Many believe Satoshi created Bitcoin simply to provide an example of how the blockchain technology can work. As I explore in Chapter 4, almost every industry and business in the world can use the blockchain technology in its specific field.

» **All blockchain activity is private.** Many people falsely believe that the blockchain technology isn't open to the public and is accessible only to its network of common users. Although some companies create their own private blockchains to be used only among employees and business partners, the majority of the blockchains behind famous cryptocurrencies such as Bitcoin are accessible by the public. Literally anyone with a computer can access the transactions in real time. For example, you can view the real-time Bitcoin transactions at www.blockchain.com.

Risks

Just like anything else in life, cryptocurrencies come with their own baggage of risk. Whether you trade cryptos, invest in them, or simply hold on to them for the future, you must assess and understand the risks beforehand. Some of the most talked-about cryptocurrency risks include their volatility and lack of regulation. Volatility got especially out of hand in 2017, when the price of most major cryptocurrencies, including Bitcoin, skyrocketed above 1,000 percent and then came crashing down. This pattern repeated itself in the 2022 market crash. While these crashes provide investing opportunities for those who missed the boat the previous years, they can be painful for those who invested at the peak and have to remain patient for the markets to move back up.

Regulations are another major topic in the industry. The funny thing is that both lack of regulation and exposure to regulations can turn into risk events for cryptocurrency investors. I explore these and other types of risks, as well as methods of managing them, in Chapter 3.

Gearing Up to Make Transactions

Cryptocurrencies are here to make transactions easier and faster. But before you take advantage of these benefits, you must gear up with crypto gadgets, discover where you can get your hands on different cryptocurrencies, and get to know the cryptocurrency community. Some of the essentials include cryptocurrency wallets and exchanges.

Wallets

Some *cryptocurrency wallets*, which hold your purchased cryptos, are similar to digital payment services like Apple Pay and PayPal. But generally, they're different from traditional wallets and come in different formats and levels of security.

REMEMBER

You can't get involved in the cryptocurrency market without a crypto wallet. I recommend that you get the most secure type of wallet, such as hardware or paper wallets, instead of using the convenient online ones. Flip to Chapter 7 to explore how these wallets work and how you can get them.

Exchanges

After you get yourself a crypto wallet (see the preceding section), you're ready to go crypto shopping, and one of the best destinations is a cryptocurrency exchange. These online web services are where you can transfer your traditional money to buy cryptocurrencies, exchange different types of cryptocurrencies, or even store your cryptocurrencies.

WARNING

Storing your cryptocurrencies on an exchange is considered high risk because many such exchanges have been exposed to hacking attacks and scams in the past. When you're done with your transactions, it's recommended to move your new digital assets to your personal, secure wallet. On the flip side, when storing all your crypto in a wallet, you become the only person responsible for them. Meaning you could lose your assets if there's a theft in your house or if your housekeeper mistakenly throws your wallet into the trash along with a pile of papers. This is why some investors spread their cryptocurrency assets among a combination of hard wallets and online wallets provided by exchanges.

Exchanges come in different shapes and forms. Some are like traditional stock exchanges and act as an intermediary — something crypto enthusiasts believe is a slap in the face of the cryptocurrency market, which is trying to remove a centralized intermediaries. Others are decentralized and provide a service where buyers and sellers come together and transact in a peer-to-peer manner, but they come with their own sets of problems, like the risk of locking yourself out. A third type of crypto exchange is called *hybrid,* and it merges the benefits of the other two types to create a better, more secure experience for users. Flip to Chapter 6 to review the pros and cons of all these types of exchanges and get to know other places where you can go cryptocurrency shopping.

Communities

TIP

Getting to know the crypto community can be the next step as you're finding your way in the market. The web has plenty of chat rooms and support groups to give you a sense of the market and what people are talking about. Here are some ways to get involved:

>> **Crypto-specific Telegram groups:** Many cryptocurrencies have their very own channels on the Telegram app. To join them, you first need to download the Telegram messenger app on your smartphone or computer; it's available for iOS and Android.

FINDING ME ONLINE

I often share my investing strategies and the latest updates on my social media. Come and say hello to me on one of the social media platforms below! Always beware of my impersonators. My *only* accounts are:

- Instagram: @investdiva
- Facebook: facebook.com/kianadanial
- TikTok: @KianaDanial
- YouTube: youtube.com/investdiva
- Twitter: @KianaDanial

>> **Crypto chat rooms on Reddit, BitcoinTalk, or Discord:** BitcoinTalk (bitcointalk.org), Discord (discord.com), and Reddit (www.reddit.com) have some of the oldest and hottest crypto chat rooms around. You can view some topics without signing up, but if you want to get involved, you need to log in. (Of course, Reddit and Discord aren't exclusive to cryptos, but you can search for a variety of cryptocurrency topics.)

>> **TradingView chat room:** One of the best trading platforms out there, TradingView (www.tradingview.com) also has a social service where traders and investors of all sorts come together and share their thoughts, questions, and ideas.

WARNING

Be aware that many scammers target these kinds of platforms to advertise and lure members into trouble. Keep your wits about you!

TIP

If you're looking for a fun, done-with-you community to help you with your investments (without having to pay a financial advisor), check out my most popular free Masterclass at investdiva.com/masterclass and claim your 30-day free access to our Premium Investing Group here: investdivapig.com.

Making a Plan Before You Jump In

You may just want to buy some cryptocurrencies and save them for their potential growth in the future. Or you may want to become more of an active investor and buy or sell cryptocurrencies more regularly to maximize profit and revenue. Regardless, you must have a plan and a strategy. Even if your transaction is a one-time thing and you don't want to hear anything about your crypto assets for the next ten years, you still must gain the knowledge necessary to determine things like the following:

» What to buy

» When to buy

» How much to buy

» When to sell

The following sections give you a quick overview of the steps you must take before buying your first cryptocurrency.

If you're not fully ready to buy cryptocurrencies, no worries: You can try some of the alternatives to cryptos that I describe in Part 3, such as NFTs, mining, stocks, and more.

Select your cryptos

Over 20,600 active and non-active cryptocurrencies are out there at the time of writing, and the number is growing. Some of these cryptos may vanish in five years. Others may explode over 1,000 percent and may even replace traditional cash. In Chapter 8, I go through all different types of cryptocurrencies, including the most famous ones right now, such as Ethereum, Ripple, Cardano, Monero, and Chainlink.

As I discuss in Chapter 9, you can select cryptocurrencies based on things like category, popularity, ideology, the management behind the blockchain, and its economic model.

Because the crypto industry is pretty new, it's still very hard to identify the best-performing cryptos for long-term investments. That's why you may benefit from diversifying among various types and categories of cryptocurrencies in order to manage your risk. By diversifying across 15 or more cryptos, you can stack up the odds of having winners in your portfolio. On the flip side, overdiversification can become problematic as well, so you need to take calculated measures. Flip to Chapter 10 for more on diversification.

Analyze, invest, and profit

When you've narrowed down the cryptocurrencies you like, you must then identify the best time to buy them. For example, in 2017 many people started to believe in the idea of Bitcoin and wanted to get involved. Unfortunately, many of those people mismanaged the timing and bought when the price had peaked. Therefore, they not only were able to buy fewer bits of Bitcoin (pun intended), but they also had to sit on their losses and wait for the next price surge.

Now, I'm not saying that by going through Part 4 of this book, you're going to become some sort of new-age Cryptodamus. However, by analyzing the price action and conducting proper risk management, you may be able to stack the odds in your favor and make a ton of profit in the future. Alongside reading this book, you can grab my free risk-management toolkit (investdiva.com/masterclass) and dive into the world of cryptocurrencies in style and with confidence.

MY CRYPTO JOURNEY

I first got introduced to Bitcoin back in 2011, when Bitcoin's price was a mere $11. My friend, M.C., recommended that I add Bitcoin to my portfolio. I said "No way Jose, that's way too risky!"

Do I kick myself for not listening to my friend's advice back in 2011?

Yes and no.

Yes, because I can obviously see how much I would have made if I bought even one Bitcoin at $11 and held it throughout the years. That would be $23,000 at the time of writing.

But I'm also at ease with my decision not to invest when I didn't know anything about Bitcoin. I'm glad I didn't blindly listen to someone (however much I trusted them) without understanding the exact risks involved and knowing whether this investment matched my risk tolerance and moral beliefs. If I had gone in blindly, there's a very high chance I would have made another mistake down the road and potentially ended up at a loss.

Investing with confidence is the foundation of my portfolio management and has now helped me build an over-$5 million investment portfolio for my family.

Unfortunately, back in 2011 there was no *Cryptocurrency Investing For Dummies* book I could read to educate myself about this new form of investment. That's why I now find it to be my responsibility to spread the education and help you understand the ins and outs of the crypto world, so that by the end of this book, you can make an informed, confident decision for yourself.

IN THIS CHAPTER

» Comparing cryptocurrencies
to traditional investments

» Building capital appreciation

» Boosting income potential

» Empowering people with
cryptocurrencies

Chapter **2**

Why Invest in Cryptocurrencies?

Whether you're a seasoned investor who has been exposed only to investment assets other than cryptos or you're just starting to invest (in anything!) for the first time, you're probably wondering why you should consider including cryptocurrencies in your portfolio. You've probably heard about Bitcoin. Heck, you may have even heard of other cryptocurrencies such as Ethereum and Litecoin, or meme coins like Dogecoin. But what's the big deal about all these funny-sounding coins anyway? Is Litecoin just a very light coin that won't take much space in your physical wallet? Is Dogecoin the type of money your pet can pay its bills with? Is a Bitcoin made of bits and pieces of other valuable coins? Why on earth should you invest in bits of coins?

You can read all about the different types of cryptocurrencies, what they're made of, and what their purpose is in Chapter 8. Here, I give you a general overview of the market as a whole. That way, you can decide whether the cryptocurrency industry is the right route for you to grow your wealth.

Cryptocurrency investing may make sense for many investors, for a growing number of reasons — from things as simple as diversification to more exciting stuff like taking control of your own money without relying on central banks, or joining the revolutionary movement toward the future of technology and infrastructure. In this chapter, I show you some exciting features of this (fairly) new investment kid on the block.

TIP

Although you can read this book in any order, I encourage you to read Chapter 3 right after this one. That's where I explain the other side of the coin, which involves the risks surrounding cryptocurrencies.

Diversifying from Traditional Investments

Diversification is the good ol' "don't put all your eggs in one basket" thing. You can apply this advice to literally anything in life. If you're traveling, don't put all your underwear in your checked luggage. Put an emergency pair in your carry-on in case your luggage gets lost. If you're grocery shopping, don't buy only apples. Even though they say "an apple a day keeps the doctor away," you still need the nutrition in other kinds of vegetables and fruit.

You can go about investment diversification in so many ways. You can diversify with different financial assets, like stocks, bonds, commodities, real estate, and so on. You can diversify based on industry, like technology, healthcare, and entertainment. You can allocate your investment by having multiple investment time frames, both short-term and long-term (see Chapters 19 and 20 for details). Adding cryptocurrencies to your investment portfolio is essentially one way of balancing that portfolio. Especially because the cryptocurrency industry is vastly different from traditional ones, this diversification may increase the potential of maximizing your portfolio's growth. One of the main reasons for this higher potential is that the cryptocurrency market may react differently to various geopolitical and financial events.

In the following sections, I explain more by briefly looking into some of the traditional markets and exploring their differences from the cryptocurrency market. (Find out more about diversification in Chapter 10.)

Stocks

The stock market gives you the opportunity to take a bite of the profits a company makes. By buying stocks of that company, you become a part-owner of that firm. The more stocks you buy, the bigger your slice of the cake. And of course, the higher the risk you face if the whole cake is thrown out in the garbage.

The stock market is perhaps one of the most appealing investment assets. Novice investors may pick up a stock or two just because they like the company. For most investors, the charm of stock investing is the possibility that the prices will increase over time and generate significant capital gains. Some stocks even provide you with a periodic income stream through something called *dividends*.

(I explain more about capital gains and dividend income in Chapter 3.) Regardless, for most stocks, the dividends paid within a year are nothing compared to the increase of the stock's value, especially when the economic environment is upbeat.

REMEMBER

This is precisely what stocks and cryptocurrencies have in common: When their respective markets are strong, you can generally expect to benefit from price appreciation.

Make no mistake, though, both markets have their bad days and sometimes even bad years. The stock market has a longer history that can guide investors through navigating the future. For example, even though it may not always seem like it, bad days happen less often than good ones. Figure 2-1 shows that for the 100 years between 1922 and 2022, the Dow, one of the main stock market indexes, ended the year at a lower price only 32 percent of the time (32 years). The other 68 years, it went up.

FIGURE 2-1:
Dow Jones
100-year
historical chart
by year.

© Macrotrends.net

However, stock investing naturally has some disadvantages. For example,

>> **Stocks face different types of risks.** Even the most awesome stocks have risks that you can't easily eliminate, such as the following (see Chapter 3 for details):

- Business and financial risk
- Purchasing power risk
- Market risk
- Global pandemic risk
- Government control and regulations
- Foreign competition
- The general state of the economy

>> **The stock selection process can be a pain in the neck.** You have literally thousands of stocks to choose from. Predicting how the company will perform tomorrow can also be very difficult. After all, the price today only reflects how the market participants feel about the current or future state of the company or that industry.

TIP

By investing in the cryptocurrency market, you may be able to balance out some of the preceding risks. The cryptocurrency selection process is also different from that of stocks, as I explain in Chapter 9.

The final disadvantage of stock investing, however, is similar to that of crypto investing. They both generally produce less current income than some other investments. Several types of investments, such as bonds, or investing in yourself and starting a side hustle, pay more current income and do so with much greater certainty.

TECHNICAL STUFF

Rightly timed, crypto investing can produce an enormous return on investment (ROI). For example, if you bought 1 Bitcoin in 2019 when the first edition of this book came out (and Bitcoin's price was at $3,409) and sold your Bitcoin in November 2021 when Bitcoin reached $68,009 in price, you would have made $64,600. That's a 1,895 percent ROI in just 2 years! However, there is a very small likelihood that anyone could time the market like that. By contrast, the best-performing stock in the same time period, Tesla, had a 2,950 percent ROI. Both assets have since fallen from their highs at the time of writing this book.

Bonds

Bonds are also known as *fixed-income securities*. They're different from cryptocurrencies and stocks in that you loan money to an entity for a period of time, and you receive a fixed amount of interest on a periodic basis. Hence its categorization as "fixed income."

Just like with cryptocurrencies and stocks (see the preceding section), you can also expect capital gains from bonds. But these capital gains work a bit differently. Because the companies issuing bonds promise to repay a fixed amount when the bonds mature, bond prices don't typically rise in correlation with the firm's profits. The bond prices rise and fall as market interest rates change.

Another similarity among bonds, cryptocurrencies, and stocks is that they're all issued by a wide range of companies. Additionally, many governmental bodies issue bonds. So if you're looking to diversify only within the bonds market, you still can choose from a range of relatively safe ones to highly speculative ones.

Compared to cryptocurrencies and stocks, bonds are generally less risky and provide higher current income. But they still are subject to a variety of risks. Some of the risks involved with bonds investing are similar to those of cryptocurrencies and stocks — namely, purchasing power risk, business and financial risk, and liquidity risk. Bonds have an additional type of risk known as the *call risk* or *prepayment risk.* Call risk is the risk that a bond will be *called,* or retired, long before its maturity date. If the bond issuer calls its bonds, you'll have to find another place for your funds.

REMEMBER

The potential for very high returns on bonds is much lower compared to cryptocurrencies and stocks, respectively. But the risk involved with bonds is also comparatively lower. You can find more about cryptocurrency risks in Chapter 3.

Foreign exchange (forex)

Have you ever traveled to another country? Have you noticed the exchange booth in the airport allowing you to exchange your country's currency to your destination country's currency? Did you notice that depending on the rate, you could either lose or gain money when you do the transactions between the two currencies? Congratulations! You have now understood the forex market!

In the early 2000s, many retail investors got introduced to online forex trading. By participating in the forex market, you buy and sell currencies in hopes for a profit. Not cryptocurrencies, but fiat currencies such as the U.S. dollar, the euro, the British pound, the Australian dollar, or any other currency any government issues. A *fiat currency* is a country's legal tender that's issued by the government.

REMEMBER

This market was my first exposure to the online financial market. But after years of practicing forex trading, I have now realized that as a retail investor, the risks involved and the time required to be a successful forex trader is not worth the reward. Since then, I have liquidated all my forex portfolios and focused on other types of investing. Even so, if you're still interested in learning more about forex, you can check out my book, *Invest Diva's Guide to Making Money in Forex* (McGraw-Hill, 2013), and read the rest of this section.

TECHNICAL STUFF

Participating in the forex market as an investor mainly consists of short-to-medium-term trading activity between different currency pairs. You can buy the euro versus the U.S. dollar (the EUR/USD pair), for example. If the euro's value appreciates relative to the U.S. dollar's, you make money. However, if the U.S. dollar's value goes higher than the euro's, you lose money.

Analyzing the forex market needs a very different approach when compared to stock and cryptocurrency analysis. When looking at the forex markets, you need to focus on the issuing country's economic state, its upcoming economic figures such as its *gross domestic product* (GDP, or the value of the goods produced inside the country), unemployment rate, inflation, interest rate, and so on, as well as its political environment.

However, just like the cryptocurrency market, you need to trade forex in pairs. In my online education course, the *Invest Diva's Make Your Money Work For You PowerCourse* (learn more at investdiva.com/masterclass), I compare these pairs to dancing couples — international couples who push each other back and forth. Traders can make money by speculating which direction the couple will move next. You can see this metaphor in Figure 2-2, where the Australian dollar (AUD, or Mr. Aussie) is dancing against the U.S. dollar (USD, or Ms. USA).

© InvestDiva.com

FIGURE 2-2:
Forex metaphor: Australian dollar dancing against U.S. dollar.

You can apply a similar concept to the cryptocurrency market. For example, you can pair up Bitcoin (BTC) and Ethereum (ETH) against each other.

TECHNICAL STUFF

Technically, when you buy Bitcoin (or anything else for that matter, like a house, clothes, or food) using your fiat currency like the U.S. dollar, you're *pairing them* up in your act of exchange. That's why you need to measure their relative value against each other and see if the potential return is worth your investment.

TIP

You can also consider cryptocurrencies as a cross between stocks and forex. Though many investors invest in cryptocurrencies for capital gain purposes, you can also trade different cryptocurrencies against each other, the way you can in the forex market. I explore cross-cryptocurrency trading in Chapter 10.

Precious metals

Time to compare one of the most recent manmade means to buy stuff (cryptocurrencies) to one of the most ancient ones! No, I'm not going back all the way to *bartering*, where people exchanged their goods and services to fulfill their needs. In the following sections, I talk about the stuff with a bling. Before the advent of paper money, precious metals such as gold and silver were long used to make coins and to buy stuff.

REMEMBER

The precious metals comparison is actually the best argument when someone tells you cryptocurrencies are worthless because they don't have any intrinsic value. In fact, this is why most Bitcoin enthusiasts believe Bitcoin is way more valuable than gold.

Getting a little background

Back in the days of bartering, people would exchange stuff that provided real value to their human needs: chickens, clothes, or farming services. Supposedly, people in the ancient civilization of Lydia were among the first to use coins made of gold and silver in exchange for goods and services. Imagine the first shopper who tried to convince the seller to accept a gold coin instead of three chickens that could feed a family for a week. This change was followed by leather money, paper money, credit cards, and now cryptocurrencies.

Some may argue that precious metals like gold also have intrinsic value. They're durable. They conduct both heat and electricity and therefore have some industrial application. I know I used some gold and silver in experiments back in the day when I was studying electrical engineering in Japan. But in reality, most people don't invest in precious metals because they're trying to conduct electricity. They primarily buy them to use as jewelry or as a store of value. Today, market sentiment mainly determines the value of gold and silver. In other words, gold (which is a type of shiny dirt!) only has value because we as a society collectively decided that gold is valuable. If an alien from a planet that's made of gold instead of dirt visits the earth, it's going to be very surprised that we treat gold as a store of value. This is true about any form of transaction. However, the anti-Bitcoiners use the exact same logic to defend their position.

To me, Bitcoin, and many other cryptocurrencies are far more than a transactional currency. I explain more in the following sections.

TECHNICAL STUFF

Silver has more use as an industrial metal than gold does. Silver is used in batteries, electrical appliances, medical products, and other industrial items. However, despite the additional demand, silver is valued lower than gold. For example, at the time of writing, silver is priced at $19 per ounce, while gold is traded above $1,751 per ounce.

Keep in mind that England didn't establish gold as its standard of value until 1816. (*Standard of value* means tying the value of the currency to its value in gold.) In 1913, the United States finally jumped on board through its Federal Reserve system. It backed its notes by gold and aimed to ensure that notes and checks would be honored and could be redeemed for gold.

Even though precious metals don't have an arguable intrinsic value, they have long been a favorite investment tool among market participants. One of the main reasons is their historical association with wealth. Often, when investments such as bonds, real estate, and the stock market go down or the political environment is uncertain, people flock to precious metals. People prefer to own precious metals at these times because they can actually physically touch metals and keep them in their homes right next to their beds. However, this is nothing more than a *feeling* of security rather than real intrinsic value.

Comparing precious metals to cryptocurrencies

Besides the fact that you need to mine in order to get your hands on precious metals and some cryptocurrencies, one key similarity between precious metals and cryptocurrencies is that both categories have unregulated characteristics. Gold has been an unregulated currency at various times and in various places. Unregulated currencies become more valuable when investors don't trust the official currency, and cryptocurrencies just seem to be another example of this trend. (I talk about cryptocurrency mining in Chapter 13.)

REMEMBER

Investing in precious metals comes with a number of risk factors you need to keep in mind. For example, if you're buying physical precious metals as an investment, you must consider their portability risk. Transferring precious metals can be expensive, given their weight, high import taxes, and the need for a high level of security. In contrast, you don't need to make a physical transfer with cryptocurrencies besides the hardware crypto wallets I discuss in Chapter 7. But moving cryptocurrencies is much faster and less expensive, even with a hardware wallet, than transferring precious metals.

On the other hand, cryptocurrency prices have been more volatile in the short time they've been available on the markets than all precious metals combined have.

One factor that gives Bitcoin enthusiasts hope for future gains is supply and demand. There are only ever going to be 21 million Bitcoins available to be mined. This number was decided by the anonymous creator(s) of Bitcoin who go by the name of Satoshi Nakamoto, and means the maximum number of Bitcoins that can be issued (or *mined*) is capped at 21 million. (I explain about mining in Chapter 13.) At the time of writing, 19 million of those Bitcoins have already been mined. This means while the demand for Bitcoin could remain the same or even go higher, the supply of Bitcoin is always going to be a fixed number. Compare that to the U.S. dollar or gold. The Fed can print new $100 bills out of thin air. We have no idea how much gold there really is. In fact, we could get hit by an asteroid made of gold, giving us enough gold to give all the people on the planet five bags full of gold; if that was ever to happen, thanks to supply and demand, the value of gold would go lower. This is also the reason why many investors consider Bitcoin to be a hedge against inflation.

Gaining Capital Appreciation

Capital appreciation refers to the increase in the price or value of cryptocurrencies. And it's one of the reasons many investors (and noninvestors, for that matter) look to jump on the cryptocurrency train. Initial Bitcoin owners sure waited years before they saw any sort of capital appreciation. Personally, I was one of the skeptics of the whole thing. Back in 2012, one of my investor friends in Switzerland told me to buy some Bitcoin. I decided not to invest in Bitcoin because I didn't feel confident in its value . . . a decision that makes sense from a risk management point of view but cost me a ton of profit. I started investing in cryptocurrencies when the price of Bitcoin had surged significantly. However, using my Invest Diva Diamond Analysis (IDDA) research, and thanks to the ups and downs in the cryptocurrency markets, I was able to find more affordable cryptocurrencies that were expected to have similar capital appreciation and to identify bargain prices to Bitcoin and other digital assets that suit my risk tolerance. I explain how the IDDA works in Chapter 9 and in my free 90-minute Masterclass at investdiva.com/masterclass.

In the following sections, I look at the history of capital appreciation for cryptocurrencies and discuss their growth potential — a big reason to consider investing in them.

With great expectations of capital appreciation and huge growth potential come great expectations of capital losses. That's why I strongly recommend reading Chapter 3 before starting your investing activity in the cryptocurrency market.

Knowing it's a wild ride

WARNING

The gains and losses in the cryptocurrency market have been a wild ride. Even as the industry becomes more established, we still witness multiple bubbles and crashes in most cryptocurrencies. Most of the bubbles are created by hype and FOMO (Fear of Missing Out), and most of the crashes have been created out of FUD (Fear, Uncertainty, and Doubt).

This simply indicates that the cryptocurrency market is still largely driven by emotions. While this can be said about any market, the cryptocurrency market, still in its infancy and largely a myth to the general public, is more sensitive to investors' feelings. I know this because I only ever get asked to go on national TV and talk about crypto when either the markets are crashing or when the markets are seeing unrealistic gains. Never do they ever ask me to go on when everything is steady! The media, in that sense, has been playing a big role in adding fuel to the market fire, which impacts the uneducated investors who are simply investing based on what they hear in the news. So congratulations on picking up this book, allowing you to create a strategy that is suitable for you, your risk tolerance, and your level of confidence if you choose to invest in cryptocurrencies.

Playing "coulda woulda shoulda"

Let's play a game of "coulda woulda shoulda": How much would you have had if you invested in crypto early?

In 2013, many people bought Bitcoin as its price approached $1,000 for the first time. As you can see in Figure 2-3, shortly after, its price crashed to around $300, where it stayed for the following two years. The next big wave of growth came in January 2017, when Bitcoin's price broke above the $1,000 level.

FIGURE 2-3: Bitcoin price between 2013 and January 2017.

© tradingview.com

If you had bought one Bitcoin at $300 at the end of 2015, by January 2017 you would've had $700 worth of capital appreciation (when the price hit $1,000). But of course, the gains didn't stop there. As you can see in Figure 2-4, after the break above $1,000, Bitcoin's price managed to go all the way up to close to $20,000 by the end of 2017, when it came crashing down to a range around $6,000.

FIGURE 2-4:
Bitcoin price between 2016 and July 2018.

© tradingview.com

For people who had bought (or mined) Bitcoin when it was valued at around $300 and held on to it throughout the volatility, the crash to $6,000 wasn't that big of a deal. For every Bitcoin they'd bought at $300, they had around $5,700 worth of capital appreciation even if they didn't cash their Bitcoins in when the value reached above $19,000.

People who bought Bitcoin at around $1,000 and cashed it out at $19,000 at its 2017 peak would've made $18,000 for every Bitcoin they owned. Of course, many people who bought Bitcoin at $19,000 felt angry and thought they were scammed by investing in Bitcoin.

But those who had entered the cryptocurrency market from an Invest Diva Diamond Analysis (IDDA) approach knew that patience is a profitable virtue. They held on to their cryptocurrency assets through the 2018 to 2020 crypto winter (outlined in Chapter 3). They then enjoyed the next wave of capital gains that pushed the price of Bitcoin to almost $65,000. But once again, Bitcoin crashed, this time just touching the 2017 "hype" price of around $20,000.

Do you see the pattern? Take a look at Figure 2-5. The Bitcoin price shoots up to a new high after a period of winter or little activity. Then it comes crashing down to the same level as the previous period's high. A variation of this pattern has been playing out over and over again through Bitcoin's short life. This could give investors some insights on when to buy and when to sell to make a profit. The geek name for this is *technical analysis*. More on that in Chapter 18.

FIGURE 2-5: Bitcoin price pattern reaching new highs then crashing towards the same level of a previous high.

© tradingview.com

This means, if you bought Bitcoin at the highest price of the 2017 bubble ($20,000) and didn't do anything for five years (neither buying more at lower prices nor selling at the higher prices), you would be at a "break-even" point. Considering the increased inflation during this time period (which tends to devalue your fiat currency), this could still be considered a win.

REMEMBER

Inflation is the reason you pay a higher price for things like gas and milk than your parents did. During times of high inflation, keeping your fiat currency in the bank means that your one dollar is worth less and less every year. It's essentially like setting your money on fire. We were always told by our parents that it's a good idea to "save." But no one ever became a millionaire by investing in a savings account. That's why I'm so passionate about helping people make their money work for them through investing. Cryptocurrency is one vehicle that can take you to your financial destination and is certainly worth paying attention to.

Knowing that history doesn't always repeat itself

Many market participants compare Bitcoin and other cryptocurrencies' appreciation to the dot-com bubble from the mid-1990s and early 2000s. According to *Fortune* magazine, since its creation in 2009 until March 2018, Bitcoin saw four bear (falling) waves, where prices dropped 45 to 50 percent, typically rebounding an average of 47 percent afterward. During the dot-com bubble, the Nasdaq composite index had five of those waves, averaging 44 percent declines followed by 40 percent rebounds. Trading volume patterns are also eerily similar.

Nasdaq has clearly rallied nicely from its low in 2002. Though history and past performance aren't indicative of future behavior, crypto enthusiasts have reasons to believe that growth potential for cryptocurrencies may be similar to the Nasdaq rebound, if not better.

TECHNICAL STUFF

Most people have no clue what's really going on in the cryptocurrency market, or any market for that matter Ever since online retail trading became popular among the "non-Wall Street" crowd, most people seek their investing advice from news sources, Twitter, or TikTok gurus. Unfortunately, "They said so" is not a real investing strategy! The majority of those interested in the market are taking their cues from market noise, making it way easier for the prices to fall when the big movers downplay for their own benefit.

REMEMBER

"Going against the crowd" is one of the key pillars in my *Invest Diva Diamond Analysis (IDDA)* that I cover in Chapter 9, as well as my free *Make Your Money Work for You Masterclass* (found at investdiva.com/masterclass). When the majority of the market panics about the drops in the value of an asset, it is often the best time to stack up on it. You can say the same about the cryptocurrency market. For the cryptocurrencies with strong blockchain technology, ideology, and future growth potential behind them, once the price bottoms out, there could be a high potential for its value to go up.

Increasing Income Potential

Although gaining capital appreciation is one of the most attractive features of cryptocurrency investing (as I explain earlier in this chapter), you can also take advantage of some cryptocurrencies that pay something similar to dividends in the stock market.

A bit about traditional dividends

By definition, a *dividend* is a sum of money public companies pay their shareholders on a regular basis. U.S. corporations pay billions of dollars' worth of dividends every year. Yet in spite of these numbers, many investors (especially young ones) don't pay much attention to dividends. They prefer capital gains because the rewards can be quicker and can way exceed any amount of dividend payment.

TECHNICAL
STUFF

In the traditional stock market, companies typically pay dividends on a quarterly basis. A firm's board of directors decides how much to pay shareholders in dividends or whether to pay dividends at all. Sometimes, the directors decide to pay dividends because the stock value isn't doing so well. So they select a higher dividend rate to keep investors interested in buying the stocks.

REMEMBER

Investors with lower risk tolerance, and those approaching retirement, may prefer dividend payments to capital gains because dividend payments don't fluctuate as much as the value of stocks do. Furthermore, if the markets crash like they did in 2020, dividends can provide nice protection. The best way to accumulate dividends is to hold onto your assets long-term.

The basics on crypto dividends

During the crypto mania of 2017, many cryptocurrency platforms were quick to realize the importance of regular payments to keep investors happy. But these payments can be a bit different than traditional stock dividends. You can generate regular, passive income in the crypto market in several ways. Here are the two most popular ones:

>> **HODLing:** No, this term is not a typo for "holding," although it has a similar meaning. It was a typo on the word "HOLD" back in 2013 that turned into one of the most popular words in the crypto world. One of the reasons it became so popular could also be that it can be used as an acronym for "Hold On for Dear Life." Buying and holding the tokens of a crypto exchange (explained in Chapter 6) that pays dividends in crypto. It is the closest payment to traditional dividends. Some cryptocurrencies pay out the HODLers, who simply purchase and carry the digital coins in their wallets.

>> **Proof-of-stake (PoS):** Staking and getting passive income from crypto is a lighter version of proof-of-work in cryptocurrency mining, which I explain in Chapter 7. When you *stake* a crypto, it means you put it aside so it can't be used in the blockchain network. If you have a ton of stakes, you have a higher chance of getting paid at a random selection by the network. Annual returns for staking vary between 1 percent and 5 percent, depending on the coin.

REMEMBER

While receiving cash (or digital coins) just for holding onto your assets is pretty cool, sometimes it makes more sense to cash out and reinvest your holdings to get a better return.

WARNING

If the dividend payments sound too good to be true, beware. At the time of writing, this remains a highly irregulated industry. That means often times you don't have any protection if the exchange behind the dividend payments goes bankrupt — and you may lose all your money. This is exactly what happened with a massive collapse popular crypto exchange FTX in 2022. FTX became popular by aggressive marketing strategies and high-yield payments for parking your money with them, much higher than you would earn from parking your money in a traditional bank. Needless to say, this too-good-to-be-true frenzy came crashing down when customers rushed to withdraw their funds just to find out the exchange did not have sufficient assets in reserve to pay back its customers.

Fueling Ideological Empowerment

Just as oil is the lubricant that allows a machine to operate, blockchain technology is the lubricant that enables the cryptocurrency market. *Blockchain* is the underlying technology for cryptocurrencies, not to mention one of those breakthrough developments that have the potential to revolutionize nearly every industry in the world completely. (I cover blockchain further in Chapter 4.)

Blockchain can offer so much more as it's aiming to resolve many economic and financial problems in the world today, from dealing with the flaws of the sharing economy to banking the unbanked and underbanked. Here are some of the kinds of social good that come through cryptocurrencies and the blockchain technology.

The economy of the future

We live in an era where the *sharing economy* is exploding. The sharing economy allows people to rent out their own property for use by others. Internet giants such as Google, TikTok, and Twitter rely on the contributions of users as a means to generate value within their own platforms. If you've ever taken an Uber or Lyft rather than a taxi or rented a room on Airbnb instead of a hotel, you're a part of the sharing economy crowd.

However, the traditional sharing economy has its issues, such as the following:

>> **Requiring high fees for using the platforms.**

>> **Hurting individual users but benefitting the underlying corporation:** In most cases, the value produced by the crowd isn't equally redistributed among all who have contributed to the value production. All the profits are captured by the large intermediaries who operate the platforms.

>> **Playing fast and loose with consumer info:** Some companies have abused their power by getting access to private data without customers knowing.

As the sharing economy expands in the future, its problems will likely become more complicated.

In order to combat these issues, several companies are developing blockchain-based sharing economy platforms. These platforms are much more affordable to use and provide much-needed transparency. They limit, and sometimes completely cut out, the need for a centralized intermediary. This shift allows true peer-to-peer interactions, eliminating the 20-to-30-percent transaction fees that come with centralized platforms. Because all transactions are logged on blockchains, all users can audit the network's operations.

This approach is possible because of the decentralized nature of blockchain technology, which is ultimately a means for individuals to coordinate common activities, interact directly with one another, and govern themselves in a more trustworthy and decentralized manner.

WARNING

Some cryptocurrency transactions aren't entirely free. In many cases, every time there is a transaction on a blockchain, you have to pay the "network fees," which are funds payable to the blockchain network members who are mining your coins/transactions. If you take into consideration the time "wasted" waiting for a transaction to clear (for example, it takes anywhere from one minute to several hours for a Bitcoin transaction to reach consensus), then in reality, you may not save anything in fees by going to some blockchain applications.

Blockchain remains the fuel behind the economy of the future, and cryptocurrencies are a byproduct to pave the way by distributing the global economy.

WHY DOES FREEDOM FROM GOVERNMENT CONTROL MATTER TO ME?

You see, I was born and raised in Iran to a Jewish family five years after the 1979 Iran revolution. Before the revolution, my dad was a very successful CEO of a construction company, working on big government projects. After the revolution, the new regime who called themselves "The Islamic Republic of Iran" took over his company, all of his assets, and froze his bank accounts. They were actually going to kill him, but he somehow lucked out. Regardless, I was born to a family who was still fighting the new government to get at least some of their money back to pay for eggs and milk.

I couldn't help but think if Bitcoin existed in the 1970s and my dad had even a portion of his assets invested in it, I wouldn't have grown up watching my mom crying over our day-to-day expenses.

This is the exact reason why I finally came about to participate in the cryptocurrency market. While I first learned about Bitcoin in 2012 (when it was only $11), its value didn't fully resonate with me. It wasn't until 2016, when I got hired to do market research for a UK-based crypto news company, that I learned this about Bitcoin: No matter what happens to your government and as long as you own your own Bitcoin keys, the government can't touch your Bitcoin.

Potential hedge against inflation

The rise of Bitcoin and other cryptocurrencies as a trillion-dollar asset class in 2017 was spurred without the oversight of a central bank or monetary authority guaranteeing trust or market conduct. Unlike fiat currencies such as the U.S. dollar and the euro, most cryptocurrencies will never be subject to money printing (officially called *quantitative easing*) by central banks. Most cryptocurrencies operate under controlled supply, which means no printing of money. In fact, networks limit the supply of tokens even in cases where the demand is high. For example, Bitcoin's supply will decrease in time and will reach its final number somewhere around the year 2140. All cryptocurrencies control the supply of the tokens by a schedule written in the code. Translation: The money supply of a cryptocurrency in every given moment in the future can roughly be calculated today.

The lack of government control over cryptocurrencies can also help with lower inflation risk. History has shown over and over again that when a particular government applies bad policies, becomes corrupt, or is faced by crisis, the country's individual currency suffers. This fluctuation in the currency value can lead to the printing of more money. Inflation is the reason why your parents paid less than a dollar for a gallon of milk while you have to pay at least three dollars. How awesome would it be if cryptocurrencies can get rid of government-controlled inflation so that your grandchildren don't have to pay more for stuff than you do?

Help for the unbanked and underbanked

One of the most noble problems cryptocurrencies can solve is banking the *unbanked*. According to Cointelegraph, "2 billion people in the world still don't have a bank account. Most of them live in low- and middle-income emerging markets, but even in high-income countries, large numbers of people are unable to use banks to meet their day-to-day financial needs. This means they don't have access to the convenience, security, and interest that banks provide."

Moreover, many people are *underbanked*; they have access to a bank account but don't have adequate access to the financial services that banks can provide. Even in the United States, for example, an estimated 4.5 percent of U.S. households (approximately 5.9 million households) were unbanked in 2021. Without access to savings and credit, these people can't participate in the cycle of economic growth.

TIP

Cryptocurrencies, with the help of blockchain technology, have the potential to help the unbanked and underbanked by letting them create their own financial alternatives efficiently and transparently. All someone needs to start using cryptocurrencies such as Bitcoin and send and receive money is a smartphone or laptop and Internet connection. (Flip to Chapter 6 for an introduction on how to buy cryptocurrencies.)

IN THIS CHAPTER

» **Understanding the concept of return in crypto investing**

» **Getting to know cryptos' risks**

» **Considering cryptocurrency return versus risk**

» **Exploring different types of cryptocurrency risks**

» **Applying your risk tolerance to your investment strategy**

Chapter **3**

Recognizing the Risks of Cryptocurrencies

S o you're excited to jump on the crypto wagon, perhaps because you expect a gigantic *return* (profit) on your investment! That's basically the reward for investing. However, you can't consider return without also looking at risk. *Risk* is the uncertainty surrounding the actual return you generate.

In my investment education course, I spend a lot of time speaking about risk and how everyone should approach it individually. What may represent high risk for me may not be as risky for you due to our unique lifestyles and financial circumstances.

Cryptocurrencies have shown their fair share of volatility, which has made some investors millions of dollars while wiping out some others' initial investment. In this chapter, I look at cryptocurrencies' price volatility from 2017 to 2022. I also define cryptocurrency rewards and risk, describe different types of risk, and give you pointers on managing risk.

Reviewing Cryptocurrency Returns

Different assets generate different types of returns. For example, one source of return is the change in the investment's value. When you invest in the stock market or the real estate market, you may generate an income in the form of dividends, interest, or rent. Investors call these two sources of return *capital gains* (or *capital losses*) and *current income*, respectively.

REMEMBER

Although most people invest in the cryptocurrency market for capital gains, some cryptocurrencies actually offer current income opportunities. You get an introduction to cryptocurrency returns in Chapter 2.

Capital gains (or losses)

The most popular reason for crypto investing is to see gains in the coins' value. Some people associate the coins with precious metals such as gold. Doing so makes sense because, just like gold, a limited amount is available for some cryptocurrencies, and one way to extract many of them is to mine. (Of course, you don't need to gear up with a pickax and headlamp when mining cryptocurrencies; head to Chapter 13 for details on cryptocurrency mining.)

With that, many investors consider cryptocurrencies to be assets even though they're technically currency tokens that can be used in transactions. Most people buy these tokens in hopes of selling them when the prices rise more. If the value of your cryptocurrency token goes higher from the time you purchase, you get capital gains when you sell the token. Congrats! If the prices go lower, and you decide to sell at those lower prices, you end up with capital losses.

Income

Income is a lesser-known and higher-risk type of return in the cryptocurrency market. Income is generated from something called *crypto yields*, which are marketed to work like traditional dividends.

Traditionally, dividends occur when public companies distribute a portion of their earnings to their shareholders. Traditional types of dividends include cash payments, shares of stock, or other property.

Earning dividends in the crypto market can get a bit more complicated and way riskier. Different currencies have different operating systems and their own rules and regulations. However, the concept still remains the same. Crypto dividend payments are becoming increasingly popular among altcoins, which are the alternative cryptocurrencies besides Bitcoin. When choosing a cryptocurrency for your portfolio, you can consider looking into crypto dividends as well as the potential of capital gains (discussed in the preceding section).

Two of the most popular ways to earn crypto dividends are

>> **Staking:** Holding a proof-of-stake coin in a special wallet

>> **Holding:** Buying and holding a crypto in any wallet

I talk more about staking and holding in Chapter 7.

WARNING

At the time of writing, the majority of crypto lending platforms have gone bankrupt. That includes the popular FTX and Celsius exchanges. Their collapse and bankruptcy left many investors shirtless and the stories created a huge wave of uncertainty in the cryptocurrency market. It also gave investors another reason to look deeper into the fundamentals of their investments and avoid investing based on hype and FOMO ("fear of missing out").

Compounding

The ultimate reason to invest in online financial assets is to take advantage of compounding. *Compounding* is the process of reinvesting capital gains, interest, or dividends to generate additional earnings. It's basically the act of making your money have babies!

There are three ways you can multiply your money by compounding:

>> **Buy low, sell high:** Buying an asset at a low, then selling it at a higher price, then going back in with more money to buy at the low prices. As you do this over and over again, your investment portfolio compounds and grows larger. However, the risk associated to this type of compounding is very high, especially if you are buying low and selling high in short periods of time.

>> **Reinvest dividends or interest:** You can manually or automatically reinvest the dividend payments you receive from your cryptocurrency or stocks. This will expose you to more potential future capital gains and dividend payments.

TIP

>> **Regular contributions:** My favorite method of compounding is by increasing my income through side hustles and then investing the increased income in online financial assets such as cryptocurrencies and stocks regularly. It is the lowest risk method of compounding because it eliminates the need for timing the market price.

Risk: Flipping the Other Side of the Coin

Investment returns are exciting, but you can't consider return without also looking at risk. The sad truth about any type of investment is that the greater the expected return, the greater the risk. Because cryptocurrencies are considered riskier than some other assets, they may also provide higher returns. The relationship between risk and return is called the *risk-return tradeoff*.

REMEMBER

Cryptocurrency investing isn't a get-rich-quick scheme. You shouldn't invest in cryptocurrencies by using your life savings or taking out a loan. You must consider your risk tolerance, understand the different sources of cryptocurrency risks, and then develop an investment strategy that's suitable for you — just you, not anyone else — because you're unique, and so is your financial situation.

Also keep in mind that early Bitcoin investors waited years to see any returns. If you don't have the patience required to see meaningful returns on your investment, you may need to forget about investing altogether.

That being said, a healthy amount of risk appetite is essential not only when investing but also in life. Don't get so paranoid about risk that you just never leave the house for fear of getting into an accident!

TIP

The lowest risk, highest return investment is always an investment in yourself to learn a high-income creating skill. Because no matter where you go, no matter the economic conditions, there you are! You can always use your own skills to increase your income. So congratulations on picking up this book and investing in yourself by increasing your knowledge!

Glimpsing Cryptocurrencies' Reward versus Risk

One of the main reasons cryptocurrency investing has become such a hot topic since 2017 is the crazy surge in the value of major cryptocurrencies such as Bitcoin.

Although you may have heard of Bitcoin the most, it wasn't even among the ten best-performing crypto assets back in 2017. Bitcoin's value grew by more than 1,000 percent, but other, lesser-known cryptocurrencies such as Ripple and NEM were among the biggest winners, with a whopping 36,018 percent and 29,842 percent growth, respectively.

Where did Bitcoin stand on the performance list? Fourteenth!

These returns made investors and noninvestors alike super excited about the cryptocurrency market. By the beginning of 2018, almost everyone you knew — your doctor, your rideshare driver, perhaps even your grandmother — was probably talking about Bitcoin, whether or not the person had any experience in any sort of investing. I know my 8-year-old nephew was asking me about it.

However, as is true of any type of investment, what goes up must come down, including the cryptocurrency market. Because the cryptocurrency prices had gone up so much, so quickly, the crash was as hard and as speedy. For example, by January 2019, Bitcoin dropped back to the lows of $3,000 from highs of nearly $20,000.

This became known as *crypto winter*. All the buzz about cryptocurrency and Bitcoin shut down and many people started calling it a scam. It wasn't until July 2020 that cryptocurrency became a hot topic again as its price started to surge. By the end of 2021, Bitcoin's price had risen to over $68,000. Everyone was talking about it again, and people were catching FOMO again. Until (surprise, surprise!) the new bubble also burst, and Bitcoin's price dropped back to $20,000 as you can see in Figure 3-1. The media went quiet on Bitcoin again. But ironically, this new low was the same value as the high of 2018!

FIGURE 3-1: Bitcoin's price action versus the U.S. dollar from 2017 to 2022.

© tradingview.com

In the geeky investing world, we call this a *support level*. A support level is the price that the asset's price has difficulty going lower than in the past. In this case, in the crypto winter of 2018 to 2020, the price had difficulty breaking below $3,000.

At the time of writing in 2022, Bitcoin's price had difficulty going lower than $20,000 and the next support level for it is identified at around $13,000 and $7,000, respectively. Conducting technical analysis (flip to Chapter 18) identifies the key support levels an asset's price could drop to, so you can mitigate your risk of buying at higher prices.

Many analysts considered the great appreciation of major cryptocurrencies' value to be a bubble. This fluctuation is a heck of a roller-coaster ride in such a short period of time! The returns were great for those who invested early and took profit at the highs. But just imagine investing in the market when the prices were up and watching the value of your investment going lower and lower. That's one of the major risk factors in any type of investing and the reason people the majority of crypto investors prefer to hold their crypto assets long term instead of trying to time the market and compound by buying low and selling high.

Digging into Different Kinds of Risk

Getting educated about risk puts you right on top of your game. Knowing your risk tolerance, you can create a strategy that protects you and your wealth. The risks associated with cryptocurrencies come from many different sources. Here are the various types of crypto risks.

Crypto hype risk

While seizing opportunities is a big characteristic of wealthy people, investing based solely on hype and trending Twitter topics may not be a good thing!

The main reason cryptos have a lot of hype is that most people get lazy in educating themselves about truly understanding the underlying value of a cryptocurrency, so they blindly follow the advice of their favorite celebrity. Crypto bubbles between 2017 and 2022 were mainly caused by market hype. After the initial hype came an adjustment in the market price (which is normal) and people panicked and started selling at a loss, resulting in a crash and a crypto winter (see earlier in this chapter for more on this).

Unfortunately, this is the exact opposite of how investors should be investing. The first method of compounding (explained earlier this chapter) is "Buy low and sell high." Not the other way around!

TECHNICAL STUFF

This type of behavior became so popular that crypto geeks created their very own lingo around it. Here are a few terms:

>> **FOMO:** This crypto-geek term stands for "Fear of missing out." This happens when you see a massive surge in a crypto you don't own and you hurry in to get your hands on it as the price goes up. Hint: Don't do it! What goes up must come down, so you may be better off waiting for the hype to calm down and buy at lower prices.

>> **FUD:** This is short for "Fear, uncertainty, and doubt." You can use this in a Reddit post when you hear one of those Doctor Doomsdays talking down the market. JPMorgan Chase's CEO, Jamie Dimon, spread one of the biggest FUDs in September 2017 by calling Bitcoin a fraud. In May 2022, he said Bitcoin's slide has created a "significant upside" for crypto investors.

>> **ATH:** Short for "All-time high." Whenever the price of an asset reaches the highest point in its history, you can say, "It's reached an ATH." This is also known as a *bubble*.

>> **Bag holder:** You don't want this to be your nickname! Bag holders are those investors who bought out of FOMO at an ATH and missed the chance of selling. Therefore, they are left with a bag (wallet) filled with worthless coins.

>> **Diamond Hands:** The positive version of a bag holder! It's an investor who has high confidence in their investment and therefore refrains from selling during the downturns and stays the long course.

>> **BTFD:** This one stands for "Buy the f@#&ing dip!" When you're confident in an asset's long-term potential growth, you've got to BTFD when its price drops lower.

REMEMBER

Before falling for the market noise, arm yourself with knowledge on the specific cryptos you're considering. You have plenty of opportunities to make lots of money in the crypto market. Be patient and acquire the right knowledge instead of betting on the current hype. An investor who trades on the hype probably doesn't even have an investment strategy — unless you call gambling a strategy! You can find different methods of strategy development in Parts 2 and 4.

Security risk

Scams! Hacking! Theft!

WARNING

These issues have been a common theme in the cryptocurrency market since Bitcoin's inception in 2009. And with each scandal, the cryptocurrencies' values are compromised as well, although temporarily. Your cryptocurrency can be compromised in three main ways, which I outline in the following sections. You should definitely follow safety precautions in every step of your cryptocurrency investing strategy.

Safety check #1: Bitcoin investing schemes

If you are on any social media, you might have seen a version of this. Scammers pretend to be an influencer and offer to pay Bitcoin. This, unfortunately, has even happened to many of my followers. Every time I post content on Instagram, Facebook, YouTube, TikTok, or even Twitter, my comment section gets flooded by impersonators pretending to be me by using my photo and a version of my name or my company's name, direct messaging to my followers and offering Bitcoin in exchange for their investment.

TIP

To avoid such scams, before ever handing your money to anyone, do a quick Google search and go to the source. You can often find influencers' social media handles on their website. In my case, all my social media handles have a verified checkmark. When in doubt, always contact the customer service of the business to ensure you're not falling for a scammer. These scammers are often very skilled in making you believe they're actually who you think you're talking with.

WARNING

Crypto investing scams don't end with public social media impersonators. You can even find scammers on dating apps and other social networks where people can contact you directly via Direct Messaging (DM). These scammers typically start building trust through long-distance conversations, and then over time, they convince their victims to buy or give money in some form of cryptocurrency. After getting the money, the dating scammer disappears. These scams are also known as *pig butchering scams*, because the scam system works kind of like fattening a hog before slaughter. The scammers may open up the conversation with a simple "hello" as the first step in a process of taking the friendly chat to an online investment that will result in your money disappearing.

Safety check #2: The cryptocurrency itself

Hundreds of cryptocurrencies are already available for investments, with thousands of new ICOs (initial coin offerings) on the way (see Chapter 12 for more on ICOs). When choosing the cryptocurrency to invest in, you must educate yourself on the blockchain's protocol and make sure it is not a rug pull or a pump and dump scam:

>> A *rug pull scam* is when scammers "pump up" a new cryptocurrency project to get funding. But after they get the money, they disappear with them.

>> A *pump and dump scam* is similar to a rug pull scam, but the difference is the scammers create hype around their cryptocurrency and get people to buy, which drives its price higher. Once the price reaches a considerably high price,

the scammers start selling, reaping profits and leaving the investors with losses in a coin that has otherwise no intrinsic value.

TIP

One way to avoid falling for these scams is to read the cryptocurrency's protocol on its white paper on its website. The white paper is an official document that the crypto founders put together before their ICO, laying out everything there is to know about the cryptocurrency. Make sure you actually understand the cryptocurrency before investing in it. If the protocol or your promised return on investment is too good to be true, or you don't fully understand how it works, then stay far away from it. There's no substitute for confidence when it comes to managing your investment risks.

In Chapter 9 I explain the best ways to analyze crypto assets from a fundamental point of view, so you can progress with confidence.

Safety check #3: The exchange

Exchanges are where you can buy cryptocurrency tokens (see Chapter 6 for an introduction). You need to make sure that your crypto exchange is trustworthy and credible. Countless numbers of security incidents and data breaches have occurred in the crypto community because of the exchanges.

One of the famous initial hacks was that of Japan-based Mt. Gox, the largest Bitcoin exchange, in 2013. At the time, Mt. Gox was handling 70 percent of the world's Bitcoin exchanges. However, it had many issues, such as lack of a testing policy, lack of a version control software, and lack of a proper management. As all these problems piled up, in February 2014 the exchange became the victim of a massive hack, where about 850,000 Bitcoins were lost. Although 200,000 Bitcoins were eventually recovered, the remaining 650,000 have never been recovered.

Many exchanges have learned a lesson from this incident and are keeping up with the latest safety measures. However, exchange hacks still happen almost on a monthly basis.

REMEMBER

Centralized exchanges are the most vulnerable to attacks. Flip to Chapter 6 for methods to spot red flags in cryptocurrency exchanges.

TIP

I'm not trying to scare you with these stories. As time goes by, the market learns from previous mistakes and works on a better and safer future. However, you still need to take matters into your own hands as much as possible. Before choosing an exchange, take a look at its security section on its website. Check whether it participates in any bug bounty programs to encourage safety. These programs are deals offered by many websites, organizations, and software developers. People who find bugs can get recognition and compensation. You should also check if the exchange has insurance and uses SOC-compliant cold storage. *SOC compliance* means that a company has completed a third-party audit to show that it has certain controls in place. Another thing to check is to see whether the exchange uses a MultiSig wallet. A *MultiSig wallet* is a digital wallet that needs more than one private key to sign a crypto transaction. This means that more than one person is needed to sign the transaction for it to happen, which adds to its security. And, of course, ask the right people about the exchange. In Invest Diva's *Make Your Money Work For You PowerCourse*, we keep an eye on the latest developments in the market and keep our members informed about any shady activities (investdiva.com/masterclass).

Safety check #4: Your wallet

The final round of security check is all in your own hands because what kind of crypto wallet you use is entirely up to you. Though you don't physically carry your crypto coins, you can store them in a secure physical wallet. You actually store the public and private keys, which you can use for making transactions with your altcoins, in these wallets as well. You can take your wallet's security to a higher level by using a backup. I explore wallet safety methods more in Chapter 7.

Volatility risk

Volatility risk is essentially the risk in unexpected market movements. Though volatility can be a good thing, it can also catch you off guard sometimes. Just like any other market, the cryptocurrency market can suddenly move in the opposite direction from what you expected. If you aren't prepared for the market volatility, you can lose the money you invested in the market.

The volatility in the cryptocurrency market has resulted from many factors. For one, it's a brand-new technology. The inception of revolutionary technologies — such as the Internet — can create initial periods of volatility. The blockchain technology (see Chapter 4) and its underpinning cryptocurrencies take a lot of getting used to before they become mainstream.

REMEMBER

The best way to combat the cryptocurrency volatility risk is looking at the big picture. Volatility matters a lot if you have a short-term investing horizon (see Chapter 19) because it's an indicator of how much money you may make or lose over a short period. But if you have a long-term horizon (see Chapter 20), volatility can turn into an opportunity.

Liquidity risk

By definition, *liquidity risk* is the risk of not being able to sell (or *liquidate*) an investment quickly at a reasonable price. Liquidity is important for any tradable asset. If you trade currencies with very low volume, you may not even be able to close your trade because the prices just won't move!

Cryptocurrencies can also see episodes of illiquidity. Heck, the liquidity problem was one of the factors that led to the high volatility in Bitcoin and other altcoins described earlier in this chapter. When the liquidity is low, the risk of price manipulation also comes into play. One big player can easily move the market to his or her favor by placing a massive order.

The crypto community refers to these types of big players as *whales.* In the cryptocurrency market, whales often move small altcoins by using their huge capital.

On the bright side, as cryptocurrency investing becomes more available and acceptable, the market may become more liquid. The increase in the number of trusted crypto exchanges will provide opportunity for more people to trade. Crypto ATMs and payment cards are popping up, helping raise the awareness and acceptance of cryptocurrencies in everyday transactions.

Another key factor in cryptocurrency liquidity is the stance of countries on cryptocurrency regulations. If the authorities are able to define issues such as consumer protection and crypto taxes, more people will be comfortable using and trading cryptocurrencies, which will affect their liquidity.

When choosing a cryptocurrency to invest in, you must consider its liquidity by analyzing its acceptance, popularity, and the number of exchanges it's been traded on. Lesser-known cryptocurrencies may have a lot of upside potential, but they may put you in trouble because of lack of liquidity. I explore different types of cryptocurrencies and their characteristics in Part 2.

Vanishing risk

No, I'm not talking about disappearing into the ever-magical blockchain industry! Quite the contrary. Thousands of different cryptocurrencies are currently out there. More and more cryptocurrencies are being introduced every day. In ten years' time, many of these altcoins may vanish while others flourish.

A familiar example of vanishing risk is the dot-com bubble. In the late 1990s, many people around the world dreamed up businesses that capitalized on the popularity of the Internet. Some, such as Amazon and eBay, succeeded in conquering the world. Many more crashed and burned. Following the path of history, many of the booming cryptocurrencies popping up left and right are destined to bust.

REMEMBER

To minimize the vanishing risk, you need to analyze the fundamentals of the cryptocurrencies you choose to invest in. Do their goals make sense to you? Are they solving a problem that will continue in the years to come? Who are their partners? You can't vanish the vanishing risk entirely (pun intended), but you can eliminate your exposure to a sudden bust. Check out Part 2 for more on fundamental analysis.

Regulation risk

One of the initial attractions of cryptocurrencies was their lack of regulation. In the good old days in cryptoland, crypto enthusiasts didn't have to worry about governments chasing them down. All they had was a white paper and a promise. However, as the demand for cryptocurrencies grows, global regulators are scratching their heads on how to keep up — and to not lose their shirts to the new economic reality.

REMEMBER

To date, most digital currencies aren't backed by any central government, meaning each country has different standards.

You can divide the cryptocurrency regulation risk into two components: the regulation event risk and regulation's nature itself.

» The *regulation event risk* doesn't necessarily mean that the cryptocurrency market is doing poorly. It just means the market participants reacted to an unexpected announcement. Between 2018 and 2022, every seemingly small regulation announcement drove the price of many major cryptocurrencies and created a ton of volatility.

» At the time of writing, the U.S. Securities and Exchange Commission (SEC) and the Commodity Futures Trading Commission (CFTC) have enforced dozens of regulatory actions. Some crypto investors are happy about the regulations while others (who are mainly interested in cryptocurrencies for their decentralized nature) aren't. But at large, substantial government regulations have yet to be put in place.

REMEMBER

The future of cryptocurrency regulations seems to be bright at this writing, but it may impact the markets in the future. As the market grows stronger, though, these impacts may turn into isolated events.

Tax risk

When cryptocurrency investing first got popular, hardly anyone was paying taxes on the gains. A lot of underreporting was going on. However, as the market gets more regulated, the authorities may become stricter on taxation.

REMEMBER

As of 2022, the U.S. Internal Revenue Service treats gains on cryptocurrencies the same way it treats any kind of capital gains. That means, just like capital gains from investing in stocks, you'll have to pay ordinary tax rates on any gains realized within a year. But for assets held longer than a year, you'll pay long-term capital gains which is typically lower. In other countries, tax risk can get more complicated. Always be sure to consult with your tax accountant as you build your investment portfolio.

Flip to Chapter 23 for more details on taxes in relation to cryptocurrencies.

Exploring Risk Management Methods

The only way you can achieve your investment goals is to invest at a risk level consistent with your risk tolerance assessment. That's why I talk a lot about methods to calculate your unique risk tolerance in my Invest Diva education courses. You can measure your risk tolerance by considering objective measures like your investment goals, your time horizon for each goal, your need for liquidity, and so on. You can increase your risk tolerance by setting longer-term goals, increasing your income using methods other than online investing, lowering your need for current liquidity, and most importantly, increasing your confidence in the asset you're planning to invest in by educating yourself about it.

These things are certainly easier said than done, especially considering you never know when you're going to get hit financially. The following sections provide guidance on how to manage risk by building an emergency fund, being patient with your investments, and diversifying.

TIP

Download my free risk-management toolkit to calculate your exact risk tolerance: investdiva.com/masterclass. See the nearby sidebar for more information, too.

Build your emergency fund first

A few years ago, my family was exposed to an unpredicted financial burden. After a year of financial success for both of us, we went ahead and upgraded our budget, bought a new house in an awesome neighborhood, and added some luxury expenses we normally wouldn't go after. It was good times!

MEASURING YOUR OWN RISK TOLERANCE

If you ask a traditional financial advisor, they'd tell you your risk tolerance has two main components:

- Your willingness to risk
- Your ability to risk

But throughout my years of investing and helping my students build their investment portfolios, I've come to realize there's a missing component in calculating your risk tolerance the traditional way. And that is: your confidence in the asset you're planning to invest in.

In other words, you can indeed increase your willingness to take a risk by increasing your confidence in the asset you're investing in.

A financial planner is likely to have you fill out a risk tolerance questionnaire that measures your willingness to risk. This questionnaire evaluates your willingness to take on risk by asking about risk issues. It can help you determine whether you are risk averse or risk tolerant. A *risk averse* investor requires significantly more return in order to consider investing in a higher-risk investment. A *risk tolerant* investor is more willing to accept risk for a small increase in return.

However, to really get an understanding about the amount you can invest in the markets, you must also find out your ability to risk based on your unique financial situation and living circumstances. To calculate your risk tolerance, you must prepare your financial statements and analyze some ratios such as

- **Your emergency fund ratio:** You can calculate this by dividing your accessible cash by your monthly necessary spending. The result must be greater than 6.

- **Your housing ratio:** Divide your housing costs by your gross pay. If you live in the United States, the result must be below 28 percent.

- **Your debt ratio:** This one calculates your total debt divided by your total assets. The benchmark varies depending on your age and financial goals.

- **Your net worth ratio:** You can calculate this by dividing your net worth (which is all your assets minus your debt) by your total assets.

Using these ratios and comparing them to benchmark numbers, you can then fill out a simple questionnaire to figure out your risk tolerance.

Then an unexpected tax law change in the United States put us in a higher tax bracket than usual and took away some of our previously sought tax exemptions and deductions. Right after that, our daughter was born, and our plans to have our parents take care of her for the first six months fell through because of sudden health issues on both sides of the family. As the saying goes, when it rains, it pours — figuratively and literally. Our area got hit by a few storms, which flooded our basement, damaged our trees, and dropped a few branches on our house. We now needed an additional budget for the damages.

I tell this story simply to point out the importance of having an emergency fund, no matter what you're investing in or what your strategy is. Thanks to our emergency fund, we were able to overcome this financially challenging time and turn our focus back on raising our little bundle of joy. Of course, now we had to rebuild the fund from scratch.

TIP

You can calculate your emergency fund by dividing the value of your total immediately accessible cash by your necessary monthly expenses. That will give you the number of months you can survive with no additional cash flow. The result *must* be greater than six months. But the more the merrier. For more on risk tolerance calculation, visit investdiva.com/masterclass.

REMEMBER

You must have an emergency fund before creating an investment portfolio, let alone adding cryptocurrencies to it.

Be patient

The risks involved with cryptocurrencies are slightly different from those of other, more established markets such as equities and precious metals. However, you can use similar methods for managing your portfolio risk regardless of your investments.

The most common reason many investors lose money online is the fantasy of getting rich quick. I can say with confidence (verifiably) that the vast majority of my long-term students made money, and in many cases a lot of money. In fact, many of our students have received our $100K Diva, $500K Diva, and even Millionaire Diva awards! These are awarded to my students who have built such a portfolio using my strategies.

But if you need a shortcut, here it is: The key has been patience.

"Patience is a profitable virtue" is the mantra of the Invest Diva movement. The majority of my students' portfolio holdings has been equities and cryptocurrencies. This works because, over time, markets usually go up, even if they are more volatile in the short term. If you're super busy, you can set your portfolio to take advantage of the long-term gains instead of getting stressed over short-term ups and downs.

That being said, the patience mantra doesn't help only long-term investors. It also goes for short-term traders and speculators. While short-term trading is not something I recommend, very often, that investment or speculative position you took may go down or sideways for what seems like forever. Sooner or later, the market will take note of the sentiment and either erase losses or create new buy opportunities.

In Figure 3-2, you can see the role patience can play in an investor's returns. Of course, you'd love for the markets to just march up to your profit target (that is, exit) price level straightaway. But more often than not, it just doesn't work that way:

>> The chart on the left shows a fantasy most traders have when they buy an asset. They hope the price will march up toward their profit target within their trading time frame, whether short-term or long-term, and make them money.

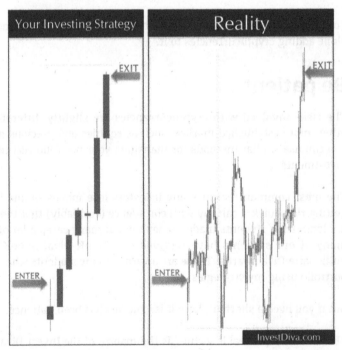

© InvestDiva.com

FIGURE 3-2:
Demonstrating why patience is a profitable virtue.

>> The chart on the right shows the reality. Traders and investors alike often see a lot of dips in the price before the market reaches their profit target. Some investors panic on the dips and call it quits. But in the end, those who were patient and held their position through the rough times win. This can be true to both short-term and long-term investors, so the chart's time frame doesn't really matter.

REMEMBER

Success follows a bumpy road. Your portfolio may even turn into negative territory at times. However, if you've done your due diligence of analyzing your investment, you must make time your friend in order to see long-term profit. See Chapter 20 for full details on long-term investing strategies.

A great example of this idea is the crash of 2008 and 2020. Almost all markets around the world, including the U.S. stock market, dropped like a hot rock because of economic issues such as the mortgage crisis in 2008 and the COVID-19 pandemic in 2020. Most people panicked and started to get out of their investments with massive losses. Had they given it some (well, a lot of) patience, they would've seen their portfolios in positive territory in around five years. By 2022, they would've more than doubled the returns on the very same investments.

Diversify outside and inside your cryptocurrency portfolio

As I note in Chapter 2, diversification is the "don't put all your eggs in one basket" rule, and this age-old investing advice remains true to the revolutionary cryptocurrency market. Besides diversifying your portfolio by adding different assets such as stocks, bonds, or exchange traded funds (ETFs), diversification within your cryptocurrency portfolio is also important. (See Chapter 10 for some diversification ideas.)

For example, Bitcoin is perhaps the celebrity of all cryptocurrencies, so everyone wants to get hold of it. But Bitcoin is also the oldest cryptocurrency, so it has some unresolvable problems. Every day, younger and better-performing cryptocurrencies make their way into the market and offer exciting opportunities. (I'm not trying to say younger is better in all facets of life. I'm talking about cryptocurrencies here, not people!)

Besides age, you can group cryptocurrencies in several different ways for diversification purposes. Here are some examples (see Chapter 8 for full details):

>> **Major cryptocurrencies by market cap:** This category includes the ones in the top ten. At the time of writing, these options include Bitcoin, Ethereum, Ripple, and Litecoin.

>> **Transactional cryptocurrencies:** This group is the original category for cryptocurrencies. Transactional cryptocurrencies are designed to be used as money and exchanged for goods and services. Bitcoin and Litecoin are examples of well-known cryptos on this list.

>> **Platform cryptocurrencies:** These cryptocurrencies are designed to get rid of intermediaries, create markets, and even launch other cryptocurrencies. Ethereum is one of the biggest cryptos in this category. It provides a backbone for future applications. Such cryptocurrencies are generally considered good long-term investments because they rise in value as more applications are created on their blockchain.

>> **Privacy cryptocurrencies:** These options are similar to transactional cryptocurrencies, but they're heavily focused toward transaction security and anonymity. Examples include Monero, Zcash, and Dash.

>> **Application-specific cryptocurrencies:** One of the trendiest types of cryptos, application-specific cryptocurrencies serve specific functions and solve some of the world's biggest problems. Some examples of such cryptos are Vechain (used for supply chain applications), IOTA (Internet of Things applications), and Cardano (cryptocurrency scalability, privacy optimizations, and so on). Some get super specific, such as Mobius, also known as Stripe for the blockchain industry, which was seeking to resolve the payment issues in the agriculture industry in 2018. Depending on the specifics of each project, a number of these cryptos may prove highly successful. You can pick the ones that are solving issues closer to your heart; just be sure to analyze their usability, application performance, and project team properly.

TIP

Depending on who you're talking to in the cryptocurrency world, people may have different opinions on the above-mentioned cryptocurrency projects. Some may even label them as *shitcoins*. This term is used to describe a cryptocurrency that is not valuable or has no immediate purpose — often altcoins or cryptocurrencies that were developed after Bitcoin became popular.

REMEMBER

One key problem the cryptocurrency market faces when it comes to diversification is that the whole market appears to be extremely correlated. The majority of cryptocurrencies go up when the market sentiment turns bullish (upward), and vice versa. Despite this tendency, you can diversify away risk in a crypto-only portfolio by adding more crypto assets to your portfolio. By investing in multiple crypto assets, or the top cryptocurrencies in each crypto category, you can spread out the amount of risk you're exposed to instead of having all the volatility of the portfolio come from one or a few assets. Flip to Chapter 10 for the full scoop on diversification in cryptocurrencies.

IN THIS CHAPTER

» **Understanding what blockchain technology is**

» **Considering current problems with blockchain technology**

» **Discovering different ways blockchain can be used**

Chapter **4**

Looking Under the Hood: Blockchain Technology

Most people have probably heard about Bitcoin more than they have blockchain. Many who *have* heard of blockchain think it's just the technology that powers Bitcoin. Although Bitcoin became one of the most famous outcomes of blockchain technology, blockchain is capable of so much more. It's perhaps one of the most interruptive technologies in decades and may change our lives forever.

REMEMBER

Simply put, the relationship between Bitcoin and blockchain is similar to the relationship between email and the Internet. To be able to send and receive emails, you need the Internet. Similarly, to be able to use any crypto, you need blockchain technology.

In this chapter, I take a look at how blockchain technology works, why it matters, and how it can impact your life in the future. Having a better understanding of blockchain technology may help reshape your view on the cryptocurrency market. That way, you can make better investment decisions in the industry.

Breaking Down Blockchain Technology Basics

Modern technologies allow people to communicate directly. You can use them to directly send emails, text messages, pictures, and videos to others without the use of an intermediary. This way, you can maintain trust with others no matter where they are in the world. Long-distance relationships aren't as hard and heart-wrenching anymore. For example, my family has maintained years and years of long-distance relationship only possible due to the advent of the Internet. I attended my sister's wedding in Los Angeles via Skype when I was in Tokyo. My Australia-based in-laws, who weren't able to travel due to a terminal illness, were able to attend our wedding in Hawaii via FaceTime.

Despite this advancement, people still have to trust a third party to complete a financial transaction. But blockchain technology is challenging this setup in a radical way. I explain the basics of blockchain technology in the following sections.

What is a blockchain, and how does it work?

Simply put, a *blockchain* is a special kind of database. According to `cigionline. org`, the term *blockchain* refers to the whole network of distributed ledger technologies. According to Oxford Dictionaries, a *ledger* is "a book or other collection of financial accounts of a particular type." It can be a computer file that records transactions. A ledger is actually the foundation of accounting and is as old as writing and money.

Now imagine a whole suite of incorruptible digital ledgers of economic transactions that can be programmed to record and track not only financial transactions but also virtually everything of value. The blockchain can track things like medical records, land titles, and even voting (as you find out later in this chapter). It's a shared, distributed, and immutable ledger that records the history of transactions starting with transaction number one. It establishes trust, accountability, and transparency.

REMEMBER

Blockchain stores information in batches called *blocks*. These blocks are linked together in a sequential way to form a continuous line. A chain of blocks. A blockchain. Each block is like a page of a ledger or a record book. As you can see in Figure 4-1, each block mainly has three elements:

>> **Data:** The type of data depends on what the blockchain is being used for. In Bitcoin, for example, a block's data contains the details about the transaction, including sender, receiver, number of coins, and so on.

>> **Hash:** No, I'm not talking about *that* kind of hash. A *hash* in blockchain is something like a fingerprint or signature. It identifies a block and all its content, and it's always unique.

>> **Hash of previous block:** This piece is precisely what makes a blockchain! Because each block carries the information of the previous block, the chain becomes very secure.

© John Wiley & Sons, Inc.

FIGURE 4-1: Three main elements of a block.

Here's an example of how a bunch of blocks come together in a blockchain. Say you have three blocks.

Block 1 contains this stuff:

>> Data: 10 Bitcoins from Fred to Jack

>> Hash (simplified): 12A

>> Previous hash (simplified): 000

Block 2 contains this stuff:

>> Data: 5 Bitcoins from Jack to Mary

>> Hash (simplified): 3B4

>> Previous hash: 12A

Block 3 contains this stuff:

>> Data: 4 Bitcoins from Mary to Sally

>> Hash (simplified): C74

>> Previous hash: 3B4

As you can see in Figure 4-2, each block has its own hash and a hash of the previous block. So block 3 points to block 2, and block 2 points to block 1. (*Note:* The first block is a bit special because it can't point to a previous block. This block is the *genesis block.*)

© John Wiley & Sons, Inc.

FIGURE 4-2:
Simplified version of how a blockchain works.

The hashes and the data are unique to each block, but they can still be tampered with. The following section lays out some ways blockchains secure themselves.

How does a blockchain secure itself?

Interfering with a block on the blockchain is almost impossible to do. The first way a blockchain secures itself is by hashing. Tampering with a block within a blockchain causes the hash of the block to change. That change makes the following block, which originally pointed to the first block's hash, invalid. In fact, changing a single block makes all the following blocks invalid. This setup gives the blockchain a level of security.

WARNING

However, using hashing isn't enough to prevent tampering. That's because computers are super-fast, and they can calculate over 100 trillion hashes per second. Technically, a hacker can change the hash of a specific block and then calculate and change all the hashes of the following blocks in order to hide the tampering.

That's why on top of the hashes, blockchains have additional security steps including things like proof-of-work and peer-to-peer distribution. A *proof-of-work* (PoW) is a mechanism that slows down the creation of the blocks. In Bitcoin's case, for example, it takes about ten minutes to calculate the required PoW and add a new block to the chain. This timeline makes tampering with a block super difficult because if you interfere with one block, you need to interfere with all the following blocks. A blockchain like Bitcoin contains hundreds of thousands of blocks, so successfully manipulating it can take over ten years! I explore more about proof-of-work in Chapter 5.

A third way blockchains secure themselves is by being distributed. Blockchains don't use a central entity to manage the chain. Instead, they use a *peer-to-peer* (P2P) network. In public blockchains like Bitcoin, everyone is allowed to join. Each member of the network is called a *validator* or a *node*. When someone joins the network, they get the full copy of the blockchain. This way, the node can verify that everything is still in order.

Here's what happens when someone creates a new block in the network:

1. The new block is sent to everyone in the network.

2. Each node then verifies the block and makes sure it hasn't been tampered with.

3. If everything checks out, each node adds this new block to their own blockchain.

All the nodes in this process create a consensus. They agree about which blocks are valid and which ones aren't. The other nodes in the network reject blocks that are tampered with. So to successfully mess with a block on a blockchain, you'd need to tamper with all the blocks on the chain, redo the proof-of-work for each block, and take control of the peer-to-peer network!

REMEMBER

Blockchains are also constantly evolving. One of the most recent developments in the cryptocurrency ecosystem is the addition of something called a *smart contract*. A smart contract is a digital computer program stored inside a blockchain. It can directly control the transfer of cryptocurrencies or other digital assets based on certain conditions. Find out more on smart contracts in Chapter 5.

Why is blockchain revolutionary?

Here are three main reasons blockchain is different from other kinds of database and tracking systems already in use.

Blockchain may eliminate data tampering because of the way it tracks and stores data

REMEMBER

If you make a change to the information recorded in one particular block of a blockchain, you don't rewrite it. Instead the change is stored in a new block. Therefore, you can't rewrite history — no one can — because that new block shows the change as well as the date and the time of the change. This approach is actually based on a century-old method of the general financial ledger.

I can explain the difference through an example. Suppose Joe and his cousin Matt have a dispute over who owns the furniture shop they've been comanaging for years. Because the blockchain technology uses the ledger method, the ledger should have an entry showing that George first owned the shop in 1947. When George sold the shop to Mary in 1976, he made a new entry in the ledger, and so on. Every change of ownership of this shop is represented by a new entry in the ledger, right up until Matt bought it from his uncle in 2009. By going through the history in the ledger, Matt can show that he is in fact the current owner.

Now, here's how blockchain would approach this dispute differently than the age-old ledger method. The traditional ledger method uses a book, or a database file stored in a single (centralized) system. However, blockchain was designed to be *decentralized* and distributed across a large network of computers. This decentralizing of information reduces the ability for data tampering.

WARNING

Blockchain attacks in the past show that data tampering can't be completely eliminated on the blockchain database as is. If 51 percent of miners decide to rewrite the ledger, it would be possible, and as a result, they can do whatever they want with the transaction: They can delay it, double-spend the coins, postpone it, or simply remove it from the block. Several blockchain networks are currently working on a custom solution for this. Even some of the traditional tech giants such as IBM have now dedicated a whole arm to blockchain services and consulting to help blockchain networks address their security and governance issues. (For more information, see: www.ibm.com/topics/blockchain-security.)

Blockchain creates trust in the data

The unique way blockchain works creates trust in the data. I get more into the specifics earlier in this chapter, but here's a simplified version to show you why. Before a block can be added to the chain, a few things have to happen:

1. A cryptographic puzzle must be solved to create the new block.

2. The computer that solves the puzzle shares the solution with all the other computers in the network. This solution is the proof-of-work I discuss briefly in the earlier section "How does a blockchain secure itself?" and more about it in Chapter 5.

3. Finally, all the computers involved in the network verify the proof-of-work. If 51 percent of the network testifies that the PoW was correct, the new block is added to the chain.

The combination of these complex math puzzles and verification by many computers ensures that users can trust each and every block on the chain. Heck, one of the main reasons I'm a big supporter of cryptocurrencies is that I trust in the blockchain technology so much. Because the network does the trust-building for you, you now have the opportunity to interact with your data in real time.

Centralized third parties aren't necessary

In my previous example of the dispute between Joe and Matt, each of the cousins may have hired a lawyer or a trusted *centralized* third party to go through the ledger and the documentation of the shop ownership. They trust the lawyers to keep the financial information and the documentation confidential. The third-party lawyers try to build trust between their clients and verify that Matt is indeed the rightful owner of the shop. (For the details of the example, check out "Blockchain may eliminate data tampering because of the way it tracks and stores data.")

The problem with centralized third parties and intermediaries such as lawyers and banks is that they add an extra step to resolving the dispute, resulting in spending more time and money.

If Matt's ownership information had been stored in a blockchain, he would've been able to cut out the centralized intermediary, his lawyer. That's because all blocks added to the chain would've been verified to be true and couldn't be tampered with. In other words, the blockchain network and the miners are now the third party, which makes the process faster and more affordable. So Matt could simply show Joe his ownership information secured on the blockchain. He would save a ton of money and time by cutting out the centralized intermediary.

This type of trusted, peer-to-peer interaction with data can revolutionize the way people access, verify, and transact with one another. And because blockchain is a type of technology and not a single network, it can be implemented in many different ways, as I explain later in this chapter.

Perusing Problems with Blockchain

The blockchain technology I describe earlier in this chapter is all sexy and revolutionary, but it sure has a bunch of problems it has to deal with before it becomes truly adapted to daily life. Here are some of the issues and barriers that blockchain has to overcome before you get too excited or too involved.

Scalability problems

Scalability is perhaps one of the most immediate problems that blockchain technology faces. Earlier in this chapter, I talk about how the blockchain secures itself, and how hackers would need a long time to be able to tamper with the system successfully. Well, this security comes at a cost for the users, too. Blockchain transactions are slow and expensive. For example, the Bitcoin network is capable of processing a maximum of seven transactions per second — for the millions of users worldwide. Additionally, to increase payment security, Bitcoin-blockchain transactions are recorded only once every ten minutes. Now imagine everyone on the planet using Bitcoins for transactions and having to wait this long for each throughput. Scary, isn't it?

However, at the time of writing, data shows that Bitcoin Lightning Network has finally solved the scalability problem. The Lightning Network is a way to make Bitcoin better. It makes it faster and easier to use. This is done by adding a second layer to the Bitcoin network and is the scaling solution that everyone in the crypto world is focused on.

TECHNICAL STUFF

Other solutions include using things like a hard fork (explained in Chapter 5), the lightning network, and sharding:

>> According to CoinDesk, "the lightning network effectively creates a layer on top of Bitcoin, enabling fast and cheap transactions which can net settle to the bitcoin blockchain." The concept "is based on a network that sits on top of the Bitcoin blockchain, and eventually settles on it. The network is comprised of user-generated channels that send payments back and forth in a secure and trust-less fashion (*trust-less* means that you don't need to trust or even know your counterparty)." Essentially, the *lightning network* takes the transactions away from the main blockchain and therefore reduces transaction fees and time.

>> *Sharding* is another proposed solution for the blockchain's scalability problem and is a concept that's widely used in databases to make them more efficient. Simply put, for cryptocurrencies sharding assigns random nodes rather than the entire network to validate a transaction on the blockchain network. The idea is that smaller sets of nodes can crunch the data faster and that the random distribution means nobody is stuck doing all the work. Sharding as a technology raises some concerns, the most basic being whether an unethical actor can manipulate a shard and whether members of a shard should be compensated.

With all the possible solutions being proposed left and right, investors can be hopeful that the blockchain's scalability problem can be solved sooner rather than later.

Environmental problems

One of the biggest problems environmentalists have with blockchains such as Bitcoin that use the PoW mining system is the amount of energy they waste at the environment's cost.

Many investors refuse to add cryptocurrencies to their portfolio purely for this reason.

According to the *New York Times*, the Bitcoin network uses around 91 terawatt-hours (91TWh) of electricity annually, which is more energy used than countries like Finland. Other sources put this number at 150TWh per year, which is more energy than Argentina, a nation of 45 million people.

That being said, in reality, calculating the carbon footprint of cryptocurrency is more complicated. As cryptocurrency and blockchain technology evolve, more efficient hardware will be introduced that requires less energy. For example, blockchains that use the proof-of-stake (PoS) method of mining new coins don't use expensive computer powers and are therefore more environmentally friendly.

TECHNICAL
STUFF

New methods of mining cryptocurrency are being introduced, such as *proof-of-burn*, which is a mix of PoW and PoS. While at the time of writing, they have not yet caught on in any significant way, such new ideas and research shows that we may at least be headed towards the right direction when solving the environmental issues caused by blockchain. In fact, the Crypto Climate Accord has gathered 250 signatures from individuals and companies who have committed themselves to reducing their carbon emissions to net zero by 2030 and eventually decarbonizing the entire cryptocurrency industry by 2040.

TIP

If you want be a part of the solution to blockchain environmental issues, check out cryptoclimate.org/solutions.

Fraud problems

The blockchain industry has had a ton of hype around it, particularly regarding the cryptocurrency market (as I talk about in Chapter 3). Some companies in the financial world are trying to take advantage of the excitement surrounding blockchain. In 2018, Nasdaq delisted one company due to concerns that the company made "public statements designed to mislead investors and to take advantage of general investor interest in bitcoin and blockchain technology." And the Securities and Exchange Commission has taken action against companies that have made false and misleading statements about blockchain technology in an effort to pump up the price of the stock. This isn't a new kind of fraud; it's the same old story where a company changes its game, takes advantage of a hot trend, and makes baseless claims to attract new investors to pump, and then dump, the stock.

WARNING

Additionally, some fraudsters have attempted to capitalize on the mystery and excitement around the term *blockchain* to target investors. Scammers have posed as legitimate websites that provide services to cryptocurrency users to target unknowing users.

The list goes on. These stories only prove the importance of being educated on the subject matter before getting too hyped up and overly involved. You have the right book in your hands to get you started with that!

Political problems

Earlier in this chapter, I talk about how blockchain technology cuts out the intermediary. Now consider how big this intermediary industry is. All the banks, brokers, lawyers, you name it — all of them make huge profits from playing the intermediary role. As of now, because the cost is distributed among millions of customers, end users usually pay very little individually. But if blockchain continues to replace these roles, it may pose a serious danger to their business — unless they join the movement, that is.

In most countries, including the United States, banks carry huge lobbying power with governments and legislators. The established financial services industry could dramatically reduce blockchain's usefulness and restrict its availability (if not kill it altogether) should it decide doing so is to the industry's benefit. But then again, the people have power, too. And the more people know about the advantages of using blockchain technology, the harder time politicians and the financial establishment will have standing in the way of its growth.

What Can Blockchain Be Used For?

The creation of the blockchain technology has piqued a lot of people's interest. Supposedly, someone called Satoshi Nakamoto invented blockchain in 2008. Blockchain's original intent was Bitcoin. Or perhaps Satoshi used Bitcoin as a tool to introduce blockchain to the masses. Regardless, soon people realized blockchain technology can be used for different purposes, such as identity verification and storing medical records. The following sections explain how a few different categories can use blockchain and, more importantly, how the cryptocurrency market uses it.

TECHNICAL STUFF

No one knows who Satoshi Nakamoto is. It can be a man, a woman, or a team of anonymous geeks. In fact, a women-on-the-block movement is out to prove that Satoshi is female!

Payments

As I cover throughout this book, money transferring was the first and most popular usage of the blockchain technology. For more than 40 years, economists have been seeking the holy grail of a digital currency that can eliminate the problem of double-spending and circumvent the issue of needing to trust an unknown third party. And then . . . bam! Satoshi's white paper was published in October 2008 and removed banks from the equation, just like that. Disregarding the scalability problem that I describe earlier in this chapter, with banks removed from transactions, most payments processed over a blockchain can be settled within a matter of seconds.

Voting

Voting fraud has been an ongoing theme in democratic, and not-so-democratic, countries. Blockchain technology can put you (and all your political debaters on social media) at ease. Digital voting through the blockchain can offer enough transparency that anyone would be able to see whether something was changed on the network. It combines the ease of digital voting with the security of blockchain to make your vote truly count.

Supply chain monitoring

Are you one of those people who must know where their food comes from? Is it organic, kosher, halal? Is there a food-borne illness you need to be aware of immediately? With the help of the blockchain, you can trace your food from its origin to your plate. It can help you make ethical, healthy choices about things you buy.

Blockchain can also help consumers view how products performed from a quality-control perspective as they traveled from their place of origin to the retailer. Furthermore, it can help businesses pinpoint their inefficiencies within their supply chains quickly. The blockchain removes the paper-based trails and locates items in real time.

Identity verification

This is an era where people are stuck between their digital identity and their actual physical presence. Credit agencies and social networks such as Facebook and Instagram act as the main gatekeepers for online identity. Meanwhile, consumers are longing for a reliable digital identity system to maintain credit records and prove who they are to employers, banks, or car rental companies without letting private corporations make money from selling their data.

To overcome this challenge, many companies are already using blockchain technology and creating a secure digital identification system that would give users a way to control their digital identities. Some examples include Microsoft's authenticator app and Deloitte's Smart Identity System.

Legal ownership of stuff

You can get into legal trouble in so many ways. Family disputes. Lost legal paperwork. Lost assets that aren't easily traceable. Most of people's assets are currently documented on paper. And as I talk about earlier in this chapter, blockchain is hard at work to keep paper, and all the intermediaries attached to it, out of the way. So if you're buying or selling land, a house, or a car, the blockchain can store titles on its network, allowing for a transparent view of this transfer and legal ownership.

Additionally, if your high-value, portable assets such as bikes, jet skis, luxury handbags, and so on are stolen, you may be able to trace them back using companies who are working on providing such blockchain-based services.

Healthcare

One major problem with medical records has been paper record keeping, which the medical sector (at least in the United States) has been trying to move away from for years. Another issue has been medical identity theft. In the United States alone, the National Healthcare Anti-Fraud Association estimates the loss owing to healthcare fraud to be about $300 billion annually.

Blockchain to the rescue! All medical information related to a patient — such as past and present ailments, treatments, and family history of medical problems — will be stored on the blockchain. This approach will make every record permanent, transferable, and accessible, which will prevent the medical records from being lost or modified. Additionally, the patient, who possesses the key to access these digital records, will be in control of who gains access to that data.

Entertainment

It's not all dull around the block. The many branches of the entertainment industry can benefit from blockchain technology, if they haven't already started. The music and esports industries are a couple of examples.

The Internet democratized content creation in the early 2000s, but a new type of intermediary has emerged in digital content. Platforms like YouTube (2.4 billion users), SoundCloud (176 million), Spotify (433 million), and Netflix (around 223 million) are now the intermediaries controlling users and artists.

This amount of control has caused a ton of disputes around artists' compensation. Even someone as famous as Taylor Swift had to go at it with Apple Music and Spotify. As artists grow increasingly disillusioned with such platforms, blockchain technology can be an exciting new option.

The blockchain can give label companies the ability to have completely encrypted records of ownership. When applied to media consumption, the technology can solve the problems surrounding content access, distribution, compensation, managing assets, and digital rights, among others.

Another example of blockchain in the entertainment industry is esports betting. Though I don't encourage this type of gambling entertainment, esports betting was pretty popular in the U.S. in 2018 and is now gaining popularity in Europe and Asia too.

Energy

Using blockchain, people can trade energy among themselves, cutting out the energy companies (yep, the intermediary or middleman.) According to Renewable EnergyWorld.com, "this shift [to peer-to-peer distribution of energy] will stimulate more renewable energy projects as a whole, ultimately forwarding our transition from carbon-emitting electricity generation. Tokenizing renewable energy allows wind, solar, and hydro producers to seamlessly connect with investors, who are willing to pay upfront for the right to consume renewable energy. As a distributed system, the middleman is removed."

Internet of Things (IoT)

The *Internet of Things* (IoT) is basically the fact that most of your stuff is connected to the Internet. For example, we control almost everything in our house, from bedside lamps to air conditioning to the microwave oven and even the baby's crib, through the Internet! While my parents were staying with us to help with our newborn, my husband would sometimes mess with them, turning off the light or TV remotely, using his phone, without their knowing. Of course, I don't think we'll get them to come back for help should we have another baby.

Besides acting as a control freak, the Internet of Things helps you send and receive data within the network of your physical devices. If you can directly integrate your physical world into computer-based systems, you may be able to reduce human exertions and improve your efficiency. According to an article in the IEEE Internet Initiative eNewsletter, "IoT capabilities are considered as 'game-changing' when combined with the concepts of big data analytics and cloud computing" (these are other hot topics of the tech world). Put it next to blockchain, and you may be taking the true next step into the future.

Chapter **5**

How Cryptocurrencies Work

I n Chapter 4, I explain how blockchain technology works. Cryptocurrencies, and more specifically Bitcoin, have been one of the first use cases for blockchain technology. That's why most people may have heard about Bitcoin more than they have about the underlying blockchain technology.

In this chapter, I go into more detail about how cryptocurrencies use blockchain technology, how they operate, and how they're generated, as well as some crypto geek terms you can impress your date or teenage kids with.

Explaining Basic Terms in the Cryptocurrency Process

Cryptocurrencies are also known as digital coins, but they're quite different from the coins in your piggy bank. For one thing, they traditionally aren't attached to a central bank, a country, or a regulatory body.

Here's an example. Say you want to buy the latest version of *Cryptocurrency Investing For Dummies* from your local bookstore. Using your normal debit card, this is what happens:

1. You give your card details to the cashier or the store's point-of-sale system.

2. The store runs the info through, essentially asking your bank whether you have enough money in your bank account to buy the book.

3. The bank checks its records to confirm whether you do.

4. If you do have enough, the bank gives a thumbs-up to the bookstore.

5. The bank then updates its records to show the movement of the money from your account to the bookstore's account.

6. The bank gets a little cut for the trouble of being the intermediary.

Now if you wanted to remove the bank from this entire process, who else would you trust to keep all these records without altering them or cheating in any way? Your best friend? Your dog walker? (I hope you didn't say the crown prince of Nigeria.) In fact, you may not trust any single person. But how about trusting *everyone* in the network?

REMEMBER

As I explain in Chapter 4, blockchain technology works to remove the intermediary. When applied to cryptocurrencies, blockchain eliminates a central record of transactions. Instead, you distribute many copies of your transaction ledger around the world. Each owner of each copy records your transaction of buying the book.

Here's what happens if you want to buy this book using a cryptocurrency:

1. You give your crypto details to the cashier.

2. The shop asks everyone in the network to see whether you have enough coins to buy the book.

3. All the record holders in the network check their records to see whether you do. (These record holders are called nodes; I explain their function in more detail later in this chapter.)

4. If you do have enough, each node gives the thumbs-up to the cashier.

5. The nodes all update their records to show the transfer.

6. At random, a node gets a reward for the work.

That means no organization is keeping track of where your coins are or investigating fraud. In fact, cryptocurrencies such as Bitcoin wouldn't exist without a whole network of bookkeepers (nodes) and a little thing known as cryptography. In the following sections, I explain that and some other important terms related to the workings of cryptocurrencies.

Cryptography

Shhh. Don't tell anyone. That's the *crypto* in *cryptography* and *cryptocurrency.* It means "secret." In the cryptocurrency world, it mainly refers to being "anonymous."

Historically, cryptography is an ancient art for sending hidden messages. (The term comes from the Greek word *krypto logos,* which means *secret writing.*) The sender *encrypts* the message by using some sort of key. The receiver then has to *decrypt* it. For example, 19th-century scholars decrypted ancient Egyptian hieroglyphics when Napoleon's soldiers found the Rosetta Stone in 1799 near Rosetta, Egypt. In the 21st-century era of information networks, the sender can digitally encrypt messages, and the receiver can use cryptographic services and algorithms to decrypt them.

What does Napoleon have to do with cryptocurrencies? Cryptocurrencies use cryptography to maintain security and anonymity. That's how digital coins, even though they're not issued by any central authority or regulatory body, can help with security and protection from double-spending, which is the risk of your digital cash being used more than once.

Cryptography uses three main encryption methods:

TECHNICAL STUFF

» **Hashing:** I talk about hashing briefly in Chapter 4, explaining how it's something like a fingerprint or signature. A *hash function* first takes your input data (which can be of any size). The function then performs an operation on the original data and returns an output that represents the original data but has a fixed (and generally smaller) size. In cryptocurrencies such as Bitcoin, it's used to guess the combination of the lock of a block. Hashing maintains the structure of blockchain data, encodes people's account addresses, and makes block mining possible. You can find more on mining later in this chapter, and in detail in Chapter 13.

» **Symmetric encryption cryptography:** *Symmetric encryption* is the simplest method used in cryptography. It involves only one secret key for both the sender and the receiver. The main disadvantage of symmetric encryption is that all parties involved have to exchange the key used to encrypt the data before they can decrypt it.

>> **Asymmetric encryption cryptography:** *Asymmetric encryption* uses two keys: a public key and a private key. You can encrypt a message by using the receiver's public key, but the receiver can decrypt it only with their private key.

Nodes

I mention nodes in the examples in this chapter and in Chapter 4. A *node* is an electronic device doing the bookkeeping job in the blockchain network, making the whole decentralized thing possible. The device can be a computer, a cellphone, or even a printer, as long as it's connected to the Internet and has access to the blockchain network.

Mining

As the owners of nodes (see the preceding section) willingly contribute their computing resources to store and validate transactions, they have the chance to collect the transaction fees and earn a reward in the underlying cryptocurrency for doing so. This process is known as *mining,* and the owners who do it are *miners.*

REMEMBER

Let me make something clear: Not all cryptocurrencies can be mined. Bitcoin and some other famous ones can. Some others, such as Ripple (XRP), avoid mining altogether because they want a platform that doesn't consume a huge amount of energy in the process of mining; power usage is one of the issues with blockchain that I bring up in Chapter 4, actually. Regardless, for the most part, mining remains a huge part of many cryptocurrencies to date.

Here's how mining works: Cryptocurrency miners solve cryptographic puzzles (via software) to add transactions to the ledger (the blockchain) in the hope of getting coins as a reward. It's called mining because of the fact that this process helps extract new cryptocurrencies from the system. Anyone, including you, can join this group. Your computer needs to "guess" a random number that solves an equation that the blockchain system generates. In fact, your computer has to calculate many 64-character strings or 256-bit hashes and check with the challenge equation to see whether the answer is right. That's why it's so important that you have a powerful computer. The more powerful your computer is, the more guesses it can make in a second, increasing your chances of winning this game. If you manage to guess right, you earn Bitcoins and get to write the "next page" of Bitcoin transactions on the blockchain.

Because mining is based on a form of guessing, for each block a different miner guesses the number and is granted the right to update the blockchain. Whoever has the biggest computing power combined, controlling 51 percent of the votes, controls the chain and can arguably win. Thanks to the law of statistical probability, the same miner is unlikely to succeed every time. On the other hand, this game can sometimes be unfair because the biggest computer power will be the first to solve the challenge equation and "win" more often. That being said, it would be very, very difficult to control 51 percent of the Bitcoin network, and even then, you wouldn't win every time, so this may not even be an issue.

Proof-of-work (PoW)

If you're a miner and want to actually enter your block and transactions into the blockchain, you have to provide an answer (proof) to a specific challenge. This proof is difficult to produce (hence all the gigantic computers, time, and money needed for it), but others can very easily verify it. This process is known as *proof-of-work*, or PoW.

For example, guessing a combination to a lock is a proof to a challenge. Going through all the different possible combinations to come up with the right answer may be pretty hard, but after you get it, it's easy to validate — just enter the combination and see whether the lock opens! The first miner who solves the problem for each block on the blockchain gets a reward. The reward is basically the incentive to keep on mining and gets the miners competing to be the first one to find a solution for mathematical problems. Bitcoin and some other minable cryptocurrencies mainly use the PoW concept to make sure that the network isn't easily manipulated.

REMEMBER

As I talk about in Chapter 4, this whole proof-of-work thing has some downsides for blockchain technology. One of the main challenges is that it consumes a lot of computing power and electricity just for the sake of producing random guesses. That's why new cryptocurrencies have jumped on an alternative wagon called proof-of-stake (PoS), covered in the next section.

Proof-of-stake (PoS)

As proof-of-work consensus started to get more heat from environmentalists, a new protocol, proof-of-stake (PoS), was created. Unlike PoW, a *proof-of-stake (PoS)* system requires you to show ownership of a certain amount of money (or *stake*). That means the more crypto you own, the more mining power you have. This approach eliminates the need for an expensive mining extravaganza. And because the calculations are pretty simple to prove, you own a certain percentage of the total amount of the cryptos available.

Another difference is that the PoS system offers no block rewards, so the miners get transaction fees. That's how PoS cryptos can be several thousand times more cost-effective than PoW ones. (Don't let the PoS abbreviation give you the wrong idea.)

Some famous PoS blockchains at the time of writing include Polkadot (DOT), Avalanche (AVAX), and Cardano (ADA).

REMEMBER

But of course, PoS also can have its own problems. For starters, you can argue that PoS rewards coin hoarders. Under the proof-of-stake model, nodes can mine only a percentage of transactions that corresponds to their stake in a cryptocurrency. For example, a proof-of-stake miner who owns 10 percent of a cryptocurrency would be able to mine 10 percent of blocks on the network. The limitation with this consensus model is that it gives nodes on the network a reason to save their coins instead of spending them. It also produces a scenario in which the rich get richer because large coin holders are able to mine a larger percentage of blocks on the network and may have an excessive influence on transaction validation.

Delegated proof-of-stake (DPoS)

The crypto world is constantly evolving, and a popular evolution of the PoS concept is the *delegated proof-of-stake* (DPoS). In this mechanism, users of the network vote and elect delegates to validate the next block. For each new block, the network chooses a limited number of delegates. For most protocols, this number is anywhere between 20 and 100. It's a bit more democratic than PoS, if you will.

WARNING

While DPoS is praised for being more democratic, there's still a chance that a network could become more centralized than traditional blockchain mechanisms. This also means voters with a larger number of staked tokens have more power, and if the power falls into the hands of bad guys, they could abuse their power. Another issue with DPoS is related to network security. Since fewer people are responsible for maintaining the network, it is easier for hackers to organize a 51 percent attack and screw the network over.

DPoS was first coined by EOS's former Chief Technology Officer, Dan Larimer, in 2014. Some other blockchains that use DPoS include TRON (TRX) and Lisk (LSK).

Proof-of-authority (PoA)

A *proof-of-authority* (PoA) consensus is all about the value of identity and reputation. The validators on a PoA blockchain don't stake coins, but instead, they stake their reputation. That means PoAs are secured by elected nodes who were voted as trustworthy entities.

This consensus mechanism is typically used by private networks and companies who want to maintain their privacy while reaping the benefits of blockchain without the need for a native currency or the need for mining. This means PoAs waste a whole lot less energy to operate.

Supply chain networks and Microsoft Azure are examples of where PoA is being implemented. Microsoft Azure is using PoA in its Ethereum-powered cloud-computing system, offering solutions for GE Aviation. In supply chain, Walmart collaborates with the VeChain blockchain to help address food safety issues and optimize product recalls.

TECHNICAL STUFF

While the other consensus mechanisms mentioned here gear towards decentralization, PoA is centralized (find out more about decentralization later in this chapter). It's primarily an attempt to improve the efficiency of traditional centralized systems. It sacrifices decentralization to achieve high output and scalability. But that doesn't mean they're immune to censorship and blacklisting.

Proof-of-history (PoH)

Also known as a *clock for blockchain*, the *proof-of-history* (PoH) mechanism aims to address the timestamp problem.

What's the timestamp problem, you ask? Let me ask you a question before answering your question:

Which came first, the chicken or the egg?

While PoH might not be able to answer that question, in our normal time-bounded world, it can prove that a transaction occurred sometime before or after an event (instead of trusting the timestamp on the transaction).

I know, the world of blockchain has lots of trust issues! That's mainly due to the fast speed at which the networks can operate and the complexity of the distributed systems.

Think of it as an international airport. For all the airplanes to operate in a timely manner and for the destination airport to know the exact time of arrival, there must be a centralized clock. With the advent of the Internet and as our communications got even faster than airplanes, there was even more need for a standardized time. For example, when you land in your new destination that has a different time zone than your departing location, your phone checks back with a centralized clock to make sure it is accurate at your new location. (Yes, your phone is pretty clever!)

TECHNICAL STUFF

PoH is like a clock that stamps transactions with a hash. This shows when the transaction happened and makes it valid. This means the network does not need to worry about verifying the time claims of nodes. They can rely on the system to do this instead. This makes it easier for nodes to process blocks and put them in the ledger. PoH, and its first web-scale blockchain, Solana, rose to fame to eliminate the "talking between validators" to agree that time has passed. Instead, each validator in PoH blockchains such as Solana has its own clock and encodes the passage of time in a sequential-hashing verifiable delay function (VDF).

How is this different from traditional blockchains such as PoW? The traditional blockchain infrastructure relies on sequential block production, but the structure could get delayed as the network waits for confirmation across the board before it can move on to the next block. According to Anatoly Yakovenko, co-founder of Solana Labs, in a PoH system, "every block producer has to crank through the VDF to get to their assigned slot and produce the block." This helps the blockchain to validate information a lot quicker and with a higher level of confidence.

REMEMBER

PoH still has its own drawbacks compared to traditional consensus systems. For one, to become a validator in a PoH system, your hardware needs to meet strict specifications described in the Solana documents (see docs.solana.com/running-validator/validator-reqs).

At the time of writing, Solana is the most famous PoH-based blockchain, and there are concerns about the extent of its decentralization competitiveness. While Solana does have features of decentralization, it appears to be more centralized than Ethereum, its biggest competitor (find out more about decentralization later in this chapter).

TIP

The PoH-based Solana blockchain is often used to build Decentralized Finance (DeFi) platforms and Non-Fungible Token (NFT) marketplaces and games. Flip to Chapters 8 and 14 for more on DeFi and NFTs.

Proof-of-importance

Proof-of-importance (PoI) was first introduced by a blockchain platform called NEM to support its XEM cryptocurrency. In some ways PoI is similar to PoS because participants (nodes) are marked as "eligible" if they have a certain amount of crypto "vested." Then the network gives a "score" to the eligible nodes, and they can create a block that is roughly the same proportion to that "score." But the difference is that the nodes won't get a higher score only by holding onto more cryptocurrencies. Other variables are considered in the score, too, in order to resolve the primary problem with PoS, which is hoarding. The NEM community in particular uses a method called "harvesting" to solve the PoS "hoarding" problem.

Here's how Investopedia defines harvesting: "Instead of each miner contributing its mining power in a cumulative manner to a computing node, a harvesting participant simply links his account to an existing supernode and uses that account's computing power to complete blocks on his behalf." (I talk about harvesting later in this chapter.)

Transactions: Putting it all together

REMEMBER

Here's a summary of how cryptocurrencies work (check out the preceding sections for details on some of the terminology):

1. When you want to use cryptos to purchase something, first your crypto network and your crypto wallet automatically check your previous transactions to make sure you have enough cryptocurrencies to make that transaction. For this, you need your private and public keys (explained in Chapter 7).

2. The transaction is then encrypted, broadcast to the cryptocurrency's network, and queued up to be added to the public ledger.

3. Transactions are then recorded on the public ledger through mining. The sending and receiving addresses are wallet IDs or hash values that aren't tied to the user identification so they are anonymous.

4. For PoW cryptos, the miners have to solve a math puzzle to verify the transaction. PoS cryptos attribute the mining power to the proportion of the coins held by the miners, instead of utilizing energy to solve math problems, in order to resolve the "wasted energy" problem of PoW. The PoI cryptos add a number of variables when attributing the mining power to nodes in order to resolve the "hoarding" problem that's associated with PoS.

Cruising through Other Important Crypto Concepts

Earlier in this chapter and in Chapter 4, I talk about basics of cryptocurrencies and how they're related to blockchain technology. I dig into more details about brokers, exchanges, wallets, and different types of cryptocurrencies in Part 2, but here I want to get a few more concepts out of the way, just in case someone starts talking to you about them. Other factors make cryptocurrencies so special and different from your government-backed legal tender, also known as *fiat currency*, such as the U.S. dollar.

Adaptive scaling

Adaptive scaling is one of the advantages of investing in cryptocurrencies. It means that it gets harder to mine a specific cryptocurrency over time. It allows cryptocurrencies to work well on both small and large scales. That's why cryptocurrencies take measures such as limiting the supply over time (to create scarcity) and reducing the reward for mining as more total coins are mined. Thanks to adaptive scaling, mining difficulty goes up and down depending on the popularity of the coin and the blockchain. This can give cryptocurrencies a real longevity within the market.

Decentralization

As I explain in Chapter 4, the whole idea behind blockchain technology is that it's *decentralized*. This concept means no single entity can affect the cryptocurrencies.

TECHNICAL STUFF

Some people claim cryptocurrencies such as Ripple aren't truly decentralized because they don't follow Bitcoin's mining protocol exactly. Ripple has no miners. Instead, transactions are powered through a "centralized" blockchain to make it more reliable and faster. Ripple in particular has gone this route because it wants to work with big banks and therefore wants to combine the best elements of fiat money and blockchain cryptocurrency. Whether non-minable currencies such as Ripple can be considered true cryptocurrencies is up for discussion, but that fact doesn't mean you can't invest in them, which is the whole purpose of this book anyway!

Harvesting

Harvesting is an alternative to the traditional mining used to maintain the integrity of a blockchain network. It was designed by a blockchain platform called NEM to generate its own currency called XEM.

According to finder.com, this is how harvesting works: "Every time someone carries out a transaction, the first computer to see and verify the transaction will notify nearby users of that transaction, creating a cascade of information. This process is called 'generating a block.' Whenever someone with more than 10,000 vested XEM generates a block in NEM, they receive the transaction fees on that block as payment." Also, as I explain earlier in this chapter, harvesting uses a PoI system rather than PoS and PoW.

Open source

Cryptocurrencies are typically *open source*. That means that miners, nodes, and harvesters alike can join and use the network without paying a fee.

Public ledger

As I explain in Chapter 4, a ledger is the age-old record-keeping system for recording information and data. Cryptocurrencies use a *public ledger* to record all transactional data. Everyone in the world can access public blockchains and see entire transactions happening with cryptocurrencies.

Note that not all blockchains use a public ledger. Some businesses and financial institutions use private ledgers so that the transactions aren't visible to the world. However, by doing so, they may contradict the original idea behind blockchain technology.

Smart contracts

Smart contracts are also called *self-executing contracts, blockchain contracts,* or *digital contracts.* They're just like traditional contracts except that they're completely digital. Smart contracts remove the intermediary between the buyer and the seller (as I talk about in Chapter 4) so you can implement things like automatic payments and investment products without the need of a central authority like a bank.

A smart contract is actually a tiny computer program that's stored and runs on a blockchain platform. Because of that, all the transactions are completely distributed, and no centralized authority is in control of the money. Also, because it's stored on a blockchain, a smart contract is *immutable*. Being immutable means that after a smart contract is created, it can never be changed again; it can't be tampered with, which is an inherited feature from blockchain technology.

However, being immutable comes with its own disadvantages. Because you can't change anything in the smart contract, that means that if the code has any bugs, you can't fix them either. This makes smart contract security more difficult. Some companies aim to combat this problem by auditing their smart contracts, which can be very costly.

As time goes by, we can expect better coding practices and development life cycles to combat smart contract security problems. After all, smart contracts are still a pretty young practice with their whole life of trial and error ahead of them.

Stick a Fork in It: Digging into Cryptocurrency Forks

What you get from a cryptocurrency fork won't fill your tummy, but it may fill your crypto wallet with some money! Many popular cryptocurrencies were born as a result of a split (fork) in another cryptocurrency like Bitcoin. The following sections explain the basics of these cryptocurrency splits and how you may be able to profit from them.

What is a fork and why do they happen?

Sometimes when a group of developers disagrees with the direction a specific cryptocurrency is going, the members decide to go their own way and initiate a *fork*. Imagine an actual physical fork. It has one long handle, and then it divides into a bunch of branches. That's exactly what happens in a cryptocurrency fork.

Some cryptocurrencies are implemented within open source software. Each of these cryptocurrencies has its own protocol that everyone in the network should follow. Examples of such rule topics include the following:

>> Block size

>> Rewards that miners, harvesters, or other network participants get

>> How fees are calculated

REMEMBER

But because cryptocurrencies are essentially software projects, their development will never be fully finished. There's always room for improvement. Crypto developers regularly push out updates to fix issues or to increase performance. Some of these improvements are small, but others fundamentally change the way the original cryptocurrency (which the developers fell in love with) works. Just as in any type of relationship, you either grow together or grow apart. When the disagreements among a group of developers or network participants intensify, they can choose to break up, create their own version of the protocol, and cause a potential heartbreak that requires years of therapy to get over. Okay, the last part doesn't really happen.

Hard forks and soft forks

Two types of forks can happen in a cryptocurrency: a hard fork and a soft fork.

Most cryptocurrencies consist of two big pieces: the protocol (set of rules) and the blockchain (which stores all the transactions that have ever happened; see Chapter 4). If a segment of the crypto community decides to create its own new rules, it starts by copying the original protocol code and then goes about making changes to it (assuming the cryptocurrency is completely open source). After the developers have implemented their desired changes, they define a point at which their fork will become active. More specifically, they choose a block number to start the forking. For example, as you can see in Figure 5-1, the community can say that the new protocol will go live when block 999 is published to the cryptocurrency blockchain.

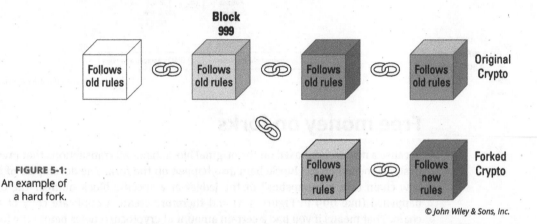

© John Wiley & Sons, Inc.

FIGURE 5-1:
An example of a hard fork.

When the currency reaches that block number, the community splits in two. Some people decide to support the original set of rules, while others support the new fork. Each group then starts adding new blocks to the fork it supports. At this point, both blockchains are incompatible with each other, and a *hard fork* has occurred. In a hard fork, the nodes essentially go through a contentious divorce and don't ever interact with each other again. They don't even acknowledge the nodes or transactions on the old blockchain.

On the other hand, a soft fork is the type of breakup where you remain friends with your ex. If the developers decide to fork the cryptocurrency and make the changes compatible with the old one, then the situation is called a *soft fork.* You can see the subtle difference in the example shown in Figure 5-2.

Say the soft fork is set to happen at block 700. The majority of the community may support the stronger chain of blocks following both the new and old rules. If the two sides reach a consensus after a while, the new rules are upgraded across the network. Any non-upgraded nodes (that is, stubborn geeks) who are still mining are essentially wasting their time. The community comes back together softly, and everyone lives happily ever after — until the next major argument, of course.

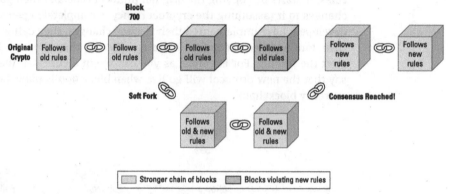

© John Wiley & Sons, Inc.

FIGURE 5-2:
An example of a soft fork.

Free money on forks

Because a new fork is based on the original blockchain, all transactions that previously happened on the blockchain also happen on the fork. The developers of the new chain take a "snapshot" of the ledger at a specific block number the fork happened (like 999 in Figure 5-1) and therefore create a duplicate copy of the chain. That means if you had a certain amount of cryptocurrencies before the fork, you also get the same amount of the new coin.

REMEMBER

To get free coins from a fork, you need to have the cryptocurrency on a platform that supports the fork before the block number at which the fork occurs. You can call this free money. But how valuable the coins are all depends how well the new fork performs and how popular it gets within the community.

A FORKING EXAMPLE: BITCOIN VERSUS BITCOIN CASH

Even the celebrity of cryptocurrencies, Bitcoin (BTC), has seen forks. One of the well-known Bitcoin forks happened on August 1, 2017. That's the birthday of Bitcoin Cash.

In this case, the developers couldn't agree on what the size for a block should be. Some wanted the block size to go from 1MB to 2MB, but others wanted to increase it even more, to 32MB.

Some people in the community loved the new big idea, while others thought the other group was crazy. So both groups decided to go their own ways. Bitcoin Cash adapted a brand-new symbol (BCH), too. People who already had BTC got the same amount of BCH added to their crypto wallets.

As of December 2022, BCH is valued at around $109, while BTC is worth over a hundred times more, around $16,000. Only time will tell whether BCH ever surpasses the original protocol's value. But hey, at least the forkers got some value out of it!

2

The Fundamentals of Investing in Cryptos

Pick an appropriate investing partner by finding an exchange or broker who's suitable for your level of involvement in the market.

Select a secure cryptocurrency wallet for your digital assets based on your needs.

Find background information on a number of current cryptocurrencies.

Identify the best cryptocurrencies to invest in at any given time.

Explore diversification methods across crypto and non-crypto assets to minimize risk in your investment portfolio.

Discover the basics of the metaverse and its impact on the cryptocurrency market.

IN THIS CHAPTER

» Looking at different methods for buying cryptocurrencies

» Understanding different types of crypto exchanges

» Discovering crypto brokers

» Exploring alternative methods of buying cryptocurrencies

Chapter **6**

How to Buy Cryptocurrencies

After you've familiarized yourself with cryptocurrencies' risks and rewards (check out Chapters 2 and 3) and have decided that cryptocurrency investing is right for you, you're ready to go crypto shopping! As you may guess, most of crypto shopping, investing, and trading occurs online; after all, we're talking about digital assets. There are ways to pay cash to purchase digital currencies, but such transactions are uncommon. I mean, sure, if you have a friend who became a crypto millionaire and is looking to sell some crypto assets, you can simply give that person your cash in exchange for the cryptocurrencies.

The most popular way to buy cryptocurrencies, though, is to go directly through an online cryptocurrency exchange. By doing so on decentralized exchanges, you'll eliminate third-party interference in your transaction. However, depending on your cryptocurrency investing goals, you may need to consider alternative methods. For example, if you're an active crypto trader, you may find a traditional cryptocurrency broker easier to use. But if you want just to buy some cryptos and park them in your wallet, a trusted online/local exchange can do the job. In this chapter, I tell you all about different types of exchanges, brokers, and other cryptocurrency providers and show you how to choose the right one(s) for your cryptocurrency goals.

REMEMBER

Choosing a method to get your hands on these hot digital assets can be a lengthy process. However, with the changing regulatory stance, increasing adoption and acceptance, and overall market confidence in cryptocurrencies, the hard work may very well pay off. Regardless of the method you use to purchase cryptocurrencies, you must have a cryptocurrency wallet ready to store your digital assets. You find out all you need to know about cryptocurrency wallets in Chapter 7.

Overviewing the Steps in Buying Cryptocurrencies

Unlike the stock market, the crypto market is open 24 hours a day, seven days a week. This means you can participate in the cryptocurrency market at a Saturday night party after consuming 10 tequila shots on an empty stomach. But I'd highly recommend that you don't do that.

REMEMBER

If you decide that buying a certain cryptocurrency is a smart investment, take the following steps to secure your position:

1. **Choose the place to buy.** You can select from cryptocurrency exchanges operating in your country, crypto brokers, or ATMs.

2. **Choose a payment method.** Most exchanges allow you to purchase crypto using the fiat currency of your country (like the U.S. dollar). One of the easiest methods to buy is connecting your bank account or other payment option to the exchange. But before being able to pay, most exchanges require personal identification methods, including pictures of your driver's license or social security card. You sometimes need to pay a fee for the transaction. The fees vary depending on your payment method and the exchange's policy.

3. **Search for the cryptocurrency you've decided to invest in.** Flip forward to Chapter 8 to discover different types of cryptocurrencies and how to select the ones that are most suitable to your risk tolerance.

4. **Select the price and the amount of cryptocurrency you'd like to invest in.** Most crypto exchanges and brokers allow you to set something called a buy limit order to purchase your crypto assets at your optimal price. By conducting technical analysis (explained in Chapter 18) and combining that with your risk tolerance (outlined in Chapter 3) you may decide to either purchase your favorite crypto asset at the current market price or to set a buy limit order to purchase at future, potentially lower prices.

COMPARING BROKERS, EXCHANGES, AND WALLETS

When you invest in stocks, your choice of where to buy them is typically very clear. Ever since online brokers became a thing, almost anyone can access the stocks listed on big stock exchanges such as the New York Stock Exchange (NYSE) and National Association of Securities Dealers Automated Quotations (NASDAQ). A broker serves as an intermediary that gives you access to financial assets so you can buy and sell.

When it comes to cryptocurrencies, however, you have more choices. Instead of using a broker as an intermediary, you can go directly to the source — the cryptocurrency exchange — to buy and sell.

The main difference between crypto brokers and a *crypto exchange* is that exchanges provide a wider selection of crypto and other digital assets. However, as a result, they sometimes charge higher transaction fees, and they may also be susceptible to cyberattacks (as it is still a new industry). At the time of writing, most cryptocurrency exchanges are expanding their services and level of security. However, the best way to protect your cryptocurrency assets is by using a crypto wallet.

In short, a *crypto wallet* is a program that allows you to store your cryptocurrency. Flip to Chapter 7 for different types of cryptocurrency wallets and how you can use them.

TECHNICAL STUFF

A *buy limit order* is kind of like pre-ordering food from your favorite restaurant. You basically tell your online broker or exchange that you want to buy an asset such as Bitcoin at a specific future price (that is lower than the current price). The broker will then automatically execute your order once the price reaches your ideal level.

Voila! You have now successfully participated in the most disruptive market since the Internet — the crypto market!

Distinguishing Crypto Exchanges

A *cryptocurrency exchange* is also called a *digital currency exchange*, or DCE for short. It's a web service that can help people exchange their cash into cryptocurrencies and vice versa. Most exchanges are more focused on providing services to help you exchange a cryptocurrency such as Bitcoin into other digital currencies like Ethereum, Dogecoin, and so on.

Most exchanges operate online. However, a number of brick-and-mortar businesses do exist; they provide customers services to exchange traditional payment methods and cryptocurrencies. Those options are similar to the currency exchange booths at international airports where you exchange your country's money into the currency of the country you're visiting.

REMEMBER

The most distinguished forms of cryptocurrency exchanges are the following:

>> **Centralized cryptocurrency exchange (CEX):** CEXs are similar to traditional stock exchanges.

>> **Decentralized cryptocurrency exchange (DEX):** DEXs aim to stay true to the pure philosophy behind the cryptocurrency industry.

>> **Hybrid cryptocurrency exchange:** Hybrid exchanges are known to be the next-generation crypto trading marketplace. They combine the best of CEXs and DEXs.

In the following sections, I give you the lowdown on CEXs, DEXs, and hybrid exchanges. Finally, I give you guidance on choosing an exchange.

Centralized exchanges

Centralized exchanges are like traditional stock exchanges. The buyers and sellers come together, and the exchange plays the role of an intermediary. These exchanges typically charge a commission to facilitate the transactions made between the buyers and the sellers. In the cryptoworld, *centralize* means "to trust somebody else to handle your money."

REMEMBER

Here's how a centralized exchange typically works:

1. You give your money to the exchange.

2. The exchange holds it for you (like a bank or a trusted intermediary).

3. You watch the prices of the available cryptocurrencies on the exchange.

4. Depending on the exchange, you can trade your *fiat* currency (a traditional currency, such as the U.S. dollar) for a cryptocurrency (such as Bitcoin). With most exchanges, however, you find better luck exchanging two cryptocurrencies for one another. I talk more about cryptocurrency pairings in Chapter 10.

5. You place your order.

6. The exchange finds a seller to match your buy order. If you're selling, the exchange finds you a buyer.

7. Ta-da! You just crypto shopped on an exchange.

Most centralized crypto exchanges have crypto/crypto pairings. But not all of them provide fiat/crypto pairings:

>> A *crypto/crypto pairing* involves exchanging one cryptocurrency (such as Bitcoin) for another cryptocurrency (such as Ethereum).

>> A *fiat/crypto* pairing involves exchanging a traditional currency (such as the U.S. dollar) for a cryptocurrency (such as Bitcoin).

WARNING

One of the main issues with centralized cryptocurrency exchanges is their vulnerability to hacks. In some past hacking scandals, however, the exchange has paid the customers back out-of-pocket. That's why choosing a centralized exchange wisely, knowing it has the financial ability to combat hackers and pay you in case it gets hacked, is important. Of course, with the popularity of cryptocurrencies, more centralized cryptocurrency exchanges are bound to pop up in the market. Some will succeed, and some may fail. Therefore, you need to pick your crypto shop wisely. I talk about methods for picking the best exchange later in this chapter.

TIP

Centralized exchanges are typically user-friendly and offer a support system to beginner investors. If you're new to crypto investing, starting at an exchange that offers fiat/crypto pairings may make the most sense.

That's precisely the reason why exchanges that provide this service have become some of the most popular ones. At the time of writing, some of the most popular centralized exchanges that offer fiat/crypto pairings include the following:

>> **Binance:** This exchange grew to become the largest crypto exchange since it was founded in 2017 (although more limited in the U.S). However, its exponential growth also brought about tons of regulatory issues, making it a risky place to use for your crypto investments. Binance offers an online crypto wallet for traders to store their assets. It also supports interest-earning services.

At the time of writing, Binance supports over 600 cryptocurrencies globally, but only 100 cryptocurrencies in the US. Binance offers almost all types of transactions.

On top of having regulatory issues, in my experience, Binance has not been the most user-friendly for beginner investors. On the bright side, it's one of the cheapest platforms to use as transaction fees are pretty low. If you use my referral link when signing up, we'll both earn $10 each after you complete $100 worth of trading in 30 days: investdivabinance.com.

>> **Coinbase:** This exchange is one of the most beginner-friendly cryptocurrency platforms and offers basic transactions, a digital wallet, and easy withdrawals. For more complicated investment methods, they also have a pro platform.

At the time of writing, Coinbase supports 179 cryptocurrencies and is insured up to $250,000. This means, in the unlikely event of hacks or scams, Coinbase exchange will pay for damages up to this amount as long as it's their fault. You can use the U.S. dollar (USD), the euro (EUR), the Australian dollar (AUD), and the British pound (GBP) to fund your account and to buy and sell cryptocurrencies.

Coinbase also offers a Visa debit card that is accepted at over 40 million merchants worldwide. If you use my referral link, we both get $10 worth of Bitcoin as a gift if you buy/sell $100 worth of cryptos with Coinbase: investdivacoinbase.com.

>> **Gemini:** Gemini was launched in 2014 by the Winklevoss brothers with high regulation standards. The exchange is focused on security and ease of use and supports over 120 cryptocurrencies.

Gemini offers a credit card that could give you up to 3 percent cash back in Bitcoin or other cryptocurrencies.

Other top cryptocurrency exchanges at the time of writing include OKX, KuCoin, Kraken, and Bitfinex. For up-to-date list of cryptocurrency exchanges, please visit here: investdiva.com/crypto-exchanges.

Decentralized exchanges

A decentralized cryptocurrency exchange (DEX) is an exchange that doesn't rely on an intermediary to hold your funds. It's a marketplace where buyers and sellers come together and process the transactions directly between one another. In other words, DEXs facilitate peer-to-peer trades.

TECHNICAL STUFF

On a decentralized exchange, you can buy and sell your crypto assets directly from other market participants. You'd be able to make the deals through things like smart contracts and atomic swaps. *Smart contracts,* as explained on Investopedia, are "self-executing contracts where the terms of the agreement between buyer and seller are directly written into lines of code." They're the underlying technology for *atomic swaps,* which enable exchange of one cryptocurrency for another without using centralized exchanges. With the DEX, smart contracts, and atomic swaps, instead of giving your cryptocurrencies to the CEX, you'll give them to an escrow that's centralized by the network running the exchange. Escrow still exists because transactions take as long as five days to clear. As a buyer, you'll have your cash taken out from your account immediately, although the funds aren't moved to the seller's account until the crypto transaction clears.

You may think that a decentralized exchange makes more sense to buy and sell cryptocurrencies on because the whole market is often billed as decentralized. Heck, cryptocurrencies became popular because they allow you to become your own bank and be in charge of your own assets. That's why many DEX fans argue that if you utilize centralized exchanges, you're essentially jeopardizing the whole point behind using cryptocurrencies.

The following sections give you more information on some of the issues facing DEXs, plus a rundown of some noteworthy DEX options.

Potential problems

Though DEXs may replace centralized exchanges completely in the future, at this point decentralized exchanges have their own problems.

WARNING

Decentralized cryptocurrency exchanges are harder to hack than centralized ones. On the flip side, you're more vulnerable to locking yourself out of your money. That means if you forget your log-in info, you may get your account locked because the system thinks you're a hacker! Other problems with DEXs include low volumes and low liquidity. *Liquidity* is how fast you can buy or sell cryptocurrencies on the marketplace. Because DEXs are less popular than centralized exchanges (at least for now), you may face more difficulty finding someone to match your buy/sell orders on a DEX. This issue is a vicious cycle because as long as DEXs are less popular, their liquidity remains low. As long as the liquidity is low, DEXs may remain less popular. That's why, at least for now, centralized exchanges are more popular than DEXs.

Additionally, most DEXs don't offer services to deposit or withdraw fiat currencies such as the U.S. dollar. They can also be expensive and slow. Everything from canceling orders to transferring crypto requires paying a fee and waiting for block confirmations; these take at least a few minutes (sometimes hours).

Popular decentralized exchanges

Regardless of possible DEX issues, the highest-ranked decentralized cryptocurrency exchanges according to traffic, liquidity, and trading volume include:

>> **Curve (Ethereum):** Curve is a popular automated market maker (AMM) platform. This platform offers a very efficient way to exchange tokens. It has low fees and low slippage. This is because it only works with liquidity pools made up of assets that have similar behavior patterns.

>> **DODO:** DODO is a decentralized exchange that uses Ethereum and Binance Smart Chain. It aims to make Decentralized Finance (DeFi) liquidity more

accessible. Unlike many other DEXs, which use an automated market maker algorithm, DODO uses its own proactive market maker algorithm.

>> **PancakeSwap:** PancakeSwap is a place where people can trade NB Chain ecosystem and one of the top DEXs by market share. The exchange employs an automated market maker (AMM) model, allowing users to trade against a liquidity pool. You can become a liquidity provider and receive LP tokens, which entitle users to a share of the exchange's trading fees.

>> **Uniswap:** With Uniswap, you can easily trade cryptocurrency tokens without having to create an account. Additionally, you can earn interest on your crypto through Uniswap's liquidity pools. Like the other DEXs, Uniswap also uses an AMM. However, Uniswap doesn't permit buying or selling of cryptocurrency. You also cannot buy crypto using regular money on this exchange — you can only use crypto that you already have in a digital wallet.

WARNING

Liquidity mining is a way to earn more money with your cryptocurrency. Some liquidity pools offer APYs (annual percentage yield) of 100 percent or more, which means you can grow your holdings by a lot. But there is also a risk that you might lose money if the value of the cryptocurrency changes while it's in the pool. This is called *impermanent loss*. This is more likely to happen with more volatile cryptocurrencies, but those are often the ones where you can earn the most money. So when you're choosing a liquidity pool, make sure you pick cryptocurrencies that are aligned with your risk tolerance and have strong fundamentals first, and then see if you can use them for liquidity mining. Flip to Chapter 3 for more on risk tolerance and attend my free Masterclass to learn how to pick the right assets for your portfolio: investdiva.com/masterclass.

Such DEXs are the purest form of decentralized exchanges. They're entirely *on-chain*, which means all orders interact with each other directly through the blockchain (see Chapter 4 for more about this technology). However, these kinds of exchanges have their own sets of problems. Many of those problems don't exist in the centralized cryptocurrency exchanges that I describe earlier; therefore decentralized exchanges are less suitable for beginner investors.

Hybrid exchanges

The hybrid approach to cryptocurrency exchanges aims to merge benefits from both centralized and decentralized exchanges to give consumers the best of both worlds. More specifically, hybrids seek to provide the functionality and liquidity of a CEX with the privacy and security of a DEX. Many believe such exchanges are the real future of the cryptocurrency trading experience. A hybrid crypto platform gives you access to *private keys* (a secret number that is used in cryptography, similar to a password; flip to Chapter 7 for more information) and allow you to trade at a lower fee.

TECHNICAL STUFF

Hybrid exchanges look to provide cryptocurrency trading services with the speed, ease, and liquidity institutional users are used to in traditional exchanges. A hybrid exchange connects its centralized elements to a network of decentralized elements. This approach allows users to access the trading platform as they do in a CEX and then engage in a peer-to-peer trading activity as they do in a DEX. The hybrid then provides confirmation and record transactions on the blockchain.

Hybrids are also called *semi-decentralized exchanges* because they incorporate both on-chain and off-chain components. An *off-chain* transaction moves your cryptocurrency value outside of the blockchain.

The first ever hybrid exchange was Qurrex (qurrex.com), which launched in 2018. The Qurrex team got together in 2016, consisting of experts who had years of experience working in the forex (foreign exchange) markets, developers of trade terminals, and founders of successfully operating stock and futures exchanges. They all saw the significant potential in applying the best practices of the traditional exchanges to create a new generation of cryptocurrency exchange, providing a harmonious merge of centralized and decentralized elements.

Another hybrid cryptocurrency exchange that's gaining attention is NEXT. exchange (https://next.exchange). If you own its native token, NEXT, you can trade between fiat and crypto pairs such as Bitcoin (BTC) versus the euro (EUR), or Ethereum (ETH) versus the U.S. dollar (USD).

How to choose an exchange

First-time investors are better off doing their research on the cryptocurrencies first and then choosing an exchange. But once you become more experienced, you can simply choose cryptos to trade based on the current market conditions.

TIP

Personally, I'm a big fan of diversification in anything. Because many of these exchanges offer different sets of pros and cons, you may be wise to diversify your cryptocurrency activities across a number of exchanges, just like what many people do when they go grocery shopping. You may go to one store for its better-quality meat but get all your pasta from another.

Security

REMEMBER

Security is one of the biggest issues in the cryptocurrency industry. Exchanges are at constant risk of hacks, frauds, and pump-and-dump schemes. A pump-and-dump scheme is when someone encourages investors to buy a crypto asset in order to artificially inflate its value (the "pumping" part) and then sells their own assets at a high price (or "dumps"). That is why one of the most important things to do before choosing your crypto shop(s) is to do your research. Word-of-mouth and online reviews on sites like Reddit or news organizations like Forbes are some of the ways to help you choose a legitimate and secure platform. Some of other safety features you must check on the exchange include the following:

>> **Two-factor authentication (2FA):** *Two-factor authentication* is a method of confirming your claimed identity by using a combination of two different factors: something the exchange knows (like your password) and something it has (like a six-digit number it sends to your mobile phone or your email address for the second step of the verification).

>> **Multi-factor authentication (MFA):** *Multi-factor Authentication* (MFA) is an authentication method that requires the user to provide two or more verification factors to gain access to a resource such as an application, online account, or a VPN. It is a more secure way to make sure that someone is who they say they are. They need to give two things that show it is them. For example, their name and a password.

>> **Cold storage for the majority of funds:** This term means the exchange stores your funds offline so risk of online hacking is lower. I explain more about this feature in Chapter 7.

>> **Proof of reserve:** This element requires the exchange to be audited to verify that the total amount of funds held by the exchange matches the amount required to cover an anonymized set of customer balances.

Supported currencies (crypto and otherwise)

When you decide which of the thousands of available cryptocurrencies are right for you, you must make sure your exchange carries them. You can read more about various crypto options in Chapter 8.

Additionally, if you're looking to purchase cryptocurrencies for the very first time, you probably need an exchange that allows you to deposit your country's fiat currency.

Some exchanges use solely cryptocurrency for purchases, and some allow you to use fiat currencies such as the U.S. dollar, the euro, or your country's currency.

Liquidity

Without sufficient liquidity, the prices and the speeds of your transactions may be compromised. After you decide which cryptocurrencies you want to purchase, make sure your exchange offers sufficient liquidity and trading volume for fast and easy transactions. Liquidity also ensures you're able to buy and sell without the cryptocurrency's price being significantly affected by big market movers. The more buyers and sellers there are, the more liquidity that exists.

TIP

The best way to measure an exchange's liquidity is to look up its most recent trading volume. Coinmarketcap.com and www.coingecko.com are two of the many cryptocurrency information websites that rank exchanges based on their volume and liquidity.

Fees

Exchanges charge their customers in a number of different ways. It would be great if they didn't, but exchanges aren't charities. Charging customers fees is precisely how they make money to stay in business. The most common method is taking a small percentage of the amount you trade. Most exchanges charge a low percentage to stay competitive, some exchanges go as low as around 0.2 percent. Often, a sliding scale decreases the fee percentage as the user's monthly trading volume rises. At the time of writing, Coinbase and Gemini charge a 1.49 percent fee for trades above $200.

REMEMBER

Paying less is always attractive, but prioritize security and liquidity over the fees. Your investment will defeat its purpose if you pay next to nothing on transaction fees and then lose all your funds in a hacker's attack. Some exchanges also have wider bid-ask spreads than others so even though the fees could be lower, you are still paying more depending on the trading pair and order type.

Ease of use

This one is especially important for newbies. You want your exchange to provide you with an easy-to-use, intuitive, and fast user interface. This factor also depends on what kind of device you want to use for your cryptocurrency investing activities. If you're always on the go, you may want to choose an exchange with great mobile app services.

A good user experience helps you take more informed and more efficient actions on the exchange. Another benefit of exchanges with great interface and mobile support is that they're more likely to grow more quickly and therefore provide more trading volume and liquidity in their markets.

Location

Depending on where you live, you may find a specific exchange that works better for you in your country than another, more popular one on an international level does. Some of the things to keep in mind are issues like which fiat currency exchanges accept and what fees they charge locals compared to international customers.

Additionally, the location of the exchange dictates the laws it has to comply with. At the time of writing, many countries don't have any specific regulations on cryptocurrencies. However, if and when they start to regulate, any restrictions may significantly affect your ability to participate in the market through the exchanges in those countries.

Method of payment

Look into the methods of payment the exchange accepts. Some exchanges require deposits by bank transfer, some use PayPal, and some accept credit and debit cards.

REMEMBER

Typically, the easier it is for you to pay, the more fees you're going to have to pay. For example, few services allow you to pay with a credit or debit card, and the ones that do will make you pay for the convenience. (Head to the earlier section "Fees" for more on fee issues; the later "PayPal" section has info on that option.)

Customer support

Poor customer support was precisely the reason I decided not to go with one of the major exchanges when I first started crypto investing. I always feel more comfortable knowing the place I'm trusting with my funds has a responsive customer support service.

You can check this factor either by directly contacting the customer support department and asking any questions that you haven't been able to find on the exchange's FAQ page or by perusing online cryptocurrency forums like BitcoinTalk (bitcointalk.org). You may find complaints about the exchanges in these forums. However, keep in mind that fast-growing exchanges often combat these complaints by improving their customer services, which is always a good thing.

TIP

Another point you may be able to find on forums is whether an exchange has spurred complaints about locking people out of their accounts. If it has, you may want to consider other options.

Trading options

Trading options are especially important for active and advanced traders. For example, depending on your risk tolerance and financial goals, you may want to have access to certain order types or margin trading. On these occasions, make sure you understand the risks involved with such trading activities (check out Part 4) before getting yourself in trouble.

Transaction limits

Most exchanges have a daily withdrawal/deposit limit. Unless you're an institutional trader who wants to make millions of transactions per day, these restrictions may not be an issue. But these limits are still something you may need to keep in mind depending on your investing style and goals. You can typically find out about the exchanges' transaction limits on their websites without having to create an account.

Understanding Crypto Brokers

If you're looking to purchase cryptocurrencies online and invest in them as an asset, then cryptocurrency exchanges are the way to go (see the previous section of this chapter). However, if you're thinking of simply speculating the price action of cryptocurrencies, then you may want to consider brokers.

As cryptocurrencies became more popular, some traditional forex currency brokers started extending their services to cryptos. But keep in mind that the concept of a "broker" doesn't really exist in pure cryptocurrency investing. You can't purchase cryptocurrencies such as Bitcoin through traditional forex brokers. Even though the brokers may carry them, all they're really providing is streaming a tradable price on their platform. That way, you may be able to take advantage of the market volatility and make (or lose) money based on your speculated trading orders.

In the following sections, I explain how traditional brokers work. Then I get into the pros and cons of utilizing them in your crypto trading activities.

REMEMBER

When you search the Internet for cryptocurrency brokers or exchanges, you often get a list that has all types mixed together. You need to take a second look to identify which is an exchange and which is a brokerage. Do this by going to each website's "About" section or simply adding the keywords "broker or exchange" next to their name in your search box.

How brokers work

Traditional brokers are market intermediaries who help traders execute trades on their platforms. They're the intermediaries between an individual retail trader and networks of big banks. Stock brokers take the order from customers and try to fill them at the best price possible. In the case of forex brokers, they typically get a price from one or multiple banks for a specific currency. They then offer you the best price they've received from their banks. You can then trade your favorite currencies based on the prices that are streaming on your broker's platform.

TECHNICAL STUFF

Such brokers operate on something called the *over-the-counter (OTC)* markets. This means that the currencies are traded via a dealer network as opposed to on a centralized exchange. The brokers unload their trading risk to third-party or internal backend warehouses called *liquidity providers*. When it comes to cryptocurrency services on their platforms, these liquidity providers are often cryptocurrency exchanges (that I talk about earlier in this chapter).

WARNING

Forex brokers mainly make money through transparent — and sometimes hidden — commission fees. Some brokers even make money when their customers lose money. That's one reason the forex industry as a whole started getting a bad reputation; some such brokers started getting caught by government regulators. I explain more about forex brokers and the scams involved with the industry in my book *Invest Diva's Guide to Making Money in Forex* (McGraw Hill, 2013). But my short, takeaway message right here, right now is if you have a low risk tolerance (based on what you calculate in Chapter 3) then you might want to stay away from trading forex!

The pros and cons of using a broker

REMEMBER

Forex brokers who provide cryptocurrency services have started hardcore marketing to advertise speculative crypto trading. Here are some of the advantages and disadvantages of trading through a broker as opposed to using a cryptocurrency exchange:

>> **Pro: You get improved liquidity.** Because the brokers get their quotes from multiple exchanges, they're able to provide increased liquidity to customers. That means you have a higher chance of getting your buy/sell orders fulfilled in a timely manner. You also may be able to get a price closer to your initial buy/sell order because the broker has multiple channels to find a buyer and seller to fulfill your order.

>> **Pro: You can start trading immediately.** If you go through an exchange, you sometimes need to wait for days before your account is confirmed. With most brokers, the account confirmation can be quicker.

>> **Con: You can't invest in cryptos as an asset.** By trading through a broker, you're simply speculating on price volatility of the market. You aren't actually purchasing or investing in the cryptocurrency market. This distinction means you don't own your cryptos even if you buy them on the brokerage account.

>> **Con: You don't have access to wallets.** For the same reason as in the preceding point, no real portfolio or wallet is available for you. This fact also means you can't realize your transfers or cryptocurrency acquisitions.

REMEMBER

In addition to these pros and cons, some conditions can be both advantages and disadvantages of trading cryptocurrencies on a broker. Of course, if you go to the brokers' websites, they've featured these characteristics as advantages. However, you must understand the risks beneath the surface, outlined in the next sections.

Pro or con: You can take advantage of a down market

This tricky advantage is one that many brokers advertise. Because you aren't actually purchasing the currencies (fiat or crypto), you can bet on the markets to go down. If the prices do go down as you predicted, you can make money.

This process is called *short-selling*. Short-selling is actually also available on exchanges and traditional stock markets as well. However, it involves a lot of risk because you need to borrow money from your broker, exchange, or whoever is providing your trading services.

Pro or con: You can trade on leverage

Trading on leverage means borrowing money from your broker to trade. With some brokers, you can open an account with $100 and then use 50-times leverage (or even more), which means you control a $5,000 account with your mere $100! But unless you're Nostradamus or have a crystal ball, using leverage can be problematic because leverage enlarges the risks of gains and losses by the same magnitude.

WARNING

Here's how leverage can make or break your account: Say you have a $1,000 account. You place a trade order without using any leverage, and you end up making $50. If you had used a 10-time leverage, you would've made $500 instead. That's awesome! But (and that's a very big but) on the flip side, if the markets go against your speculation when you're trading on that leverage, you lose $500 rather than $50, wiping half of your account. Newbie traders often wipe out their accounts completely within the first few days. Sometimes, depending on the broker's policy, investors' losses can even exceed their initial deposits, which means they actually owe the broker money!

REMEMBER

Using leverage can be an advantage if you know what you're doing and you have high enough risk tolerance to be prepared for a worst-case scenario, which means losing parts or all of your initial investment through the broker.

Here are the two traditional brokers that offer cryptocurrency trading services; I personally use them for a portion of my investment portfolio:

>> **Robinhood:** This is my favorite beginner's app thanks to its ease of use. Despite going through a rough patch of scandals in 2020, Robinhood is, like

most other brokers, regulated by the Securities and Exchange Commission (SEC) and insures your assets by up to $250,000.

Robinhood's trading app originally offered stocks and ETF (exchange-traded fund) services but now provides fiat pairings to Bitcoin (BTC) and Ethereum (ETH) alongside other cryptocurrencies.

An important note about Robinhood is that it only allows you to take a position on the cryptocurrency's price, either enter a buy or sell position with the hopes of making a profit. However, by trading on Robinhood you will not actually own the cryptocurrency asset. That means you are not able to transfer them to your own cryptocurrency wallet. If you are only interested in position trading, then Robinhood is a commission-free choice, and their app is very easy to use. If you use my referral link, we'll both get some free stocks in our portfolio: earn.investdiva.com/robinhood.

>> **Interactive Brokers:** This platform is available in over 200 countries and offers one of the largest selections of financial assets including stocks, cryptocurrencies, options, and bonds.

I personally started my stock investing journey with Interactive Brokers and continue to hold some of my assets with them. At the time of writing Interactive only lets you trade four cryptocurrencies. You can get up to $1,000 of free IBKR stock when opening an account at Interactive Brokers if you use my link. Check it out here: earn.investdiva.com/ib.

How to choose a broker

REMEMBER

You may notice the Internet has no lack of cryptocurrency exchanges and brokers! And more variations of exchanges are bound to make their way into the market. Which type of platform is best for you to buy and sell cryptocurrencies: brokers, CEX, DEX, or hybrid? Even then, which one of the many platforms in each category should you choose?

I can't answer these questions for you, but I can offer ways to cycle through some of the most important characteristics in exchanges and brokers to help you make the best decision.

The following sections note a few things to consider when choosing a cryptocurrency exchange or a broker:

>> **Make sure it's regulated.** Each country has strict international regulatory authorities that audit brokers on a regular basis to ensure their security. Your best bet is often to make sure the broker is regulated by two or more

regulatory bodies in your country. You can find regulation information on brokers' websites.

>> **Consider ease of deposit and withdrawals.** Good brokers will allow you to deposit funds and withdraw your earnings without a hassle. Brokers really have no reason to make it hard for you to withdraw your profits because the only reason they hold your funds is to facilitate trading.

>> **Make sure they have insurance.** Banks, brokers, and exchanges alike have a limited amount they guarantee to insure in the event of theft, hacks, or system breakdowns. This amount is typically $250,000 but some brokers offer more insurance. Before choosing a place to store your financial assets, confirm their insurance amount by either visiting their policy page or calling their customer service.

TIP

If your financial assets exceed the amount they insure, consider spreading your assets among various platforms. For example, I spread my over-$5 million portfolio across over seven platforms.

>> **Beware of promotions.** Some brokers have discovered that people love discount sales! So they use such promotions to attract customers. Nothing is wrong with promotions, but you must be careful because sometimes brokers use these promotions to push new traders into making risky investments or using unreliable products and signals. That's why you need to do your due diligence and know your broker before you take advantage of a promotion.

Looking at Other Methods for Buying Cryptos

I cover some of the most popular methods to purchase or invest in cryptocurrencies earlier in this chapter. However, these options aren't the only ones. Check out the following sections for a few other handy ways to buy cryptos. (I explain where to store your cryptocurrencies after you purchase them in Chapter 7.)

Funds

Many people seek exposure to the cryptocurrency market but don't want to invest in a specific cryptocurrency such as Bitcoin or Ethereum. They may be looking for an equivalent of a *mutual fund* or an *exchange-traded fund* (ETF), which tracks a basket of different assets such as stocks and indexes. (See Chapter 15 for more information.)

Several ETFs now offer direct or indirect exposure to cryptocurrency prices, stocks of digital payment companies, crypto brokers and exchanges, or blockchain technology. These funds can hold cryptocurrency future contracts or stocks of companies that are involved with crypto. Some non-U.S. ETFs even offer spot cryptocurrency in offline storage. *Spot cryptocurrency* is when you buy and sell assets right away; it is like day trading in the stock market, where people buy and sell assets within one day.

The upside of a fund is that it's somewhat diversified. That's because you get to invest in a number of popular cryptos in one fund, without the hassle of selecting just a few. The downside of most funds is their costs and restrictions.

Here are some cryptocurrency ETFs current in 2022:

>> **Amplify Transformational Data Sharing ETF (BLOK):** This ETF is focused on companies that are involved with cryptocurrencies or that offer indirect exposure to crypto prices. It has $555 million under its asset management at the time of writing.

>> **Fidelity Crypto Industry and Digital Payments ETF (FDIG):** This index tracks the performance of global cryptocurrency, blockchain, and digital payment companies. At the time of writing, FDIG owns 35 stocks and has around $16 million under its management. Three of its major holdings include Block Inc. (SQ), Coinbase Global Inc. (COIN), and Marathon Digital Holdings (MARA). This fund has a passive investing strategy for its fund. Its expense ratio is at 0.39 percent.

An *expense ratio* is a number that shows how much it costs to manage, advertise, and distribute a mutual fund or an ETF. The expense ratio is usually a percentage of the fund's average net assets.

>> **Global X Blockchain ETF (BKCH):** This is another passively managed fund that can give you exposure to companies that may benefit from the adoption of blockchain technology. This includes Bitcoin mining companies such as Marathon Digital (MARA) and leading crypto exchange Coinbase (COIN). At the time of writing, BKCH has around $80 million under management.

TIP

A quick Google search gives you a list of the newest crypto-related ETFs. Always make sure you then separately check the ETF and all its holdings. I personally don't like investing in ETFs because we never know what assets might be hidden in their basket.

I am a huge fan of moral investing and avoid investing in assets or companies that don't comply with my moral beliefs. Investing in ETFs is mainly a lazy approach to participating in the online financial markets, and with just a little bit of research you can instead create an investment portfolio that's suitable to you, your risk tolerance, your moral beliefs, and allows you to avoid paying that non-necessary management fee.

Credit card

Financial services such as Coinmama allow you to buy cryptocurrencies like Bitcoin (BTC) and Ethereum (ETH) using a credit card. But they are not available in all countries yet at the time of writing.

PayPal

Earlier in this chapter, I touch on various methods of payment cryptocurrency exchanges may offer, including transferring money from your bank account and using your credit card/debit card. PayPal is another form of online payment system that supports money transfers and serves as an electronic alternative to traditional money.

PayPal started out working on Bitcoin integration earlier than many other financial services, back in 2014. At the time of writing, Coinbase is the only exchange that accepts PayPal money transfers and this is only available to customers in the U.S. This means you can use PayPal to indirectly buy cryptocurrencies.

TIP

This type of information is constantly subject to change due to cryptocurrencies' volatile current state. The best way to stay on top of cryptocurrency news is on websites such as www.coindesk.com or simply typing the most relevant keywords into your chosen search engine. Some keywords include "how to buy cryptocurrency," "best methods to buy crypto," and "best crypto funds today."

Cash

TIP

The process for paying cash to buy cryptocurrencies such as Bitcoin is to find someone who owns cryptocurrencies and is willing to sell them in exchange for cash:

>> One place you can find buyers and sellers of cryptocurrencies for cash is localbitcoins.com. On this website, you can sign up for free, enter the amount you're looking to buy or sell, and choose your preferred payment method — in this case, cash — to find a counterpart.

>> Other sites connect buyers and sellers in a way where the seller provides bank details that let the buyer make a cash deposit at the bank. You must keep the

receipt to provide proof, and the seller can send you the Bitcoins. Some options in this vein include www.bitquick.co (part of Athena Bitcoin based in Chicago) and paxful.com (based in Delaware).

TECHNICAL STUFF If you do an Internet search on how to buy cryptocurrencies with cash, you may get directed to a mobile app called Cash App, which is indeed an app that helps you buy and sell Bitcoin from friends! However, this isn't the type of cash payment I'm talking about in this section.

Cryptocurrency ATMs

Cryptocurrency ATMs are becoming more popular. Many individuals are even trying to start their own such machines to make passive income. Bitcoin (and other cryptocurrency) ATMs work like any other ATM. The first step in the process is to find one near you, something you can do via a quick online search or at coinatmradar.com.

There are several different brands of ATMs with differing methods of verifying your ID and *cryptocurrency address* (a code in your cryptocurrency wallet). Naturally, you need to do some research in finding a secure and trustworthy ATM with a good online reputation. One simple research method is entering the ATM name on Google or Bing, and checking whether it has any negative press.

The process of buying cryptocurrencies at an ATM may vary from machine to machine. However, here are the general steps most ATMs require:

1. **Verify your identity (using an ID card, for example).**

2. **Select the cryptocurrency you want to purchase.**

3. **Provide a cryptocurrency address for deposit.**

   Chapter 7 has more on this.

4. **Select the amount of cryptocurrency you want to purchase.**

5. **Insert cash into the cryptocurrency ATM.**

6. **Confirm the operation.**

REMEMBER Some cryptocurrency ATMs even provide services to sell digital coins as well as buy. Keep in mind that these types of cryptocurrency machines aren't ATMs in the traditional sense, where they help you connect with your bank account. Instead, they're machines that are connected to the Internet and direct you to a cryptocurrency exchange in order to provide you with your cryptocurrency.

IN THIS CHAPTER

» **Understanding how crypto wallets work**

» **Distinguishing different types of crypto wallets**

» **Selecting the best crypto wallet for you**

» **Upping the security on your crypto wallet**

Chapter **7**

Using Cryptocurrency Wallets

A traditional wallet is where you keep your valuable personal items such as cash, credit cards, and identification cards. But now that you're using the most advanced, futuristic form of money (cryptos, baby!), you're going to need a brand-new type of wallet to go with it: a cryptocurrency wallet.

With a cryptocurrency wallet, you can not only store the value of your digital money but also send and receive currencies. Additionally, you can monitor your balance the way you'd do with your banking account. In this chapter, I walk you step-by-step through understanding and choosing your very first cryptocurrency wallet.

Defining Cryptocurrency Wallets

A *cryptocurrency wallet* is a software program that helps you manage your digital money. Though you may be the type of person who doesn't like to carry around traditional wallets and would rather put your cash and credit cards right in your back pocket, you must have a digital cryptocurrency wallet if you want to use any type of cryptocurrency. There's no way around it. Cryptocurrencies aren't stored in a bank reserve like other types of traditional assets such as gold and cash. Without crypto wallets, the whole idea of cryptocurrencies dies! Cryptocurrency wallets are the air that keeps the system alive.

TECHNICAL STUFF

While in theory Bitcoin is decentralized and nobody controls anything, it's in fact run by a network that's controlled and maintained by someone (whoever is hiding behind the name Satoshi Nakamoto). In other words, Bitcoin is distributed and miners are somewhat anonymous, but the actual blockchain is stored in its entirety by the network. It's so large in size that miners have maybe 30 days' worth of transactions and blocks stored on their devices; the full blockchain is actually stored somewhat centralized by the network.

A few important terms

REMEMBER

Before you get started, take a look at some geek terms that you may encounter as you explore the world of crypto wallets:

>> **Hot wallet:** A wallet connected to the Internet.

>> **Cold wallet:** A wallet that isn't connected to the Internet.

>> **Wallet address:** A number that functions something like a traditional bank account number.

>> **Public key:** A code that allows you to receive cryptocurrencies into your account or wallet. It's mathematically linked to your wallet address, but it isn't identical.

>> **Private key:** A code that's coupled with the public key to ensure your security. It's something like your own private password you use to enter your bank account in the real world.

The following section explains how some of these items work together so you can complete crypto transactions.

How a wallet works

Crypto wallets don't actually store the cryptocurrency itself; rather, they store the cryptocurrency's private and public keys. These keys are something like the PIN code you use to access your bank account.

REMEMBER

No two wallet addresses are ever the same. They're something like fingerprints. This distinction means that there is a very low chance that somebody else can get your funds by mistake. Also, you have no limit to the number of wallet addresses you can create.

WARNING

There have been cases where a wallet ID was intercepted and changed and funds went to the wrong wallet. For example, some malware recently replaced wallet IDs in the clipboard of a computer so when the user cut and pasted the IDs of the intended recipient, the wrong ones were actually pasted — that of the perpetrator.

To give you an example of what a cryptocurrency address looks like, here is the wallet address believed to belong to the creator of Bitcoin, Satoshi Nakamoto!

1A1zP1eP5QGefi2DMPTfTL5SLmv7DivfNa

As you can see, it uses a combination of numbers and letters, both uppercase and lowercase. Don't worry; as long as you have a safe and secure wallet, you don't have to memorize your crypto wallet address. Personally, I keep my wallet address and other keys in a locked document on a secure computer. You can also consider printing your keys and storing them somewhere safe that you won't forget about.

A private key does the job of a unique individual password to your individual crypto wallet address. A public key then adds an extra layer of security and ensures that your wallet can't be hacked. Here is a quick example of what the keys look like:

Private key:
03bf350d2821375158a608b51e3e898e507fe47f2d2e8c774de4a9a7edecf74eda

Public key: 99b1ebcfc11a13df5161aba8160460fe1601d541

These addresses look completely different to the eye, but the software technology knows that the two keys are specifically linked to each other. That proves that you're the owner of the coins and allows you to transfer funds whenever you want.

REMEMBER

When someone sends you any type of cryptocurrency, they are essentially signing off ownership of those cryptos to your wallet's address. To be able to spend those cryptos and unlock the funds, the private key stored in your wallet must match the public address the currency is assigned to. If the public and private keys match, the balance in your wallet increases, and the sender's balance decreases accordingly. No exchange of real coins actually occurs. The transaction is signified merely by a transaction record on the blockchain (see Chapter 4) and a change in balance in your cryptocurrency wallet.

Looking at Different Types of Wallets

First, let me clear up the difference between a traditional digital wallet and a cryptocurrency wallet. You may already be using digital wallets, also known as e-wallets, through your mobile phone. Personally, I use wallet apps for my train tickets, parking tickets, Apple Pay (a mobile payment and digital wallet service by Apple Inc. that allows users to make payments in person, in iOS apps), and Venmo (a mobile payment service you can pay your babysitter, friends, and family with).

Cryptocurrency wallets are a whole different animal; furthermore, they come in several different species catering to different needs. The following sections cover the five most popular types of cryptocurrency wallets, in order of their security level (from least secure to most).

In Figure 7-1, you can see a summary of most common crypto wallets and their examples that I share with Invest Diva students.

SUMMARY OF CRYPTOCURRENCY WALLETS

	SOFTWARE	ONLINE	HARDWARE	PAPER
PROS	User-controlled Security For POS coins, allows minting	High convenience, Accessible from any browser without needing to download the Blockchain	Protects user's private keys, which are stored on the device Can be recovered with PIN and seed	Extremely secure. Can't be hacked using digital means Great for long term storage
CONS	Must download entire Blockchain for each type of coin/token	Susceptible to key logging hacks Can't stake POS coins Unknown level of security	Doesn't support all coins/tokens Can't stake POS coins	Inconvenient to use for transactions
EXAMPLES	Electrum Armory	Blockchain MyEtherWallet	Ledger Trezor	

© John Wiley & Sons, Inc.

FIGURE 7-1: Popular cryptocurrency wallet types.

Note: According to Bitcoin Wiki, a "seed phrase, seed recovery phrase, or backup seed phrase is a list of words which store all the information needed to recover a Bitcoin wallet. Wallet software will typically generate a seed phrase and instruct the user to write it down on paper. If the user's computer breaks or their hard drive becomes corrupted, they can download the same wallet software again and use the paper backup to get their bitcoins back." A POS stands for proof-of-stake, a mining concept I explain in Chapter 5.

REMEMBER

Specific wallet brands I mention here aren't the only options available, and you shouldn't take their inclusion as a recommendation. You must do your own research to find the best options available in your area and for your needs and chosen cryptocurrencies. I discuss choosing a crypto wallet in more detail later in this chapter.

Online wallet

Online wallets may be less secure, but they do have a bunch of advantages for small amounts of cryptocurrencies. An *online* (or *web*) *wallet* allows you access to your cryptos via the Internet. Therefore, as long as you're connected to the Internet (the cloud), you can reach and store your coins and make crypto payments. The online wallet provider stores your wallet's private key on its server. The provider may send you the crypto code but store your keys and give you the ability to access your keys. Different services offer various features, with some of them linking to multiple devices such as your mobile phone, tablet, and computer.

Advantages of online wallets include the following:

>> They enable fast transactions.

>> They may be able to manage multiple cryptocurrencies.

>> They're convenient for use on the go and for active trading.

Disadvantages include these:

>> They risk your online security because of potential vulnerability to hacks and scams.

>> They risk your personal security because of potential exposure to computer viruses.

>> You aren't storing your cryptos; a third party is.

Mobile wallet

Mobile wallets are available on your cellphone through an app. You can use mobile wallets when shopping in physical stores as cryptocurrencies become more acceptable.

Note: Other types of wallets, such as online wallets (see the preceding section), offer mobile versions as well. But some wallets are specifically and only used for mobile phones.

Mobile wallets (which fall into the category of software wallets) have their advantages:

>> They can be safer than online wallets.

>> They're convenient for use on the go.

>> They offer additional features such as QR code scanning.

Some disadvantages of mobile wallets include the following:

>> You risk losing your crypto assets if your phone is lost or damaged unless you at least have your seed phrase secured some place other than your phone (so you can create a new digital wallet).

>> They run the risk of getting mobile viruses and malware.

Desktop wallet

You can download a *desktop wallet* and install it on your computer. Some argue that desktop wallets are safer if your computer isn't, or even better, has never been connected to the Internet. If a desktop computer has never been connected to the Internet, it essentially becomes a cold wallet. On the other hand, a computer that has never been connected to the Internet may expose you to malware that may automatically move from the wallet drive that you connect to the computer and infect the desktop since it's never been patched with software updates that require an Internet connection. Talk about a catch-22!

TIP

To set up your wallet on a computer that has never been connected to the Internet, you must first download the latest version of the wallet on a computer that *is* connected to the Internet. You then move the file to a USB drive or something similar in order to move it to your offline computer.

Some advantages of desktop wallets (which fall into the category of software wallets) include these:

>> They're a convenient choice if you trade cryptos from your computer.

>> You aren't storing your private keys on a third-party server.

>> If your computer has never been connected to the Internet, a desktop wallet can be safer than an online wallet.

But desktop wallets do come with some disadvantages:

>> Using your crypto assets on the go is more difficult.

>> If you connected the wallet to the Internet, it turns into a less secure hot wallet.

>> If you don't back up your computer and it dies, you lose your cryptos.

POPULAR ONLINE, MOBILE, AND DESKTOP WALLETS

Some of the cryptocurrency exchanges I mention in Chapter 6 offer online, mobile, or desktop crypto wallets where you can store the cryptocurrencies you purchase through them. Here are some of most popular ones at the time of writing:

- **Binance.us:** This wallet may be a better fit for more experienced crypto investors. Binance.us incorporates high security and is regulated by the FCA in the United Kingdom and the SEC in the United States. In April 2019, when hackers stole over $40 million in funds from the platform, Binance covered the entire amount for their customers. While the U.S. branch of Binance regulations are fierce, this is not yet true for Binance global at the time of writing. If you use my referral link when signing up, we'll both earn $10 each after you complete $100 worth of trading in 30 days: investdivabinance.com.

- **Coinbase:** Just like Coinbase exchange (see Chapter 6), Coinbase online wallet is user friendly and easy to use. It supports over 170 digital assets and offers multi-signature and two-factor authentication support. You can use the Coinbase Wallet on mobiles and tablets, as well as the Chrome extension on your computer. If you use my referral link, we both get $10 worth of Bitcoin as a gift if you buy/sell $100 worth of cryptos with Coinbase: investdivacoinbase.com.

- **Metamask:** This decentralized online wallet was launched in 2016. With the advent of non-fungible tokens (NFTs), covered in Chapter 14, the Metamask wallet became even more popular. This wallet is mainly used for storing Ethereum (ETH) and can be linked to most NFT market places. The wallet supports thousands of decentralized applications and is compatible with other blockchain solutions and Web3 networks, including Polygon, Binance Smart Chain, and Avalanche. On a desktop,

(continued)

(continued)

you can use the MetaMask wallet on Google Chrome, Microsoft Edge, Mozilla Firefox, and Brave browsers. On mobiles you can use Metamask on Android or Apple devices. You can download the Metamask Wallet here: `metamask.io`.

- **Trust Wallet:** This wallet is owned by Binance, and it has one of the most user-friendly mobile apps for storing your crypto. According to their website, it supports over 160,000 coins and tokens. Just for holding your cryptocurrency, you can earn up to an 11 percent Annual Percentage Rate (APR) in 12 different cryptos. Like Metamask, Trust Wallet is also popular with NFT and decentralized app enthusiasts. You can check out Trust Wallet here: `trustwallet.com`.

Always beware of the amount of risk you're willing to take to gain high APR earnings. Risk and reward are directly correlated, and when companies promise such high earnings, there's always a risk involved. Flip to Chapter 3 to calculate your risk tolerance.

Hardware wallet

A *hardware wallet* can arguably be one of the safest types of crypto wallets out there. These wallets store your private keys on a device like a USB drive. You're still able to make online transactions, but the wallets are offline most of the time, so you can consider them cold wallets.

TIP

For security purposes, a hardware wallet is an absolute must (and a bare minimum) for large crypto amounts. Keeping a ton of your assets on other, less secure types of wallets increases your risk of unrecoverable hacking attacks. Even safer than hardware wallets are paper wallets, which I talk about in the next section.

Here are some advantages of hardware wallets:

>> They're one of the safest crypto wallet options.

>> They're great for storing large amounts of cryptocurrencies that you don't want to use on a day-to-day basis.

Some disadvantages of hardware wallets include the following:

>> They're the most expensive type of wallet.

>> They aren't as user-friendly as other wallets, especially for beginners.

Paper wallet

A *paper wallet* is a super cold crypto wallet. To use it, you print out your private and public keys. You can send funds by transferring the money to the wallet's public address, and you can withdraw or send your currencies by entering your private keys or by scanning the QR code on the paper wallet.

Some of the advantages of paper wallets include these:

>> They're ultra hacker-proof.

>> You don't store them on a computer, mobile phone, or third-party server.

Paper wallets do have some disadvantages, though:

>> They aren't user-friendly for non-geeks.

>> They're harder to use for day-to-day transactions than other wallet types are.

>> They can catch fire.

POPULAR HARDWARE AND PAPER WALLETS

Some of the most popular hardware wallets to store your cryptocurrency include, at the time of writing:

- **Ledger:** Ledger Nano S hardware wallet (priced at $99) is one of the most popular and highly rated secure wallets out there. I personally use Ledger hardware wallets to store my cryptocurrency assets. While it is not the most user-friendly wallet out there, it has kept my crypto secure. You can also connect your wallet to their mobile app, Ledger Live, to track your crypto assets and their value as the market goes up and down. If you use my personalized link you can get the best deal: `earn. investdiva.com/ledger`.

- **Trezor:** This is another popular hardware wallet, storing your cryptocurrency with a high level of security. The maker of this wallet is a part of SatoshiLabs and is head-quartered in Prague, Czech Republic. This wallet is on the pricier side, and pairs with your mobile app through Trezor Suite. You can check them out here: `trezor.io`.

Paper wallet generators include bitaddress.org and paperwalletbitcoin.com (one of the oldest BTC paper wallet generators that still remains active at the time of writing). Another popular choice offering a variety of crypto-related services is Bitcoin.com. It has gained recognition recently and provides different services, including wallets, an exchange, and crypto news. You can create a paper wallet using their wallet generator: `paperwallet.bitcoin.com` (notice the dot after "paperwallet" in this address).

Choosing a Crypto Wallet

Depending on your cryptocurrency needs and goals, you may need more than one type of cryptocurrency wallet. Personally, I use cold wallets to store my larger crypto reserves and hot wallets for active trading. Regardless, you can choose your cryptocurrency wallet(s) based on different characteristics, some of which I discuss in the following sections.

REMEMBER

Make sure you've gathered everything you need to know about a given wallet before committing to getting one.

Based on security

REMEMBER

Even if you're an active crypto trader, I recommend that you have a super secure cold wallet where you store your larger amounts of crypto assets. As I note earlier in this chapter, online wallets aren't the most secure option, however convenient they may be. You can always transfer your assets to an online wallet if you need immediate access to your cryptocurrencies for an investment/shopping opportunity.

Another point to keep in mind is that the most secure hardware wallets are normally the most expensive ones. So you should calculate whether spending that much money for a particular wallet makes sense for the amount of crypto you're going to store in it.

Some questions you must ask before choosing the most secure wallet include the following:

>> What sort of authentication does the wallet use?

>> Is the website secure?

>> What do online reviews say?

TIP

CoinCentral.com, 99Bitcoins.com, and CryptoCompare.com are among the websites that provide an annual crypto wallet review. I normally check with two or more websites before making a decision.

Based on your crypto ownership

Not all crypto wallets can handle your different types of cryptocurrency assets. In fact, some wallets are purpose-built for just one cryptocurrency; many cryptocurrencies have their own official wallets, which can handle only that one crypto.

For example, Bitcoin-specific hot wallets include Bitcoin Core Wallet (bitcoin.org/en/choose-your-wallet), Mycelium (wallet.mycelium.com), and Electrum (electrum.org/#home). For Ethereum, you have options such as Ethereum Wallet (www.ethereum.org), MetaMask (metamask.io) and MyEtherWallet (which is a paper wallet; see www.myetherwallet.com). If you're not planning to diversify among other types of cryptocurrencies, a singular official cryptocurrency wallet may be right for you. Most of the time, you can find the official wallet of a cryptocurrency on the company's website.

Multicurrency wallets are an option for people who want to hold more than one cryptocurrency. The majority of online wallets provided on the exchanges (introduced in Chapter 6) give you the opportunity to store and transact among multiple cryptos. However, if you're using these wallets to store your crypto assets, know that your wallet security may be compromised.

WARNING

I do *not* recommend leaving a large amount of coins in an online exchange wallet.

TIP

Coinomi (www.coinomi.com) is a popular multicoin mobile wallet. It supports more than 200 different digital tokens and a number of blockchains. It's a great multiasset cryptocurrency wallet, but at this writing, it's available for mobile devices only. Exodus (www.exodus.io) is another multicoin wallet, available only on desktop. Your private keys remain secure on your device and never leave it. Exodus can even encrypt the private keys for you.

Based on transaction fees

If you're planning to do a lot of crypto shopping and use digital coins on the go, you may need to be mindful of the transaction fees you're paying along the way. This point is especially true for active traders. If you're a day trader and you're paying more on transaction fees than what you're making in the market, doesn't that defeat the purpose of trading?

Based on anonymity

Anonymity is an extra layer of security you can take into consideration when choosing a crypto wallet. If you use an anonymous wallet, you can separate your personal information from your funds, therefore making it harder for anyone to track down your cryptos and potentially steal them. This factor is something that can be very personal. Some wallets offer full anonymity, while others don't. If anonymity is something that's really important to you, choose among more-private wallets. Note that prioritizing anonymity may affect transaction fees and the price of the wallet.

To find the latest, most popular anonymous wallets, you can simply search the term "anonymous cryptocurrency wallets" on your favorite search engine. Anonymous wallets come in the forms of mobile, hardware, software, and so on. With that, you can have one or more anonymous wallets based on your needs. Some of the popular anonymous wallets at the time of writing include these:

>> **BitLox:** This hardware Bitcoin wallet ensures both security and anonymity. It's capable of holding over 100 wallets with the ability to create millions of addresses for each wallet. Check it out here: www.bitlox.com.

>> **Electrum:** This desktop Bitcoin wallet appears to be one of the most trusted software wallets by the cryptocurrency community. Check it out here: electrum.org/#home.

>> **Samourai:** This wallet is a mobile Bitcoin wallet. According to the Samourai website, the aim is to "to keep your transactions private, your identity masked, and your funds secure." You can check out the company here: samouraiwallet.com.

Keeping Your Wallet Secure

After you've selected the cryptocurrency wallet(s) aligned with your goals, you want to actively keep your investment safe. No matter how secure a wallet is, you still need to take personal steps to enhance that security, just like you'd do with your traditional personal wallet. Because you may be storing a higher value in your cryptocurrency wallets, keeping them safe becomes that much more important. This effort is basically the price you pay for wanting to manage your own money without having to rely on third parties, governments, and big banks. Here are some tips on keeping your wallet safe.

Back up your wallet

WARNING

A famous *Sex and the City* episode has main character Carrie Bradshaw losing her journalism portfolio because she didn't back up her computer. Don't let that happen to your crypto portfolio. Back up your cryptocurrency wallets just like you back up your photos, work files, and computer data.

REMEMBER

A backup of your wallet can protect you against computer failures and many human mistakes. It can also allow you to recover your wallet if your mobile phone or computer is stolen. Of course, you need to keep your backup wallet in a safe place, away from your original wallet. And make sure you back up regularly to ensure that all recent crypto addresses are included in your original wallet.

Additionally, you should also consider keeping a backup of PIN codes, usernames, and passwords if your wallet provides these features. This measure is just in case it has been long enough for you to forget these things. Personally, I keep a hidden file with these items on a secure local cloud for our personal use that is almost impossible to hack.

Have multiple wallets

It's diversification time, baby! If you're having a hard time choosing among the many secure wallets, don't worry. Keeping your assets across multiple wallets is actually a great practice anyway. That way, if any of your wallets are somehow compromised, you don't go bankrupt of cryptocurrencies.

TIP

A good combination is using two or more hardware wallets for larger crypto amounts, with the rest of your smaller amounts spread across mobile, desktop, or online wallets, depending on your everyday use of cryptocurrencies. Of course, all these need to have their own specific backups (as I explain in the preceding section).

Add more security levels

You can add to the security level of your wallets in a number of ways. Here are some suggestions:

>> **Use two-factor authentication (2FA).** If your wallet allows it, *two-factor authentication* is a great way to take the security of your wallet to the next level. It's simply a double authentication of who you are, though it can be done in different ways. Personally, I use the Google Authenticator app, which provides a six-digit code that changes every minute and is unique to you.

>> **Encrypt your wallet.** Encrypting your wallet or your smartphone allows you to set a password for anyone trying to withdraw any funds. This act helps protect against thieves, though it can't protect against keylogging hardware or software (which tracks your keystrokes). You should also consider encrypting your backups. *Note:* Some methods to encrypt may need a bit more technical familiarity. The best way to encrypt your wallet is to contact your wallet provider for more information.

>> **Use a strong password.** A strong password must contain letters, numbers, and punctuation marks and must be at least 16 characters long. Avoid passwords that contain only letters, only numbers, or only symbols. Recognizable English words are also a no-go because they're easy to break.

TIP

You can make a very long, strong password by memorizing a pattern on your keyboard instead of selecting a word. For example, start from the left side of the keyboard and type, top to bottom, the keys along the lines of this pattern (using the shift key after the last lowercase letter): 1qaz2wsx!QAZ@WSX. It's an extremely strong password, and you don't have to memorize it! Of course, if you try to log in to your software from a mobile phone, things can get complicated.

Update your software

REMEMBER

If you're using mobile or desktop wallets, make sure you're using the latest version of the wallet's software. Reputable companies constantly send stability and security fixes. By updating your software regularly, you can make sure that you're using the newest safety features that can prevent problems from minor to severe. (Updating your wallet's software isn't the same as backing it up, which I discuss in the earlier section "Back up your wallet.")

Remember where you hide it!

This suggestion may sound a bit silly, but you have no idea how many times I've tried to hide something valuable, just to lose it forever! If you're one of those people who hides things so well that even you can't remember where they are, make sure you choose a location you won't forget. If you lose your cryptocurrency wallets, you may very well lose your shirt as well in the long run.

Chapter **8**

Different Types of Cryptocurrencies

By now, you probably have heard of the cryptocurrency that started it all: Bitcoin. But Bitcoin is hardly the only famous or even investment-worthy cryptocurrency out there anymore. Heck, some people even think that Bitcoin may be the worst cryptocurrency to own or to invest in. So many other digital coins are available that have made massive improvements to the Bitcoin model to avoid its disadvantages.

TIP

Personally, I still see value in Bitcoin for various reasons: It is the only truly decentralized cryptocurrency, which can give you the ultimate control over your wealth and free you from governments globally. It is a *category king* (it created an entirely new industry and is the most well-known in its category) and has value simply for its brand recognition. There's only ever going to be 21 million Bitcoins out there so if it remains a Category King, its value has nowhere to go but up due to the law of supply and demand. However, there are investors who'd rather avoid investing in Bitcoin due to its high energy consumption, slow and costly transactions, and lack of real utility.

In this chapter, I go over some of the most famous cryptos as of 2022. But because the cryptocurrency market is ever-changing, I explain how you can navigate your way through all the up-and-coming cryptos for years to come.

Different Types of Cryptocurrency

If you've scrolled through any crypto-related article, you may have caught them referring to cryptocurrencies in different terms such as coins, altcoins, and tokens. While some people use these terms interchangeably, there's an actual difference between them.

The following sections present a quick overview of what each term really means.

Coins

Coins are the native cryptocurrencies of the specific blockchain they run on (for more on blockchains, check out Chapter 4). For example, Bitcoin is a coin because it runs on the Bitcoin blockchain. Since Bitcoin was the first ever cryptocurrency, all other coins that are native to a blockchain are considered alternative coins. Therefore, in the world of cryptocurrency, "coin" *only* refers to Bitcoin.

REMEMBER

Some people also consider Ethereum to be a coin as it was the second cryptocurrency out there and it runs on its own blockchain. As cryptocurrencies gained popularity in the 2010s, most other cryptocurrencies were formed as a result of Bitcoin or Ethereum forks — a splitting from the original blockchain (explained in Chapter 5). As blockchain is becoming more mainstream, there are many more novel blockchains popping out.

Altcoins

All cryptocurrency coins other than Bitcoin (and for some people, Ethereum) that run on a native or their own independent blockchain are called *altcoins*. Examples include Litecoin, Dogecoin, and Binance Coin.

TECHNICAL STUFF

The first ever altcoin was Namecoin, which was created in April 2011. Namecoin is a decentralized open-source information registration and transfer system.

Tokens

Tokens are a digital representation of an asset or utility in a blockchain. They usually reside on top of another blockchain (rather than their own independent blockchain). Tokens are meant to serve a different purpose to money, which is what coins and altcoins are all about. They can represent any asset that's fungible. Being *fungible* means that you can replace it with an identical item. For example, you can interchange your 100-dollar bill for any other 100-dollar bill. This makes it fungible.

Tokens can represent all fungible and tradable assets, from commodities to loyalty points and cryptocurrencies. You can even *tokenize* real estate.

REMEMBER

To figure out if you're dealing with a crypto coin or token, you need to find out if the cryptocurrency has its own blockchain. If it does, then it's a *coin*. If it doesn't, but operates on an existing blockchain, then it's a *token*.

Celebrating Celebrity Cryptocurrencies by Market Cap

One of the fastest ways to navigate through popular cryptocurrencies is to check out their ranking based on their *market capitalization,* or *market cap.* Traditionally, market cap is the value of a company that's traded on the stock market. You can calculate it by multiplying the total number of shares by the present share price.

In the cryptoworld, market capitalization shows the value of all units of a specific cryptocurrency that are for sale right now. To calculate a cryptocurrency's market cap, simply multiply the cryptocurrency's current price by its *circulating supply.* Circulating supply is the best approximate number of coins that are circulating in the market and in the general public's hands.

Market cap = Price × Circulating supply

REMEMBER

Knowing about a crypto's market cap and its ranking versus other coins is important because that info can quickly show you how popular the coin is and how much money you may be able to make from it. You can find out about all cryptocurrencies' market caps by visiting websites such as coinmarketcap.com, www.cryptocompare.com, coincodex.com, and www.coingecko.com.

WARNING

Market cap can't tell you everything about a cryptocurrency's investment potential. Lots of other factors, such as forks, regulation, rumors, blockchain, community, utility, mission, and so on, can affect a cryptocurrency's value. I talk more about analyzing a cryptocurrency's performance in Chapter 9.

WARNING

A higher market cap isn't necessarily a good thing. Investors who can take higher risks may prefer cryptocurrencies with a lower market cap because those may offer more room for the market cap to increase. However, if you want to play it safe and avoid volatility or vanishing risk (as I explain in Chapter 3), you may prefer going with cryptocurrencies with a higher market cap.

With a knowledge of what role a coin's market cap plays in the industry, you can start to evaluate cryptocurrencies based on that metric. I discuss Bitcoin and other major cryptocurrencies in the following sections.

Bitcoin

Ranking number one on the list, Bitcoin was developed in 2008. As of September 2022, Bitcoin's market cap is around $385 billion. For comparison, when I wrote the first edition of this book in October 2018, Bitcoin's market cap was $115 billion. So even though at the time of writing Bitcoin has technically crashed from its 2021 all-time highs, its value has tripled within these four years!

A bit of Bitcoin background

TECHNICAL STUFF

An entity called Satoshi Nakamoto invented Bitcoin. Satoshi claimed to be a man living in Japan, born on April 5, 1975. I was actually living in Japan, completing my studies in electrical engineering in Tokyo, when Bitcoin hit the scene. I can tell you that Bitcoin wasn't really a big thing in Japan at that time. That's why most speculation about the true identity of Satoshi points to a number of cryptography and computer science experts of non-Japanese descent living in the United States and various European countries.

But Satoshi's anonymity isn't really a big deal, because Bitcoin (and most other cryptocurrencies, for that matter) are supposed to be open source and decentralized, as I explain in Chapter 5. In fact, according to Bitcoin.org, no single person or entity "owns the Bitcoin network much like no one owns the technology behind email." Bitcoin users around the world control Bitcoin, with the developer improving the software and the forkers making some radical changes. However, the main idea behind Bitcoin and Bitcoin's protocol can't be changed.

Almost ten years after Satoshi published Bitcoin's white paper, Bitcoin's market cap went up to as much as $320 billion by the end of 2017. If you had invested $100 to buy one Bitcoin in 2011 (something my investor friends told me to do that I ignored), you would've had $20,000 worth of Bitcoin by the end of 2017. Of course, many initial investors bought more than one Bitcoin at the time, which is exactly how all those Bitcoin millionaires were made. If you had bought 100 Bitcoins in 2011, by the end of 2017 they would have been worth $2 million.

But by the time everyone started talking about Bitcoin, it went crashing down to around $120 billion and stayed there until 2020. Then came another Bitcoin boom which brought its market cap to over $1 trillion! Then it fell back down but this time to the highs of 2017. Throughout the rollercoaster ride over the years, however, Bitcoin has maintained its number one ranking among all other cryptocurrencies. The main reason behind this position may be that most people have heard a lot (relatively speaking) about Bitcoin but not so much about other cryptocurrencies. So even though they have several hundred other altcoins to choose from, even some that may be better long-term alternatives to Bitcoin, most newbies who want to get involved in the market start out with Bitcoin.

Another reason for Bitcoin's huge market cap is its accessibility. I can pretty safely say that all cryptocurrency exchanges (see Chapter 6) carry Bitcoin. But not all exchanges list all altcoins, at least for now.

Bitcoin characteristics

Here are some main features of Bitcoin:

>> Bitcoin's trading symbol is BTC.

>> Bitcoin is minable.

>> Coin creation occurs through proof-of-work (PoW; see Chapter 5).

>> Transaction time is between 30 minutes and 24 hours.

>> Transactions aren't fully anonymous.

>> Bitcoin is decentralized.

>> Mining Bitcoin requires a lot of (wasted) energy.

TIP

Because Bitcoin has been the superstar of all cryptocurrencies, it tends to pull the entire market along. Generally speaking, the whole market sentiment follows the volatility of Bitcoin in longer-term time frames (with many past exceptions). You can use this piece of information in technical analysis for investing, as I cover in Chapter 18. You can find out more about Bitcoin on its website, bitcoin.org.

Ethereum

Move over Bitcoin, here enters Ethereum! Celebrity cryptocurrencies such as Bitcoin and Ethereum were often criticized for their mining process and the amount of wasted energy they required to exist; that was until September 15, 2022, when Ethereum successfully made an upgrade to its entire network, cutting down its energy consumption by more than 99 percent. Ethereum has maintained its number two rank behind Bitcoin based on coin market cap over the years and at the time of writing. With that, it is safe to say that Ethereum is a major cryptocurrency. As of September 2022, its market cap is around $177 billion . . . a significant jump from its $23 billion market cap when I was writing the first edition of this book in 2018.

WARNING

Remember that past performance is not indicative of future results!

REMEMBER

In mid-September 2022, Ethereum went under a major shift to improve the security and scalability of its blockchain network. These improvements were referred to as Ethereum 2.0 or ETH2.0 before September 2022. This new version uses a different method to verify transactions, called proof-of-stake instead of proof-of-work. Then, something called The Merge happened in September 2022, when the old Ethereum (ETH1.0, the one that's been around since the beginning), joined the new Ethereum (ETH2.0). Now that they have merged, there is only one version of Ethereum.

Brief Ethereum background

Compared to Bitcoin, Ethereum is a younger currency; Russian American Vitalik Buterin proposed it in 2013. It's almost five years younger than Bitcoin, which in the cryptoworld is still a big deal.

TECHNICAL STUFF

Buterin was born in 1994. That's the year the Cranberries sang their hit song "Zombie" and two years before the Backstreet Boys and Spice Girls became famous. If this math makes you feel old, imagine how Bitcoin's Satoshi must feel.

Ethereum uses the old Bitcoin's wisdom and philosophy, but it has a different purpose and capability. According to its website, www.ethereum.org, "Ethereum is a decentralized platform that runs smart contracts." As I explain in Chapter 5, *smart contracts* allow people to create agreements without an intermediary. Ethereum creates these smart contracts by employing the same blockchain technology as Bitcoin. Just as Bitcoin's blockchain and network validate Bitcoin ownership, Ethereum's blockchain validates smart contracts, which the encoded rules execute.

Ethereum versus Bitcoin

Once people learned about the underlying technology that supports Bitcoin, they were eager to utilize it for purposes other than a decentralized payment network. Ethereum was proposed as a network for creating tamper-proof contracts and applications. This means Ethereum is technically not a competitor of Bitcoin, but a complement to it. The main difference between Ethereum and Bitcoin is that Ethereum wants to be the place users go to execute their decentralized applications. In fact, its goal is to be a sort of massive, decentralized computer that executes smart contracts. That's why many other cryptocurrencies can run on the Ethereum platform. The Ethereum blockchain forms a decentralized network where these programs can be executed.

Bitcoin is different in this sense. It was the granddaddy of all crypto and its goal is to radically change the definition of money as we know it and introduce us to a new type of money that operates outside of the control of any government or centralized institution. Its platform gets the miners to compete and solve the complicated blockchain math problems I talk about in Chapter 4. The first one who solves the problem is the winner and gets rewarded. But miners can use Ethereum's platform as a co-working space to create their own products. They get compensated for providing the infrastructure so that inventors can cook their own new types of products.

TIP

In fact, even major technology players like Intel and Microsoft and financial behemoths like J.P. Morgan and Credit Suisse are using the Ethereum platform to create new stuff of their own. Along with other giant founding members, various blockchain start-ups, research groups, and Fortune 500 companies have created a group called the Enterprise Ethereum Alliance (EEA). By September 2022, the alliance had more than 500 members, including Accenture, AMD, Credit Suisse, Dash, Fedex, Pfizer, Samsung, and Toyota, to name a few. You can find out more about the EEA at entethalliance.org.

Ethereum characteristics

Here are some main attributes of Ethereum:

>> Ethereum's token symbol for investors is ETH.

>> Ethereum is minable.

>> Coin creation used to be through PoW, but after its September 2022 update, Ethereum got rid of the PoW mechanism and is now using a new mechanism called proof-of-stake (PoS) that gets rid of puzzles and mining and thus reduces the network's energy consumption by 99.9 percent.

>> Transaction time can be as little as 14 seconds, although it can go higher based on confirmation requirements.

>> Transactions aren't fully anonymous.

>> Ethereum is arguably less decentralized than Bitcoin, although different crypto enthusiasts may have different takes on this.

Ripple

During the first crypto bubble/crash era between 2017 and 2020, Ripple was the third largest cryptocurrency by market cap. It even surpassed Ethereum at the beginning of 2018, temporarily ranking number two. However, after getting into trouble with the U.S. Securities and Exchange Commission (SEC) in 2020, its ranking has dropped to number seven at the time of writing. Regardless, it remains a project with many enthusiasts in its community, a unique mechanism, and governmental issues making it worthy of being mentioned in this book.

Some Ripple background

The idea of Ripple actually goes all the way back to 2004. That's way before Satoshi and Bitcoin. In 2004, Ryan Fugger founded a company called RipplePay. According to blog.bitmex.com/the-ripple-story, the idea behind the protocol was a "peer-to-peer trust network of financial relations that would replace banks." (If that sounds familiar, that's probably because it's also how blockchain works, as I discuss in Chapter 4.)

By 2011, Ripple's target demographic started paying attention to Bitcoin, which was just becoming popular and was doing a better job as a peer-to-peer payment network than Ripple. Ripple's architecture started to shift when an early Bitcoin pioneer, Jed McCaleb, joined the Ripple network in May 2011. Others joined the Ripple bandwagon as time went by.

Finally, Ripple's XRP, a cryptocurrency that also acts as a digital payment network for financial institutions, was released in 2012, according to their website, ripple.com/xrp. Like many other cryptocurrencies, XRP is based on a public chain of cryptographic signatures. That being said, Ripple is very different from traditional cryptos like Bitcoin and even Ethereum.

REMEMBER

Some people don't consider Ripple a true cryptocurrency. Also, Ripple as a company and Ripple the cryptocurrency are two different things, although they're connected. Ripple the company does business as Ripple Labs, Inc., is a money transfer network designed to serve the needs of the financial services industry, and provides global payment solutions for big financial institutions using blockchain technology. Ripple the cryptocurrency, which trades as XRP, is the native cryptocurrency on the Ripple network that is used with some of the company's payment systems to facilitate transactions on the network.

Ripple versus Bitcoin

Here are some of the key differences between these two cryptocurrencies:

>> **Purpose and usage:** Bitcoin is a cryptocurrency based on a decentralized blockchain intended as a means for payment for goods and services. Ripple (XRP) runs on the XRP ledger, a blockchain that uses a distributed consensus mechanism via a group of bank-owned servers. XRP's main utility is to allow fast transactions between big financial institutions.

>> **Ownership and decentralization:** As I talk about earlier in this chapter, Bitcoin is owned by no particular person or entity, and Bitcoin the cryptocurrency is pretty

much the same as Bitcoin the open-source platform. That's why Bitcoin is highly decentralized and open source, owned by a community that agrees on changes. This setup can make upgrades tough and is why Bitcoin has had a ton of forks (hard and soft; see Chapter 5) in its history.

By contrast, Ripple is a private company called Ripple Labs, with offices all over the world. Ripple's digital asset (cryptocurrency) is called XRP and is also owned by Ripple Labs. The company constantly looks to please everyone (especially its partners) and come up with consensus, which can allow for faster upgrades. It has an amendment system with which the developers seek consensus before making changes to the network. In most cases, if an amendment receives 80 percent support for two weeks, it comes into effect, and all future ledgers must support it. Basically, Ripple is a democracy that tries to avoid hard forks and nasty splits!

TIP

You can find out more about Ripple and its most recent updates at `ripple.com`.

>> **Transaction speed and fees:** This area is where Ripple really starts to shine. Bitcoin's transaction speed can sometimes go up to an hour depending on fees. And the fees can reach $40 depending on demand.

Ripple's transactions, on the other hand, can settle in as little as four seconds. Fee-wise, even when the demand was super high at the end of 2017, Ripple's transaction fees averaged $0.007 — a fraction of that of Bitcoin. XRP transactions are faster than Ethereum but not faster than Solana, a cryptocurrency that became an investor favorite in 2021.

TIP

You can compare different cryptocurrencies' historical transaction fees at `bitinfocharts.com/comparison/transactionfees-btc-xrp.html`.

>> **Number of transactions per second:** At any given second, you can make around ten Bitcoin transactions. Enter Ripple, and raise the number to 1,500. Although some Bitcoin forks aim to resolve this issue, at the time of writing Ripple appears to be ahead of the game.

>> **Coin amount limits:** Bitcoin and other minable cryptocurrencies have finite numbers of coins, which come into the market only through mining. But XRP is limited to the 100 billion coins in circulation now, largely to appeal to Ripple's (the company's) biggest clients, which are large financial institutions.

Ripple characteristics

The following list gives you a summary of Ripple's main features:

>> Ripple's token symbol for investors is XRP.

>> Ripple's XRP isn't minable. No miners whatsoever.

>> Coin creation and algorithm processing happens through consensus, *not* PoW.

>> Transaction time can be as little as four seconds.

>> Transactions can be made anonymous.

>> Ripple isn't fully decentralized.

>> Energy cost per transaction is minor.

REMEMBER

Because these unique features are so different from Bitcoin's, some people believe Ripple's XRP isn't truly a cryptocurrency. Ripple is actually a strange hybrid of a *fiat currency* (the traditional form of currency backed by a local government, such as the U.S. dollar) and a traditional cryptocurrency. This deviation is because Ripple primarily has been seeking to serve financial institutions like American Express instead of focusing on the spread of Ripple's XRP among everyday users. This may very well change in the future.

Cardano

Cardano entered the cryptocurrency game as an alternative to Ethereum by (surprise, surprise) the cofounder of Ethereum, Charles Hoskinson, in 2015. Both Ethereum and Cardano have the same goal of providing a platform for other applications and building a connected and decentralized system.

Cardano considers itself as an updated version of Ethereum, however, at the time of writing, Cardano still remains under construction. Regardless of that, Cardano and Charles Hoskinson have been able to gain momentum, which has brought Cardano's cryptocurrency, ADA's market cap, into the top ten largest cryptocurrencies.

TIP

Check out my interview with Cardano founder Charles Hoskinson to learn more about the network: investdiva.com/charles-hoskinson-interview-from-ethereum-to-cardano-and-iohk.

Cardano versus Ethereum 2.0

Cardano is a direct competitor to Ethereum and especially the new version of Ethereum. Ethereum 2.0 moved the platform from a PoW system (which is what Bitcoin uses) to a PoS system (which is what Cardano uses). You can use both Cardano and Ethereum for peer-to-peer transactions and run custom programming logic (also known as *smart contracts*). Here are some of the differences between the two:

- **Coin limitation:** Ethereum has no coin limitation. Kind of like oxygen that can be produced by trees, Ethereum can produce an unlimited number of ETH coins only capped on an annual basis. That means Ethereum can grow by 4.5 percent per year. However, Cardano has a total limited supply of 45 billion tokens. Some may argue that having a supply limit may increase the coin's value.
- **Scalability:** Cardano and Ethereum are both dedicated to managing smart contracts and decentralized apps. However, Cardano focuses on functionality by using a dual-layer design. Ethereum focuses on mass adoption by using a single-layer solution.

Cardano characteristics

Cardano's main traits include the following:

- Cardano's token symbol for investors is ADA.
- Cardano works on a PoS system.
- Transaction time is around five minutes.
- Transactions are comparatively anonymous, but if you purchase from an exchange or a trading platform, they will know your details.
- Cardano is decentralized.
- Cardano is one of the most eco-friendly coins, and only uses an estimated 0.00277429 terawatt-hours per year. Compare that to Bitcoin, which uses an estimated 127 terawatt-hours. This makes Cardano 47,200 times more energy-efficient than Bitcoin!

TIP

Most crypto enthusiasts typically argue that their platform is the best. The best way to go about your investment strategy may be to diversify your assets not only between these options but also among the other categories of cryptocurrencies I cover in this chapter. Find out more about diversification in Chapter 10.

Other top ten major cryptos

In the preceding sections, I introduce some of the most well-known cryptocurrencies that also have some of the largest market capitalizations on average. But being famous doesn't mean they're necessarily better. In fact, many analysts and investors believe some of these celebrity cryptocurrencies may vanish within ten years (as I explain in Chapter 3). For example, in the first edition of this book, I had Litecoin listed in the top ten, but at the time of writing, Litecoin has dropped to number 23 based on market cap, and there's not much clout going on about it. Also, having a bigger market cap doesn't necessarily mean having a brighter future. Their current popularity may just be the proverbial 15 minutes of fame, and they may therefore have lower growth opportunities compared to those that are less known.

REMEMBER

Chances are that if anything should happen to a core cryptocurrency, a hard fork may come along that saves it. As I explain in Chapter 5, if you've already invested in a cryptocurrency when it forks, you get the same amount of new coins anyway. That's why I've recommended to my Premium Investing Group (Invest Diva PIG) members in 2017–2018 to start their cryptocurrency portfolio by first diversifying among the top ten largest ones by market cap and then getting into other, different categories.

One of the biggest cryptocurrencies in 2021–2022 was Dogecoin, for example, which got a lot of hype from Elon Musk and his followers. Personally, I believe Dogecoin only has value because Elon Musk said so! At the time of writing, Dogecoin doesn't solve any core problems, besides making crypto fun. When it comes to long-term investing, I prefer to invest in projects that solve a tangible problem. Regardless, Dogecoin has remained in the top ten list by market cap.

Table 8-1 shows some cryptocurrencies (listed alphabetically) that were on the top 20 list more consistently during 2022. Please note that I have not personally invested in some of these cryptocurrencies.

TABLE 8-1 **Some Top Twenty Cryptos as of 2022**

Crypto	Symbol	Description
Avalanche (www.avax.network)	AVAX	Another of Ethereum's competitors that aims to have a higher transaction output while not compromising scalability.
Binance Coin (www.binance.com)	BNB	The cryptocurrency of the largest global crypto exchange in the world, Binance.
Chainlink (https://chain.link)	LINK	One of the first networks to allow the integration of off-chain data into smart contracts, and one of the major players in the data procession field.
Dogecoin (dogecoin.com)	DOGE	A popular Internet meme coin that features a Shiba Inu on its logo. It started as a joke and was promoted by Tesla CEO Elon Musk during 2021–2022.
Polkadot (polkadot.network)	DOT	The leading protocol for Web3, a decentralized Internet of blockchains that can be interoperable with each other.
Solana (solana.com)	SOL	Launched in March 2020 in Switzerland, Solana is one of the fastest growing blockchains focused on decentralized finance (DeFi).

Top 100 major cryptos

You can dive into the top 100 major cryptocurrencies and still not find *the one* you want to have a long-term relationship with. At this point, selecting cryptocurrencies that match your portfolio really becomes like online dating. You've got to make some decisions based on first impressions and then go on dates (start making small investments and do more research) to discover whether a currency is worthy of a bigger chunk of your crypto portfolio.

TIP

You can find the list of all cryptocurrencies ranked based on their market cap at any given time here: coinmarketcap.com.

Cryptocurrencies by Category

As an alternative to selecting cryptocurrencies by market cap, the best way to truly diversify your portfolio, for both value and growth purposes, may be to go about selecting cryptocurrencies by category. After you've flipped through the categories and selected the finalists that best fit your risk tolerance (see Chapter 3), you can then move on to the advanced techniques I discuss in Chapters 9 and 10 and in Part 4.

Here are some of the most popular cryptocurrency categories and the leading cryptos in each space. I cover these based on their popularity and total market cap as of 2022. Some popular cryptocurrency categories include the following:

» Decentralized finance

» Utility

» Exchange

» Payment

» Privacy

» Stablecoins

» Platform

» Fintech/finance

» Legal/property

» NFTs/collectibles

» Metaverse

- » Gaming/gambling
- » Supply chain
- » Transportation
- » Medical/healthcare

The following sections describe just a few examples of these categories in the exciting cryptocurrency world; you may recognize some of the currencies from their coverage earlier in this chapter. Other people may categorize these cryptos differently.

REMEMBER

Keep in mind that some categories are hotter as of this writing, but others may have become more popular by the time you get this book in your hands. Also know that some cryptos are hybrids of multiple categories and are hard to fit in only one box. You can find the latest different crypto categories by searching "cryptocurrency categories" on your favorite search engine.

Decentralized Finance (DeFi) cryptos

Decentralized finance (DeFi) aims to allow anyone with access to the Internet to lend, borrow, and bank without going through traditional intermediaries. DeFi is an unregulated financial system that many people believe will potentially revolutionize the way we conduct financial transactions.

WARNING

However, because DeFi is still primarily unregulated, investors do not enjoy the same protection that they do in traditional financial markets. That being said, despite some risks, the benefits of DeFi could be considered numerous because of the sheer level of transparency involved in transactions and no banks or other financial institutions are needed to oversee your money.

Ultimately, DeFi works to replace the traditional role of financial systems through its smart contracts. In summary, any cryptocurrency that has its main focus on finance or decentralization can be considered a DeFi.

Here are some examples of DeFi Cryptos:

- » **Avalanche (AVAX):** Avalanche is a smart contract-capable blockchain platform which focuses on lightning-fast transaction speed, low costs, and overall eco-friendliness. Avalanche is aiming to deliver an easily scalable blockchain that doesn't sacrifice security or decentralization. See www.avax.network.

- >> **Uniswap (UNI):** Uniswap is the largest decentralized exchange (or DEX) operating on the Ethereum blockchain. It allows worldwide users to trade crypto without involving an intermediary. See `uniswap.org`.

- >> **Chainlink (LINK):** Chainlink is a decentralized oracle network that provides real-world data to smart contracts on the blockchain. Smart contracts are pre-determined agreements on the blockchain that evaluate information and then automatically execute when certain specific conditions are met. LINK tokens are therefore the digital asset token used to actually pay for services on the network. Chainlink's sophisticated technology has so far proven to be one of the most important pillars of the DeFi and wider crypto ecosystem. See `https://chain.link`.

Utility cryptos

Utility tokens are a type of cryptocurrency designed to be used for a specific purpose in a certain ecosystem. Utility tokens allow users to do certain things on a specific blockchain network or decentralized application.

REMEMBER

Utility tokens are different from other kinds of tokens, as they can only be used in certain ecosystems. For example, the Basic Attention Token or BAT is useful only on the Brave Browser. BAT can be used to tip content creators on the Brave Browser or in other applications that have a BAT wallet. You also need to understand that BAT doesn't have any other use than being traded for its value. It's just like other utility tokens. Utility tokens are also pre-mined and created in a certain quantity which is determined by the team behind the project.

Exchange-specific cryptos

Exchange-specific cryptos are the cryptos that (mainly) the cryptocurrency exchanges introduce and use. You can think of these cryptos as incentives that bring people to the exchanges' platforms.

To select the best exchange-specific cryptocurrency, you can consider taking the steps I introduce in Chapter 6 for choosing the best cryptocurrency exchange.

Here are a few examples of these currencies:

- >> **Binance Coin (BNB):** Issued by Binance exchange, Binance Coin runs on the Ethereum platform and has a strict maximum limit of 200 million BNB tokens. See `www.binance.com`.

>> **KuCoin Shares (KCS):** KuCoin Shares is just like Binance Coin but for the KuCoin exchange. See www.kucoin.com.

>> **FTT Token (FTT):** FTT is the utility token on the FTX exchange. It can be used to reduce trading fees on the exchange or serve as collateral against futures positions. See ftx.com.

>> **Cronos Token (CRO):** Cronos (CRO) is a utility token designed by Crypto.com and issued on the Crypto.com exchange to facilitate transactions within its blockchain and is a full-service decentralized finance provider and exchange. See crypto.com.

Payment cryptos

Payment cryptos are by far the biggest category in terms of total market cap. In this group, you find cryptocurrencies that mainly aim to be used as a store of value, transaction, and payments, just like fiat currencies like the U.S. dollar. Examples of cryptocurrencies that fall into this category include these:

>> Bitcoin (BTC)

>> Litecoin (LTC)

>> Bitcoin Cash (BCH)

>> OMG Network (OMG)

>> Dash (DASH)

>> Ripple (XRP)

>> Tether (USDT; https://tether.to)

>> Algorand (ALGO)

>> Stellar (XLM)

TIP

With Bitcoin as the pioneer, no wonder this category started out so popular. But as I say multiple times throughout this book, blockchain technology can be applied to so much more than just payment systems, so be on the lookout for the next big thing within other hot categories!

Privacy cryptos

Privacy cryptos are heavily focused toward transaction security and anonymity, a lot more than those in the payment category are. In fact, the idea that Bitcoin and other cryptocurrencies in the payment category are fully anonymous and untraceable is a common misconception. Many blockchains only disguise users' identities while leaving behind a public record of all transactions that have occurred on the blockchain. The data in the ledger often includes how many tokens a user has received or sent in historical transactions, as well as the balance of any cryptocurrency in the user's wallet.

WARNING

Privacy cryptos can be a bit controversial because authorities see them as an illicit tool that criminals could use to engage in illegal activities, such as money laundering. Nonetheless, some of them have gained popularity. Here are some examples:

>> **Monero (XMR):** Monero is the most famous privacy crypto as of 2022.

>> **Zcash (ZEC):** Zcash is similar to Monero but has a different protocol (set of rules). See https://z.cash.

>> **Decred (DCR):** Decred is a cryptocurrency primarily designed for community input, open governance, privacy, and sustainable funding for development. It also operates a hybrid consensus mechanism. See decred.org.

Stablecoin cryptos

Stablecoins are a type of cryptocurrency, a digital asset whose value is directly linked (*pegged*) to an external and generally stable asset class such as a specific fiat currency like the U.S. dollar or gold. The cryptocurrency market is fairly volatile and stablecoins can therefore offer a less risky way of storing money on the blockchain as they maintain a predictable price range.

REMEMBER

Stablecoins are used completely differently than other cryptocurrencies that people tend to buy as an investment. They are often used to send money digitally to another party in the world. They are also used as a way of transferring your own funds between cryptocurrency exchanges as well as storing funds on an exchange so that you can quickly use them to purchase other cryptocurrencies. Some online platforms even allow you to lend out your stablecoins in order to earn high rates of interest.

Here are some popular examples of stablecoins:

>> **Tether (USDT):** Tether is designed to provide a stable price point at all times. The Tether stablecoin was created to function as the internet's Digital Dollar, with each token being worth $1.00 USD and backed by $1.00 USD in physical reserves. See tether.to/en.

>> **USD Coin (USDC):** USD Coin is another popular stablecoin like Tether and shares similar characteristics. USDC is often described as potentially a safer stablecoin as it places huge emphasis on transparency of its fully backed reserves as well as great effort to comply with government regulation and audits. See www.circle.com/en/usdc.

>> **Binance USD (BUSD):** BUSD is a stablecoin founded by Paxos and Binance. It is a regulated, fiat-backed stablecoin pegged to the U.S. dollar. For every unit of BUSD, there is one U.S. dollar held in reserve. The supply of BUSD is pegged to the U.S. dollar at a ratio of 1:1. As an example, when the price of the U.S. dollar rises or falls, the price of BUSD also does in equal amounts. This is the most traditional model of stablecoin. See www.binance.com/en/busd.

Platform cryptos

Platform cryptos are also referred to as *decentralized application protocol cryptos, smart contract cryptos,* or a hybrid of all three. In this category, you can find cryptocurrencies that are built on a centralized blockchain platform; developers use them to build decentralized applications. In other words, such cryptocurrencies act as platforms where people build upon blockchain applications (and thus other cryptocurrencies).

TIP

In fact, some analysts suggest you may want to forget about payment cryptocurrencies and invest in crypto platforms instead. They're generally considered good long-term investments because they rise in value as more applications are created on their blockchain. As blockchain technology becomes more mainstream, the number of applications and their usage will increase, along with the price of such coins.

The most famous example in this category is Ethereum (ETH). Others include the following:

>> **NEO (NEO):** A smart contracts ecosystem similar to Ethereum, NEO wants to be a platform for a new smart economy. NEO is China's largest cryptocurrency.

>> **Lisk (LSK):** Lisk is a smart contracts platform similar to Ethereum but based on JavaScript. See https://lisk.io.

>> **EOS (EOS):** Another smart contracts platform similar to Ethereum, EOS has performance and scalability benefits.

>> **Icon (ICX):** Icon wants to "Hyperconnect the World" by building one of the largest decentralized global networks. See https://m.icon.foundation.

- » **Qtum (QTUM):** Qtum is a Singapore-based Ethereum and Bitcoin hybrid. See `qtum.org`.

- » **VeChain (VEN):** VeChain is a blockchain-based platform that gives retailers and consumers the ability to determine the quality and authenticity of products they buy. See `www.vechain.org`.

- » **Ark (ARK):** Ark wants to provide an all-in-one blockchain solution for developers and start-ups. See `https://ark.io`.

- » **Substratum (SUB):** Substratum wants to create a new generation of Internet. See `substratum.net`.

These are just a few of hundreds of cryptocurrencies that are emerging in this category.

Finance and fintech cryptos

Here I group pure financial cryptos with financial technology (fintech) cryptocurrencies. These cryptos facilitate the creation of a financial system for the blockchain and for people around the world:

- » **Ripple (XRP):** Ripple is a blockchain payment system for banks, payment providers, digital asset exchanges, and other companies. It's designed to move large amounts of money quickly and reliably. See `ripple.com`.

- » **Stellar (XLM):** Stellar aims to develop the world's new financial system. It's building an open system where people of all income levels can access financial services. See `www.stellar.org`.

- » **OMG Network (OMG):** OMG Network is designed to enable financial services for people without bank accounts. It works worldwide and with both traditional money (fiat currency) and cryptocurrencies. See `https://omg.network`.

- » **Quoine (QASH):** Quoine wants to solve the liquidity problem in the cryptocurrency market through its LIQUID platform. See `quoine.com`.

- » **Bancor (BNT):** Bancor lets you convert between two cryptocurrencies of your choice without another party. See `www.bancor.network`.

- » **Crypto.com (CRO) (formerly Monaco, MCO):** This cryptocurrency-funded Visa debit card allows you to spend your coins on everyday purchases. See `crypto.com`.

Legal and property cryptos

More cryptocurrencies are emerging in the two categories of legal and property cryptos. But because they're related, I've grouped them together here for now. Here are a couple of examples:

>> **Polymath (POLY):** Polymath helps provide legal advice for token investors and smart contract developers. See https://polymath.network.

>> **Propy (PRO):** Propy solves problems of purchasing properties across borders when using fiat currencies or cryptocurrencies. It's the first company to ever sell a property on the blockchain and using Bitcoin. See propy.com.

Other up-and-coming property cryptocurrencies include REAL and REX, but at the time of writing they're way down on the cryptocurrency market cap ranking list.

NFTs and collectibles cryptos

NFTs (non-fungible tokens) are cryptographic assets on a specific blockchain with unique identification codes and metadata that distinguish them from each other. NFTs are therefore not able to be replicated but they can represent collectible real-world items, the most popular and well-known being artwork. For more on NFTs, see Chapter 14.

Here are a few of examples of NFT related crypto coins/tokens:

>> **Flow (FLOW):** Flow is a blockchain platform that allows for fast, low-cost transactions and supports smart contracts. It powers blockchain applications including NBA Top Shot, a non-fungible token (NFT) offering. See flow.com.

>> **Chiliz (CHZ):** Chiliz is an Ethereum token that powers Socios.com, a platform that lets users trade tokens to show their support and appreciation for professional sports teams. It runs on an Ethereum-based Chiliz blockchain and the token effectively serves as currency which allows users to purchase NFTs at Chiliz's Socios fan token marketplace. See www.chiliz.com/en.

>> **ApeCoin (APE):** ApeCoin is a token that serves many functions within the APE ecosystem, which is made up of individual token holders and the products and services utilizing the token. It's closely affiliated with an NFT project known as the Bored Ape Yacht Club (BAYC), a hugely successful and highly valuable collection of 10,000 uniquely different cartoon-styled ape drawings each with their distinctive look! See apecoin.com.

Metaverse cryptos

The integration of Metaverse cryptos with blockchain infrastructure enables them to make virtual items exchangeable for real economic value beyond the confines of the metaverse. These cryptocurrencies are especially popular in the gaming world.

The metaverse is the perfect collision between the physical world and digital worlds when virtual reality and augmented reality bridge the gap and allow the physical and virtual worlds to interact closely.

Here are some examples:

>> **Decentraland (MANA):** Decentraland is a virtual-reality blockchain-based platform. It allows for a virtual world where users can buy, develop, and sell virtual land and estates (LAND) as well as gaining access to Avatar wearables and names in the Decentraland Marketplace. See decentraland.org.

>> **The Sandbox (SAND):** The Sandbox is an Ethereum-based metaverse and gaming ecosystem where users can create, share, and monetize in-world assets and many other different types of gaming experiences. Users have the option of buying and selling virtual land and creating virtual communities, as well as purchasing NFT collections and digital avatar accessories. See www.sandbox.game/en.

Gaming cryptos

Gaming cryptos are cryptocurrencies that are used on gaming platforms. These platforms reward gamers with cryptos for playing games or being active on the platform.

Crypto gaming tokens are special items that represent gaming assets, such weapons, skins, skills, and customizations. Some of the famous gaming coins at the time of writing include Decentraland (MANA), Sandbox (SAND), and Axie Infinity (AXS).

Other crypto categories

Blockchain technology can be used in almost any project including supply chain, transportation, and the medical industries. For example, for the supply chain industry, the blockchain technology is a way to make sure that companies can track all types of transactions more securely and transparently. This is important because it can help companies figure out where products came from and where they are now. Every time a product changes hands, the transaction is documented on the blockchain, creating a permanent history. This can be helpful for companies that work together on one platform because it reduces the time delays, costs, and human error associated with transactions.

Blockchain technology is also used for many purposes in the healthcare industry, including securing patient data and managing the pharmaceutical supply chain.

TIP

You can always learn about the most recent developments in each crypto category by searching the name of the category and adding "crypto" on your favorite search engine. My team and I also regularly update our most recent strategies here: investdivapig.com.

IN THIS CHAPTER

» **Using IDDA to identify the best cryptos**

» **Flipping through thousands of cryptos with fundamental analysis**

» **Selecting the right cryptos for you through market sentiment analysis**

» **Pinpointing the best time to buy and sell**

Chapter 9

Identifying Top Performing Cryptocurrencies

I n Chapter 8, I open a huge window to all the different categories of cryptocurrencies because this whole industry isn't just about Bitcoin or a few other famous cryptos you may have already heard of. Having so many options to choose from is exciting! But just like dating in the digital age, having too many options can be tricky. You're always keeping an eye open for the next best thing.

The good news is that you can have multiple "right" cryptocurrencies for you. But swiping through so many cryptocurrencies can become challenging, especially if you don't know exactly what you're looking for.

In this chapter, I guide you through finding your best crypto match(es) by introducing you to my golden strategy development method, the Invest Diva Diamond Analysis (IDDA).

Introducing the Invest Diva Diamond Analysis

Most individual investors learn one or two methods for analyzing the markets before pulling the trigger and actually executing an investment strategy. For example, most newbie investors rely on things like technical analysis and their favorite economic news anchors on TV. Unfortunately, depending on only one type of analysis can be incredibly dangerous.

REMEMBER

Enter the Invest Diva Diamond Analysis (IDDA)! The IDDA suggests analyzing the markets from five different points, as you can see in Figure 9-1:

1. Intentional analysis

2. Capital analysis (personal risk management)

3. Fundamental analysis

4. Technical analysis

5. Sentimental (market sentiment) analysis

FIGURE 9-1:
Five points of
the Invest
Diva Diamond
Analysis (IDDA).

© John Wiley & Sons, Inc.

Flip to Chapter 3 to read about risk management (part of the capital analysis point); for a comprehensive Masterclass on the IDDA, please visit `investdiva.com/masterclass`. In the rest of this chapter, I discuss fundamentals and market sentiment analysis and introduce technical analysis to help you pick the right cryptocurrencies at the right prices for your portfolio. Here's a brief overview of these concepts:

>> **Fundamental analysis:** As a fundamental analyst, you look at the fundamental value a blockchain or cryptocurrency project produces, and evaluate data from facts to rumors to decide whether that asset is worth buying.

>> **Technical analysis:** As a technical analyst, you look at how an asset's price has been performing, identify the past key psychological prices the market as a whole has been eyeing, and then you make an investment decision that is right for you.

More specifically, you analyze the price action of your favorite cryptocurrency to see the best time to jump into a relationship and a good time to call it quits. You can see the history of the crypto price actions on something called *charts* that are available on your cryptocurrency exchange. (Head to Chapter 18 to discover all the dirty secrets about technical analysis methods.)

>> **Sentimental analysis:** *Market sentiment* gauges the emotions and attitudes of traders in the market about a specific asset. Using sentimental analysis, even non-animal-lovers in the investing world compare market expectations to bulls and bears.

REMEMBER

If traders expect upward price movement of a specific security, the sentiment is said to be *bullish*. On the contrary, if the market sentiment is *bearish,* most traders expect downward price movement.

TECHNICAL STUFF

I first introduced the Invest Diva Diamond Analysis (IDDA) investment strategy development method in my book *Invest Diva's Guide to Making Money in Forex* (McGraw-Hill Education, 2013). I no longer trade forex but this very method then became the key strategy for investing in other assets such as stocks and cryptocurrencies for all my clients and students, from investing.com and Nasdaq to my own educational products for universities in New York and for our very own Invest Diva Movement that has now served over 300,000 students. (Check out some of our student success stories here: investdivareviews.com.)

Using Fundamental Analysis to Pick Cryptocurrencies

Fundamental analysis is the art of making sense of all the gossip, stories, and facts about an asset, the problems its solving, its long-term value, whether or not it's going to be relevant in the time frame you'd want to be invested in it, its financial situation, and upcoming risk events that may move the market. You can apply the same fundamental analysis approach you'd use for stocks to cryptocurrencies. Going back to the dating metaphor at the start of this chapter, finding the right crypto category is like picking your type in a significant other. Except in this case, you should most certainly think with your brain. And maybe a little bit with your gut feeling. But nothing more than that (if you catch my drift). Here are some methods you can use to cherry-pick the best crypto assets for you.

Go with what you know

Going with what you know is a golden yet simple method also used in the stock market. If you've already been exposed to certain types of cryptocurrencies or, better yet, used them in real life and have liked their performance, consider adding them to your portfolio. In the stock market, for example, many newbie investors make several profitable investments by simply observing their own buying habits. If they prefer to buy from healthier fast-food services like Chipotle (CMG on the New York Stock Exchange, or NYSE) rather than McDonald's (NYSE: MCD), they may consider adding CMG to their portfolio.

Similarly, say you notice that your favorite online store has already added a cryptocurrency payment option to its checkout page and you place an order with it smoothly. That success may be an indication that the trading volume for that cryptocurrency will increase in the future, and the crypto may become a valuable asset for your portfolio.

TIP

Investing in what (or who) you know is by far my favorite investing strategy development method. This goes far beyond investing in online financial markets. Think about who you know the most about . . . who would that be? It's likely that the one person you know the most about in the world is yourself. That's why on the top level of the Invest Diva Movement, we prioritize investing in yourself. Investing in yourself can mean investing in your health, your relationships, or learning high-income generation skills that can increase your wealth. For example, you are right now investing in yourself by reading this book to learn about the next generation of investing (congratulations!). As you accumulate high-income-producing skills, no matter what direction the world or the economy goes, you are always going to be there for yourself. For more about investing in yourself to acquire high-income producing skills and building generational wealth, visit wealthdiva.com.

Choose the right categories

In Chapter 8, I talk a huge deal about crypto categories and where you can find them. Certain categories perform better at certain times in the overall market, not just the crypto market. So, for example, if you notice that the decentralized finance (DeFi) sector is heading higher in equities and that everyone is talking about artificial intelligence (AI), you may want to consider browsing through the AI category and finding cryptocurrencies that are involved with it.

Another way to pick the best categories for medium-term investments is to choose from categories that are already outperforming the overall market. I'm not talking about a category that did well just today but rather something that either has been doing well for a few months or even years or is showing signs of picking up. You can pick the hottest category as your top pick and then add on the second and third ones for diversification purposes. I talk more about diversification in Chapter 10.

REMEMBER

The cryptocurrency categories may not always follow the rest of the market. Because cryptocurrency is a very new industry to begin with, you may find opportunities in it that you may not necessarily find in the more traditional equities market. Heck, the crypto industry may turn into a safety net if the stock market crashes.

TIP

Exchange traded funds (ETFs) normally consist of a basket of a number of assets in the same category. They're super popular in the equities market because they make the choosing process much easier. They're also cheaper to purchase than their big, fancy hedge-fund equivalents, mutual funds.

Personally, I'm not the biggest fan of ETFs or Index Funds because it doesn't give me enough control over my portfolio. Investing in Index Funds is kind of like taking the bus: If you don't have a driver's license, you better take the bus because if you drive a car, you're likely gonna crash. But if you have educated yourself on investing principles (like you're doing now), you might consider building your own portfolio. Investing in individual assets is like driving your own car. You don't have to stop at every bus stop, you have more control over the route you take to reach your destination, and you can even have multiple destinations as you please!

Check out cryptos' websites

Whether you have a number of cryptocurrencies in mind based on your own experience or you've picked a category and now want to choose the best crypto within that sector, you must now start a more detailed analysis on your finalists.

If you've ever watched *The Bachelor* or *The Bachelorette* on TV (guilty as charged — I'm addicted), you're probably already familiar with the process. You start out with around 30 potential matches for your portfolio. By the time you're down to the three or four finalists, you're ready to see what their worlds are all about. In the cryptocurrency world, the company's website is the equivalent of the TV hometown dates. Here are a few ideas to consider when you're picking your crypto sweethearts that don't involve visiting their high schools and getting a grilling from their families.

Flip through their white papers

A *white paper* is something like a business proposal for new cryptocurrencies. It includes everything potential investors need to know about the crypto, such as technology, purpose, financial details, and so on. More-established cryptocurrencies may already have a page that breaks down all this critical information into easy-to-understand video clips and cool infographics on tabs titled "About" or "How It Works." For others, you may just need to find the white paper on the website and try to digest the information by reading. The good news is that white papers are often written in a language that people who aren't experts in the field can understand.

Identify their teams

No one really knows who created Bitcoin, but the rest of the cryptocurrencies out there normally have a team behind them who guide the company and its blockchain technology (see Chapter 4). The team behind the crypto is important even if its platform is completely open source, which means anyone can access and modify it.

REMEMBER

When you invest in anything, whether it's stocks, a new start-up, or a hot date, understanding the background and how it came to life can play a major role. Here are some things to look for in the management:

>> Bios

>> Resumes

>> Experience in the field

In addition to the core management, I also like to check the backgrounds of the members of the board of advisors if the company has it. You normally can find such information on the company's website, under tabs labeled things like "About Us" or "Our Team."

TIP

When you invest in a cryptocurrency, you're essentially investing in a start-up company, an entrepreneur, and its community of people. Sometimes these entrepreneurs are young with no qualifying resume, just like Facebook's Mark Zuckerberg or Ethereum founder Vitalik Buterin. That's when the creator's personality can become a factor in your decision making. As Mark Cuban (*Shark Tank* investor and Dallas Mavericks owner) told CNBC, "When you invest in an entrepreneur, you get the personality. And if that's not appropriate or you don't think it's right, buy another stock" (or in this case, crypto).

Playing the devil's advocate here, I think it's also important to remember that the leader of any movement (whether it's a company, a blockchain, or a government) is essentially the "attractive character" that has the power to either attract or repel the kind of people they want in the community as defined by their culture. Sometimes, the more polarizing an attractive character, the stronger the community, and therefore the greater the chance of success.

Browse their partnerships

If you're not willing to take a lot of risk, seeing who in the industry has put their trust in the hands of the cryptocurrency you're considering buying is very important. More established blockchains have been able to team up with traditional giants like IBM and Microsoft and banks like Goldman Sachs. These companies have expert analytic teams perform due diligence before jumping on board with new investments and partnerships. Having reputable partners can be a sign that the company is solid and on the right track to get ahead of the competition.

Another good thing about having partners in the traditional world is that the cryptocurrency may have a higher chance of getting accepted by the masses. If a cryptocurrency has established partnerships with other companies, they are normally listed under a tab named "Our Partners" or "About Us."

Familiarize yourself with their technology

Many cryptocurrencies are tokens from blockchain companies with multiple products. Well-developed websites walk you through their technology and their products in a not-so-intimidating way. The more you get to know the products and the technology behind the cryptocurrency, the easier you can make your decision about the finalists on your cryptocurrency list. Chapter 5 can be your go-to "cryptionary" along the way.

Check out their contribution to society

What problems are your shortlist cryptocurrencies trying to solve? Does it matter to you? Are they just here to get rich quick, or do they have a long-term plan for the betterment of society? Finding an answer to these questions can also help you narrow down your list of finalists. Companies like Ripple describe their social contributions under a subtab called "Ripple for Good." Other companies often use a similar format or simply put their core social contributions first thing on their home page.

Analyze their road maps

Many companies behind cryptocurrencies have sections on their websites dedicated to their road maps: where they come from, what they've achieved, and what they're planning to accomplish in the future. If available, road maps are a great way to discover a ton of fundamental information about the crypto in a few minutes.

Get to know their community

A big part of peer-to-peer blockchains and their tokens are the people. People are the heart and soul of crypto projects and oftentimes they are also the cause of creating hype and FOMO ("Fear Of Missing Out") around a specific crypto project. Often these communities of people become so passionate about their own projects that they start bashing the other projects.

TIP

I recommend keeping emotions away from making investment decisions and looking into the communities from above, taking notes on what they stand for, and deciding if they are aligned with your own values and moral beliefs.

Get involved

You can take the previous step to the next level and start participating in the communities. Just like dating, the more you get involved, the more you get to know about the dirty secrets. The majority of cryptocurrency platforms love to increase their followings and encourage people to get involved right there on their websites. Depending on the cryptocurrency, getting involved can mean anything from mining (see Chapter 13) to joining its social forums or even starting a new cryptocurrency project on its blockchain platform (like Ethereum)! Of course, getting involved also means investing more of your time, so you need to find a balance there.

Trying Technical Analysis to Select Cryptos

When you've got your heart set on a few cryptocurrencies to add to your portfolio, you're ready to decide the best time to buy them. The golden rule to any type of investment comes down to four important words:

"Buy low, sell high."

REMEMBER

But how can you decide when the price is at its lowest point to buy? That's where technical analysis, the third point of IDDA, comes in. *Technical analysis* is the art of using history to predict the future. Read on here for a brief introduction to price action and the best price analysis methods (but also check out Part 4, where I dive deeper into technical analysis):

>> **Technical analysis basics:** So many fabulous tools and gadgets can help you understand the historical movements and patterns of a cryptocurrency's price. By discovering how each pattern and indicator works, you can have a higher accuracy in predicting future price actions. Flip to Chapter 18 to explore some of the most important chart patterns and indicators that can help you develop your winning investment strategy for your favorite cryptocurrency.

>> **Recent price action:** Although the current price of one coin isn't a very good indicator of a cryptocurrency's overall value, analyzing the price action becomes *very* important when you're trying to figure out when to buy and sell. You can check the most recent price action of your selected cryptocurrency on websites such as `coinmarketcap.com` to see how much the price has dropped or surged in the past day, week, or even months. Analyzing recent price action is more important for short-term traders who are looking to get in and out of the market more rapidly, say within a day or a week. Chapter 19 has more on short-term trading strategies.

>> **Big picture:** If you're a long-term investor like I am, you may find looking at the big picture more useful in your technical analysis. Many cryptocurrencies are too young to have a well-developed price history, but you still can use similar techniques by comparing older cryptocurrencies in the same category and applying big-picture analysis to the new ones. In Chapter 20, I discuss technical analysis methods for long-term investors.

Choosing Cryptos with Sentimental Analysis

After you've done the essential background check on your prospective cryptocurrencies, you can move on to the fifth point of IDDA, sentimental analysis. *Sentimental analysis* is the study of the love–hate relationship with cryptocurrencies and traders.

Key sentimental elements

Without getting too sentimental, here are some essential elements to check before setting your heart on your favorite cryptocurrencies.

The crypto community

The company behind the cryptocurrency can play a role in the direction the crypto goes, but the network that participates in the currency's blockchain technology (see Chapter 4) is an important key to its success. Many cryptocurrencies directly depend on the participation of their communities, like miners and developers. Most of the crypto communities have their own forums on places such as the following:

>> Reddit (www.reddit.com)

>> Bitcointalk (bitcointalk.org)

>> Steemit (steemit.com)

These forums are great not only because they give you a sense of what type of people are involved in the cryptocurrency but also because you can find out more about the cryptocurrency itself.

TIP

More and more cryptocurrencies use their Telegram or Discord channels as a way to communicate with their userbase. To join, you must download the Telegram app on your mobile phone (telegram.org) or Discord (discord.com), respectively.

Exchanges that carry the crypto

REMEMBER

As I discuss in Chapter 6, cryptocurrency exchanges are a big part of the whole ecosystem. You want to make sure your cryptocurrency exchange carries your cryptos of choice, but choosing cryptos that are listed on many different exchanges is also a good idea. Most exchanges choose the cryptocurrencies they carry carefully. Finding your finalists on many different exchanges may be a sign that many exchanges have found that crypto to be valuable enough to carry. Therefore, the demand for it may be higher, and you may be able to do more with your investment. You can discover which exchanges carry your crypto of choice on websites such as coinmarketcap.com.

For example, say you want to know which exchanges carry Ripple's XRP. After selecting Ripple's XRP on coinmarketcap.com, go the tab labeled "Markets," as shown in Figure 9-2; you may need to scroll down the web page a bit to find it. There you can view the full list of exchanges that carry XRP.

Volume

TIP

Volume means how much cryptocurrency got traded in a specific time frame. It's important because it tells you how easily you can buy or sell that cryptocurrency. The higher the volume, the more easily you can trade it off. You can check and compare cryptocurrency volume on websites such as www.cryptocompare.com and coinmarketcap.com, where they show the number of coins that have been traded in the last 24 hours. You can also examine which exchanges had what volume. Generally, the biggest and most popular coins are traded the most. But if you're trying to choose a cryptocurrency within a specific category (and not simply going for the celebrity cryptos), trading volume can be a very important indicator in making your decision.

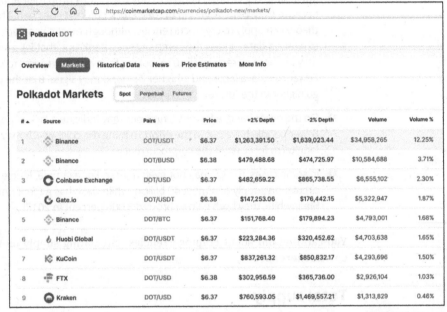

© CoinMarketCap.com

FIGURE 9-2: Locating exchanges that carry Polkadot (DOT) on coinmarketcap. com.

Coin market capitalization

One of the fastest ways to navigate through cryptocurrencies is to check out their ranking based on their *market capitalization*, or *market cap*. A bigger market cap shows a higher value of all units of a specific cryptocurrency that are for sale right now. This metric can again come handy when you're trying to select "the one" within a specific category of cryptos. For more on market capitalization analysis, flip to Chapter 8.

Circulating supply

Circulating supply (CS) is the number of coins or tokens that people have mined or that companies have generated. The key is that the circulating supply number shows you how many of these coins are currently in the market and that the general public has access to.

You can look at the importance of the CS in a couple of different ways:

>> Some crypto investors believe less is more in terms of the CS. That's if you look at it as an oversupply issue. Any market generally moves based on a principle called *supply and demand*. For example, when stores have a lot of apples and not enough people to buy them, they drop their apple prices because they want to get rid of their stock before it goes bad. The same theory can apply to cryptocurrencies. Although most coins don't have an expiration date (unless the company goes bankrupt, that is), a smaller CS may be more attractive if you're looking to invest short-term to medium-term. Fewer coins available and a higher demand may signal that the prices may go higher in the future.

>> On the other hand, a lower CS number may indicate a lack of popularity. Fewer people have put in the effort to mine the coin, which may impact the long-term forecast of the cryptocurrency.

>> In some cases, the CS may not even matter. For example, Ripple's XRP has a circulation supply of almost 40 billion, while Dash has a CS of only 8 million. Meanwhile, they both gained around 3,000 percent in 2017!

You can find out about cryptocurrencies' circulating supply on websites such as coinmarketcap.com.

Total supply

TECHNICAL
STUFF

When you add the newly mined cryptocurrencies to the circulating supply (see the preceding section), you get the *total supply* number. In other words, total supply is the total number of coins currently in existence, not just those circulating. For several reasons, some coins are reserved or locked and aren't sold in the public market. Total supply doesn't really impact a coin's price and isn't more important than the circulating supply. I just threw it out here in case you come across it on a website and wonder what it is.

Stuff to check in the news

The news has the power to make someone or something so incredibly popular. Just take a look at reality stars or the latest Instagram sensation.

The same thing goes for cryptocurrencies. The media was behind the whole cryptocurrency hype and bullish market sentiment of 2017 and then again in 2021. Just like you may do a quick cyber check about your potential date before agreeing to meet, you may want to consider looking into the following about your finalist coins.

Recent coverage

TIP

Has your finalist been in the news a lot lately? Is it a hot topic? If the answer is yes, find out whether the news coverage is organic or paid. Of course, crypto companies are aware of the impact of the media, so they pay a ton of money to popular search engines to bring them right up on top of the search results ranking system. Some crypto news providers include CoinDesk (www.coindesk.com), NewsBTC (www.newsbtc.com), Nasdaq (www.nasdaq.com/topic/cryptocurrency), and of course, investdiva.com/investing-guide/category/cryptocurrencies.

Another way you can approach this task is to simply go to the "News" tab on your search engine. When you search a topic on Google, for example, you're automatically directed to the "All" tab, which includes everything, from advertisements to news and general information. Find the "News" tab, and you'll get the relevant news coverage that's less likely to be paid ads.

WARNING

Just because a crypto asset is getting a ton of hype, it doesn't mean it's worthy of your investment. Sometimes, hyped up cryptocurrencies simply become a pyramid where the price goes higher and higher for no other reason than FOMO, and the last person who buys at the highest price becomes the victim. This happened during the NFT (non-fungible token) craze of 2021 with all the Bored Ape NFTs being sold to celebrities for millions of dollars, just for the whole thing to crash down and the status of owning an NFT immediately wiped out. See Chapter 14 for more on NFTs.

Upcoming events

TIP

You can look for upcoming events in the early stages of finding your crypto soulmate or right at the very end:

>> For the first method, you can check out websites such as coinmarketcal.com and www.newsbtc.com/crypto-calendar and see which cryptos have a busy lineup of announcements and events that may impact the crypto in a positive way. Then take the other approaches I talk about earlier in this chapter to see whether that crypto is right for your portfolio.

>> For the second method, compile the list of your finalists, and then you can either check the cryptocurrency's website to see whether it has a blog where it shares its upcoming events or check out the third-party crypto calendars for additional information.

Of course, you can also combine both approaches.

Negative press

Public Relations 101 says any press is good press. The reason for that is that people tend to enjoy reading about negative stuff more. Then they get passionate about it and are more likely to remember the entity associated with the bad press in the future — but not necessarily in a bad way anymore. That certainly is the mentality of some celebrities, who believe any coverage of them, good or bad, will bring them positive outcomes in the long run.

And it certainly can be true in cryptocurrency investing as well. During the period when the negative press is a hot topic, the prices are likely to plummet. However, contrary to what you may think, that exact period may be a good time to purchase because everyone is likely dumping the asset. Catch them when they're down, and go to the top with them. A perfect romantic fairy tale, eh?

WARNING

Buying during negative press works only if all the other IDDA analysis points indicate the cryptocurrency is worthwhile long-term. If the negative press consists of something ultra-damaging that the crypto is unlikely to recover from, then go ahead and pass.

IN THIS CHAPTER

» **Understanding how diversification helps your portfolio**

» **Exploring long-term diversification methods with cryptos**

» **Seeing short-term diversification strategies for cryptocurrencies**

Chapter **10**

Diversification in Cryptocurrencies

I talk a lot about diversification throughout this book, specifically in Chapters 3, 8, and 9, and in my education products and seminars. In this chapter, I get to the bottom of what diversification means for your crypto portfolio, why it's important, and how you can manage your portfolio's risk by properly diversifying your assets.

Breaking Down Some Basics on Diversification

Small investors regularly hear about the topic of diversification for their personal stock portfolio. One of the first things a financial expert tells you when you want to get started with investing is "don't forget to diversify!" You don't want to put all your eggs in one basket, regardless of whether that basket is stocks or cryptos. The following sections dig into what that really means, especially for cryptocurrency investing.

What is traditional diversification?

When you're building your personal stock portfolio, *diversification* often means having more than one or two stocks. The most conventional diversification method in a personal stock portfolio is to have around 15 to 20 stocks that are spread across different industries.

REMEMBER

When you diversify among industries, assets, or investment instruments that aren't correlated, you're less likely to see major drops in your portfolio when one of the categories is doing poorly. Diversification doesn't guarantee you have no risk of losses, though. It just reduces that risk if done correctly.

TIP

While diversification appears to be a logical general rule to follow, throughout my years of investing I have come to realize that nothing beats having confidence in your investment. Investing in what you know and what you are confident about not only increases your risk tolerance, but also prevents you from having unnecessary stress when the markets move against you. In other words, diversifying by investing in assets you don't really know much about, just for the sake of diversifying, is not recommended.

How does diversification reduce risk?

You encounter two types of risk in a stock portfolio: unsystematic and systematic. *Unsystematic risk* is the type of risk that you can mitigate by combining multiple industries into one portfolio. Unsystematic risk includes the following:

>> **Business risk:** This risk is associated with a company's earnings and its ability to meet its financial obligations. This risk is also tied to the company's industry, as sometimes all the businesses within a category are exposed to a similar degree of uncertainty.

>> **Country risk:** This is the risk of political and economic instability in the country where the company does business.

>> **Default risk:** This is the risk that a company isn't able to repay its debt and therefore is subject to default.

>> **Executive risk:** This risk is associated with the moral character of the executives who run the company. If they get into legal or ethical trouble, the company's stock may suffer both short term and long term.

>> **Financial risk:** This risk is associated with the amount of leverage (a measure of the amount of debt) a company uses in its financial structure. The more

debt the company has, the more leverage it's using, and therefore the higher the risk.

>> **Government/regulation risk:** This is the risk that a country may pass a new law or regulation that negatively impacts the industry that a company is in.

Systematic risk you can't get rid of simply by diversifying across various industries. That risk category includes

>> **Market risk:** The risk that the market moves against your position due to various reasons, such as political reasons, social reasons, or general change in market sentiment

>> **Exchange rate risk:** The risk that the exchange rate goes higher or its movements negatively impact your investments

>> **Interest rate risk:** The chance that changes in interest rates adversely affect the asset's value

>> **Political instability risk:** The risk that political uncertainties or changes negatively impact the market

>> **Reinvestment risk:** The chance that you won't be able to reinvest your funds at a favorable rate of return

>> **Event risk:** The chance of something unpredictable (like bankruptcy and hacker attacks) happening to the company/exchange/broker/wallet that holds your asset, therefore contributing to negative market fluctuation

Traditional diversification in a stock portfolio helps reduce unsystematic risk. This is when things get interesting. You can't diversify away systematic risk within your stock portfolio, but how about diversifying across other markets? This approach is actually how I got into investing in the first place during the crash of 2008. (You can read about the details in the nearby sidebar "My foray into forex.")

REMEMBER

As we get closer to the next inevitable stock market crash, I think adding unconventional investment instruments such as cryptocurrencies to your portfolio is more important than ever. Here's why: At the time of writing, the cryptocurrency market couldn't be more different from the traditional markets. It's new. It's unregulated, and therefore traditional systematic risks such as political instability or interest rate risks don't really apply to it. In fact, investors may well see cryptocurrencies as a safety net for when things go south in other markets during a major economic crisis.

MY FORAY INTO FOREX

In 2008, I was a mere college student studying electrical engineering at a university in Tokyo. I had no idea how the financial markets operated. But all I could hear was that the stock market was crashing and that the U.S. dollar's value was dropping versus the Japanese yen. That refers to the *exchange rate risk* portion of systematic risk (see "How does diversification reduce risk?" in this chapter). No amount of diversification could prevent the exchange rate risk in a U.S. stock portfolio, but investors did have one avenue to take advantage of the falling U.S. dollar: selling it against the appreciating Japanese yen. It was a brand-new investing opportunity called *forex* (short for the *foreign exchange market*).

That's exactly what I did (with the help of a friend), which led me to doubling my initial investment within a month while the rest of the market was crashing down. As a college student, making $10,000 within a month in a crashing market was enough for me to want to ditch my electrical engineering degrees (and six years of education!) and get on with finance and investing.

The rest is history. I came to New York to pursue my new dream and ended up empowering more women to join the movement in this male-dominated industry. Since then, I have stopped trading forex and have instead expanded my personal portfolio to stocks, exchange-traded funds (ETFs), and cryptocurrencies.

Using Cryptocurrencies in Long-Term Diversification

When it comes to adding cryptocurrencies to your portfolio, keep the following two types of long-term diversification in mind:

>> Diversifying with non-cryptocurrencies

>> Diversifying among cryptocurrencies

Here's a bit more about these two types of crypto diversification. (I talk more about diversification from traditional markets such as stocks, bonds, and forex in Chapter 2.)

Diversifying with non-cryptocurrencies

You have so many financial instruments to choose from when you consider diversifying your portfolio across the board. Stocks, commodities, precious metals, and bonds are just a few examples. As I explain in Chapter 2, each of these assets has its unique traits. Some assets' inherited risks can offset the risks of the other ones through long-term market ups and downs. The following sections provide guidance on how to use cryptos and non-cryptos together in the long term.

REMEMBER

No single golden diversification rule works for all investors. Diversification percentages and the overall mix greatly depend on the individual investor and his or her unique risk tolerance, as I talk about in the sidebar in Chapter 3 and in my free Masterclass (investdiva.com/masterclass).

TIP

The more risk you're willing to take, the higher the chances of a bigger return on investment, and vice versa. If you're just starting out and have a lower risk tolerance, you may consider allocating a bigger portion of your portfolio to bonds and then systematically adding stocks, precious metals, and cryptocurrencies. For tips on calculating your unique risk tolerance, check out the sidebar in Chapter 3.

Some background on trading fiat currencies

Fiat currencies are the traditional money that different countries' authorities declare legal. For example, the U.S. dollar is the official currency of the United States. The euro is the official currency of the European Union and its territories. The Japanese yen is backed by Japan. You get the idea.

The *foreign exchange market*, or *forex*, is a huge market where traders trade these fiat currencies against one another. Even though I no longer trade forex due to its high risk, time consumption, and low ROI compared to other types of income creating activities, having a bit of a background in forex can help you better understand the cryptocurrency market and how you can trade the different types of currencies against one another, especially in the shorter time frames. I compare this market to a big international party where all the couples are made up of partners from different regions. So if one is the Japanese yen (JPY), her partner may be the euro (EUR). I call them Ms. Japan and Mr. Euro. If one is the U.S. dollar (Ms. USA), her partner can be British, Portuguese, or Japanese.

In the forex market, these international pairs get together and start "dancing." But oftentimes, the paired-up partners aren't compatible, and their moves aren't correlated. For example, every time Ms. USA makes a good move, her partner screws up. Every time her partner picks up the rhythm, she's stuck in her previous move. These incompatibilities gain some attention, and a bunch of people who are watching the dancers start betting on which of the partners is going to screw up next. Those folks are the forex traders. You can watch this forex metaphor in action in my video here: investdiva.com/forex-coffee-break-with-invest-diva-education-course-info.

REMEMBER

The point is that when trading currencies — fiat or crypto — you can only trade them in pairs. For example, you can trade the U.S. dollar (USD) versus the Japanese yen (JPY); this is the USD/JPY pair. You can trade the Australian dollar (AUD) versus the Canadian dollar (CAD); that's the AUD/CAD pair.

Quote currency versus base currency

When trading currency pairs, the *base currency* is listed first, and the *quote currency* is listed second. Which currency in a given pair is the base currency and which is the quote currency is normally fixed across the trading markets. For example, when talking about trading the U.S. dollar versus the Japanese yen, the currency of the United States always comes first, followed by the currency of Japan (USD/JPY). In the EUR/USD pair, the euro always comes first, followed by the U.S. dollar.

REMEMBER

These set patterns have nothing to do with whether a certain currency's country is more important or whether one currency in a pair is more popular than the other. It's just how the trading crowd sets things up. The system doesn't change, which means everyone is on the same page and navigating through the pairs is easier.

As the base and quote come together, the currency pair shows how much of the quote currency is needed to purchase one unit of the base currency. For example, when USD/JPY is trading at 100, that means 1 U.S. dollar is valued at 100 Japanese yen. In other words, you need 100 Japanese yen (the quote currency) to buy 1 U.S. dollar (the base currency).

The same concept applies to cryptocurrency pairs. Many cryptocurrency exchanges offer a select number of quote currencies, mainly popular ones such as a fiat like the USD and cryptos such as Bitcoin, Ethereum, and their own exchange cryptos. Then they offer trading opportunities versus all the hundreds of other cryptocurrencies they may carry versus these quote currencies. I talk more about this topic later in this chapter.

Trading cryptos versus fiat currencies

Similar to the forex market, you can trade cryptocurrencies versus other currencies. The most common approach at the time of writing is trading them versus a fiat currency, typically the one backed by the country you live in. For example, in the United States, most people trade Bitcoin versus the USD. They don't really think of it as trading these currencies in pairs because it feels a lot like buying a stock. But the fact is that when you buy Bitcoin using the U.S. dollar in hopes of capital gain, you're essentially betting that the value of Bitcoin will move higher against the U.S. dollar in the future. That's why if the U.S. dollar decreases in value (not only against Bitcoin but also against other currencies) at the same time that Bitcoin increases in value, you're likely to make more return on your investment.

This is where diversification can help you reduce your trading risk. As I explain in the later section "Diversifying among cryptocurrencies," most cryptos are correlated to Bitcoin in shorter time frames. That's why you can diversify your portfolio with the fiat currencies you trade them against. For example, if you think that at the time you're trading, the U.S. dollar and the Japanese yen aren't correlated, you can open up two Bitcoin trades: one versus the U.S. dollar and one versus the Japanese yen. Of course, in order to do so, you should make sure your exchange or broker carries these different fiat currencies and offers such trading opportunities.

WARNING

Speculating the markets and short-term trading carries a lot of risk. It may not be suitable for all investors, and you may end up losing all your investment. Before deciding to trade such assets, you should carefully consider your investment objectives, level of experience, risk tolerance, and risk appetite. Also, you should *not* invest money that you can't afford to lose. (If you're still curious, I delve more into short-term trades later in this chapter and in Chapter 19.)

Diversifying among cryptocurrencies

The majority of cryptocurrency exchanges offer a wider selection of cross-crypto pairs than they do fiat/crypto pairs. In fact, some exchanges don't even accept any type of fiat currencies altogether. That's why many traders have no choice but to trade one cryptocurrency against another. This is also called *cross-crypro trading*. Bitcoin (BTC) versus Ethereum (ETH) gives you the BTC/ETH pair, for example.

As you can imagine, the thousands of different cryptocurrencies available to trade mean the mixes and matches can be endless. Many cryptocurrency exchanges have categorized these mixes by creating different "rooms" where you can trade the majority of the cryptos they carry versus a number of more popular cryptos. For example, as you can see in Figure 10-1, the Binance exchange has created four rooms or categories for the main cross-cryptos: Bitcoin (BTC), Ethereum (ETH), Binance Coin (BNB), and Tether (USDT). By clicking on each of these categories, you can trade other cryptos versus the selected quote currency that I talk about earlier in this chapter.

TIP

When trading currency pairs, fiat or crypto, the best bet is always to pair a strong base currency versus a weak quote currency and vice versa. This way, you maximize the chances of that pair moving strongly in the direction you're aiming for.

FIGURE 10-1:
Binance exchange cryptocurrency pairing options.

© Binance.com

As I talk about earlier in this chapter, the reason you diversify your portfolio is to reduce its exposure to risk by including assets that aren't fully correlated. The big problem about diversifying within your cryptocurrency portfolio is that, at least at the time of writing, most cryptocurrencies are heavily correlated to Bitcoin. On most of the days where Bitcoin is having a bad day, the majority of other cryptocurrencies (that are not stablecoins or exposed to extreme media hype) are, too. Figure 10-2, for example, shows a snapshot of the top 12 cryptocurrencies on August 18, 2018. All are in red. In fact, 94 out of the top 100 cryptocurrencies by market cap were plummeting that day. (*Market cap* shows the value of all units of a crypto that are for sale right now; head to Chapter 8 for more on this topic.) In the crypto market, this type of short-term market correlation has become the norm.

Fast forward to December 2022, and the correlation between Bitcoin and other cryptocurrencies is still going strong (see Figure 10-3). During the second week of December 2022, for example, the majority of the top 15 cryptocurrencies surged. The only exceptions were Tether (a stablecoin that isn't supposed to move that much), Binance Coin (an exchange coin that was having a lousy PR month due to scandals), and Dogecoin (a meme coin).

REMEMBER

Such correlations are typically more substantial long term compared to the short term. This is also one key reason short-term trading cryptocurrencies is riskier than many other financial instruments. Considering long-term investments when adding cryptocurrencies to your portfolio may be best. That way, you can reduce your investment risk by diversifying within different crypto categories.

© CoinMarketCap.com

	Cryptocurrencies ▾	Exchanges ▾	Watchlist				USD ▾	Next 100 →	View All
#	Name	Market Cap	Price	Volume (24h)	Circulating Supply	Change (24h)	Price Graph (7d)		
1	Bitcoin	$110,649,855,082	$6,426.55	$4,110,066,055	17,217,625 BTC	-1.73%			
2	Ethereum	$30,275,258,926	$298.55	$1,815,655,842	101,409,291 ETH	-3.57%			
3	XRP	$13,067,008,532	$0.331882	$500,290,020	39,372,399,467 XRP *	-6.18%			
4	Bitcoin Cash	$9,727,259,913	$562.26	$438,890,267	17,300,163 BCH	-1.91%			
5	EOS	$4,681,414,809	$5.17	$864,785,525	906,245,118 EOS *	-4.09%			
6	Stellar	$4,271,146,076	$0.227530	$79,898,204	18,771,755,700 XLM *	-2.51%			
7	Litecoin	$3,313,730,889	$57.23	$253,969,516	57,903,334 LTC	-4.81%			
8	Tether	$2,719,405,730	$0.908995	$3,359,590,344	2,722,140,336 USDT *	-0.10%			
9	Cardano	$2,631,037,998	$0.101478	$107,934,610	25,927,070,538 ADA *	-5.37%			
10	Monero	$1,596,232,879	$97.75	$33,423,127	16,329,214 XMR	-0.48%			
11	TRON	$1,439,869,668	$0.021900	$146,381,621	65,748,111,645 TRX *	-3.63%			
12	Ethereum Classic	$1,393,191,044	$13.41	$298,225,868	103,884,149 ETC	-6.22%			

FIGURE 10-2: Correlation between the top 12 cryptocurrencies and Bitcoin as BTC drops.

© CoinMarketCap.com

#	Name	Price	1h %	24h %	7d %	Market Cap	Volume(24h)	Circulating Supply	Last 7 Days
1	Bitcoin BTC	$18,078.93	0.22%	1.73%	7.32%	$347,723,995,749	$19,494,285,597 1,079,916 BTC	19,233,662 BTC	
2	Ethereum ETH	$1,339.41	0.05%	1.04%	9.54%	$163,908,761,051	$5,726,606,491 4,273,441 ETH	122,373,866 ETH	
3	Tether USDT	$1.00	0.00%	0.00%	0.00%	$65,977,597,652	Stablecoin 25,687,	11 USDT	
4	USD Coin USDC	$1.00	0.00%	0.00%	0.00%	$45,169,784,724	$2,679,792,639 2,679,492,353 USDC	45,165,946,711 USDC	
5	BNB BNB	$272.55	0.03%	0.82%	3.91%	$43,599,183,487	$1,021,773,561 3,749,104 BNB	159,967,832 BNB	
6	XRP XRP	$0.3931	0.07%	0.50%	2.56%	$19,808,412,669	$807,876,385 2,053,496,671 XRP	50,395,461,568 XRP	
7	Binance USD BUSD	$0.9999	0.04%	0.02%	0.03%	$19,978,7	Exchange Coin 5,978,7		
8	Dogecoin DOGE	$0.09182	0.43%	0.41%	4.46%		Memecoin 4,731,		
9	Cardano ADA	$0.3133	0.02%	0.07%	0.67%	$10,801,958,749	$225,413,614 719,575,777 ADA	34,475,058,303 ADA	
10	Polygon MATIC	$0.9292	0.20%	0.40%	6.79%	$8,116,215,166	$259,808,795 279,328,163 MATIC	8,734,317,475 MATIC	
11	Polkadot DOT	$5.35	0.26%	1.44%	0.37%	$6,130,521,083	$187,159,600 35,030,007 DOT	1,146,739,346 DOT	
12	Dai DAI	$1.00	0.05%	0.02%	0.03%	$5,857,303,937	$206,789,276 206,812,575 DAI	5,857,248,754 DAI	
13	Litecoin LTC	$79.43	0.37%	0.24%	2.20%	$5,633,261,179	$406,144,428 5,148,190 LTC	71,827,169 LTC	
14	Solana SOL	$14.55	2.34%	5.72%	6.26%	$5,334,253,664	$247,746,487 17,503,278 SOL	366,559,831 SOL	
15	TRON TRX	$0.05634	1.29%	3.66%	8.00%	$5,186,292,338	$211,864,066 3,785,431,564 TRX	92,046,245,067 TRX	

FIGURE 10-3: Correlation between the top 15 cryptocurrencies and Bitcoin as BTC surges.

EXCHANGE TRADED FUNDS OR INDIVIDUAL ASSETS?

Exchange-traded funds (ETFs) are the lazy approach to investing. While it may save you from having to do the proper research on individual assets, it also takes away your control over what you're investing in and how much you're allocating to each individual asset. Personally, it is very important for me to only invest in assets that are aligned to my moral beliefs. When you invest in an Index Fund or an Exchange-Traded Fund (ETF), you will never fully know what asset the fund managers may sneak into the basket. If you have to stay on top of everything that's happening in the fund, you might as well invest in each asset individually and become your own money manager!

On the bright side, as the cryptocurrency market continues to develop, the diversification methods can also improve, and the whole market may become less correlated to Bitcoin.

Tackling Diversification in Short-Term Trades

If you've calculated your risk tolerance based on the information in Chapter 3 and the results are pretty aggressive, you may want to consider trading cryptocurrencies in shorter time frames. Here are some suggestions to keep in mind. To read more about developing short-term strategies, flip to Chapter 19.

WARNING

>> **Beware of commissions.** Cryptocurrency trading exchanges generally require lower commission and transaction fees than brokers who offer forex or stocks. But you shouldn't completely ignore the commission cost to your wallet. When day trading, you may end up paying more in commission than what you're actually making by trading if you trade way too often, getting in and out of trades way too fast without calculating your returns! Also, as I talk about in Chapter 6, cheaper isn't always the best option when choosing an exchange. You always get what you pay for.

TIP

>> **Keep expanding your portfolio.** Some people invest a lump sum in their investment portfolios and then either wipe it out in dangerous day-trading actions or get stuck in a strategy that's working but isn't maximizing their returns. A healthy portfolio requires nourishment. Consider leaving a monthly investment fund aside out of your paycheck in order to expand your portfolio and make your money work for you.

>> **Observe the rule of three.** You have a ton of options when trading currencies. You can mix and match crypto/crypto and fiat/crypto pairs like there's no tomorrow if your account size lets you. However, the key in having a healthy diversified portfolio is to avoid double-dipping the same quote currency in your trades. Try to limit your open short-term positions against each quote currency to three. For example, trade one crypto versus Bitcoin, another versus Ethereum, and a third versus your exchange's cryptocurrency. This approach also helps you keep your portfolio at a reasonable size so it's not too big to monitor.

Chapter **11**

The Role of Cryptocurrency in the Metaverse

"The meta-what?"

To get a good understanding of what the metaverse is, let's first take a look at the word itself. Meta is a prefix that means "beyond," and "verse" comes from "universe," making up the word metaverse. Metaverse therefore means beyond the universe.

REMEMBER

The metaverse is a truly interactive and immersive environment that has the ability to connect communities and different worlds. It is the next platform on which we can work, live, connect, and thrive. In simple terms, the *metaverse* is a space where people can interact and participate with each other inside a shared virtual universe. In the metaverse, we have digital versions of ourselves (known as *avatars*). People — or rather their avatars — are able to engage in a shared virtual space, talk to each other, play different games, hang out together, watch movies, and even browse the Internet.

The possibilities are almost endless! The metaverse is supposed to be a much more fun, immersive, and interactive Internet experience when compared to the relatively flat 2D and heavily text-based experience that most of us are used to online. The metaverse is designed to be a real awakening for our senses! It brings with it a world in 3D, a world of texture, dimension, and vibrant colors.

You can do many more things in the metaverse than you can do in the real world because you do not have any physical constraints on your abilities, your location, or the way that you can interact. People can meet, watch shows, visit virtual museums, ride in virtual parks, earn and spend virtual currency, and go to websites all within the same metaverse.

This chapter looks at how the metaverse will affect our future lives, how it uses blockchain technology, and what its impact is going to be on cryptocurrency. It's a bit of a crystal-ball chapter!

Looking into the Future: How the Metaverse Will Change Our Lives

Before looking at the role that blockchain and cryptocurrency have to play in the metaverse later in this chapter, you first need to understand some key sectors that are being transformed by the introduction of the metaverse . . . and how this will potentially change all of our lives.

The metaverse is like the next natural evolution of the Internet. It is therefore inevitable that as time progresses, it will likely start to play a bigger role and have a greater impact on our lives.

At the moment, gamers are the people who are typically getting the most out of what the metaverse has to offer. They are able to enjoy a much more engaging and intense experience with video games such as Roblox, Fortnite, and Minecraft than earlier generations of gamers could have ever imagined.

So gaming is likely the most obvious frontier for the metaverse to become linked to. However, eventually, the idea is that the metaverse will probably host something for everyone. Similar to the Internet as we currently know it, the metaverse will allow for commercial activity, the exchange of ideas, as well as an array of recreational activities. The metaverse will be versatile for sure and will ultimately give rise to endless opportunities to help our ever-changing world evolve, adapt, and thrive.

With this in mind, let's take a look at some key sectors in which the metaverse is likely to affect our lives both now and in the future. Each sector will be virtualized, allow for greater opportunities, accelerated results, and a brand-new virtual economy.

Education

Education is a sector in which the metaverse can play a crucial and defining role. We currently use web browsers by default in our day-to-day use of the Internet, but our ability to enter different virtual worlds will become the foundation of the educational metaverse.

The metaverse will improve education in ways previously unimaginable because students will be able to actually see what they are studying rather than purely reading text about it. As unique human beings, we all learn and absorb information in different ways. The introduction of the metaverse into the educational sector would allow students to engage in different ways and at a higher level with their learning.

As students study and enter pages of their virtual textbooks, examples would be able to be brought to life in 3D to help students more easily understand particularly complex topics. The power to see and visualize something is often considered to be a more powerful and immediately memorable way of learning compared to just reading.

Imagine a situation where you would be able to be fully present (virtually) inside the topic or environment that you are learning about. How incredible would that be? This type of interactive and realistic learning environment would allow students to learn and interact from literally anywhere in the world.

TIP

This is one of the metaverse sectors that excites me the most. One of our goals in my company, Invest Diva, is to also be able to offer our investment education services in the metaverse. See our progress here: investdiva.com/metaverse.

Communication

Communication is another sector that is being transformed by the metaverse, and the only thing you will need is a virtual reality (VR) device and your own virtual reality avatar!

The metaverse gives you the opportunity to create your own unique online identity through your avatar and then interact with anyone from literally anywhere in the world inside of a shared virtual environment. You'll be able to see people's different facial expressions as well as read their body language!

It doesn't stop there though. Communicating in the metaverse allows people to meet up with each other in what is perceived to be a more physical way. We are all used to communicating via video calls from computers or smartphones at the moment, but the metaverse allows us to see other people right there in front of us as if they were actually standing next to us in the same virtual room.

The metaverse makes communication a much more interesting, immersive, and engaging experience. The way you communicate with others for work could change to the point where you wouldn't even need to leave your home to commute to a physical office. Imagine the time and cost saved on this one factor alone as well as the huge saving in overall efficiency.

Business

Following on from communication, the metaverse is again changing how we conduct business. Having the ability to work from anywhere in the world is a powerful proposition for people and businesses. Commuting costs and business-related travel expenses would be a thing of the past.

Virtual team meetings in the same virtual shared space in the metaverse allow people to work together in real time irrespective of their physical location. Strong bonds and working relationships between team members could quickly be established despite working remotely in a way that is just not entirely possible through a screen alone.

Businesses would be able to measure increasing improvements in productivity by working this way. Team members would be able to sit at the same virtual table together and work on projects from their homes. Working in the metaverse would also allow you to change your virtual setting to suit you literally on demand. All of your working files could easily be accessed and shared directly from within your metaverse profile.

REMEMBER

The increased networking opportunities that the metaverse presents would be enormous. You'll be able to look people directly in the eyes, shake their hands (using ultrasonic waves), and actually feel the grip of their hands.

Entertainment

Film and television have transformed the way that we have entertained ourselves for decades. However, the metaverse will change the entertainment industry forever in an even more profound way. As we become immersed inside of new virtual worlds of entertainment, motion pictures will eventually become obsolete as we will have the ability to be right there, in and amongst the action inside the film ourselves.

The metaverse will completely transform things like concerts and sporting events. Things like queuing and seating capacity will never be an issue. Virtual tickets will become the norm and you'll always be able to watch your chosen event from the comfort of your own home as well as experience all of the excitement of your chosen event from the best virtual seat in the house.

The metaverse is a win-win scenario for the entertainment industry because it will bring a huge increase in value to consumers as well as increased revenue opportunities for entertainers.

Gaming

Gaming is being completely revolutionized by the metaverse. Rather than just playing video games, in the future we will actually be able to experience them firsthand in a much more dynamic, interactive, and immersive way.

The user experience opportunities for gaming are almost unlimited but here are a few of the greatest and most exciting enhancements for gamers in the metaverse:

>> Play-to-earn (P2E) has become a popular feature.

>> Players have the ability to profit from and own their in-game assets.

>> Players can experience a greater sense of satisfaction and accomplishment from being fully immersed within the virtual games they play.

TECHNICAL
STUFF

Play-to-earn really is a phenomenal evolutionary element to gaming in the metaverse. To be able to reward players with cryptocurrency and various digital assets that can ultimately be "cashed out" and exchanged for money is an enticing proposition. Players are able to buy, sell and, trade items with other players as well as have the option to earn an income.

Games such as The Sandbox, Axie Infinity, Star Atlas, Illuvium, and Zed Run already integrate a play-to-earn element within a metaverse environment, and is likely a key reason for their successes so far.

Travel

Have you ever wondered if time travel would be possible in your lifetime? Thanks to the metaverse, both time travel and teleportation may become a reality.

The metaverse will give us the option of how and when we would like to travel without many of the physical, price, and time restrictions that can be a barrier for many people when considering traditional travel.

Here are some of the key benefits that may enhance travel in the metaverse future:

>> Taking a trip (teleporting) wherever you want to without time and space restrictions.

>> Lowering the cost to travel in the metaverse.

>> Traveling to places that are out of reach for traditional forms of travel (space, for example).

>> Removing the need to pay for a plane ticket, a hotel, or food!

Real estate

You might not have thought this was possible, but a completely practical application of the metaverse exists in the real estate industry, and it is starting to unlock a world of new and exciting opportunities in this space.

Here are some of the ways that the metaverse is changing real estate:

>> Virtual real estate investing, more choice of properties, easier process, faster, less hassle

>> Virtual reality technology allowing you attend a physical open-house viewing

>> Buying, selling, and trading virtual properties quicker and cheaper compared to traditional real estate

Properties in the metaverse are stored on the blockchain as NFTs (non-fungible tokens). NFTs are unique cryptographic tokens that exist on a blockchain and cannot be replicated. They can represent real-world items such as artwork and real estate, and I discuss NFTs in detail in Chapter 14.

This means that you could go to an online marketplace such as Opensea (https:// opensea.io) where properties are available for sale, and purchase them with the click of a button. The blockchain deals with the transfer of ownership, contracts, and the distribution of any fees that are associated with purchasing virtual real estate.

A great example of a well-known brand operating in the metaverse is Gucci. They decided to purchase some digital land in The Sandbox metaverse with a view to providing a new immersive virtual store for their shoppers as well as selling collectible NFTs.

Understanding the Role of Blockchain in the Metaverse

The metaverse allows us to participate in various forms of immersive virtual worlds. However, the reality is that as people socialize and interact, they are inevitably going to want to enhance their experience through different types and choices of transactions.

REMEMBER

Blockchain technology (see Chapter 4 for more details) therefore very quickly becomes absolutely essential for developing an ecosystem in the metaverse, where individuals can create and monetize decentralized assets as well as own them. Away from the constraints of centralized institutions, blockchain applications in the metaverse provide easy access to a digital space where transactions can take place.

REMEMBER

The role of blockchain in the metaverse is inextricably linked. It provides so many solutions to how a virtual environment needs to operate successfully. With features such as payments, governance, digital proof of ownership, accessibility, and interoperability, it becomes obvious and inevitable that blockchain technology is needed to support and extract the best possible user experience in the metaverse. The combination of blockchain and the metaverse allows for unlimited possibilities for both of these different concepts to thrive but especially when combined.

The next sections explore some of the main future roles of blockchain in the metaverse.

Application of NFTs

One of the most significant primary use cases for the role of blockchain in the metaverse is to facilitate the application of NFTs (see Chapter 14 for more about NFTs). It is understandable that people want to replicate real-world experiences in the digital world; this is a natural evolution of people's behavior.

In order for this to happen, it is important to have replicas of real physical-world commodities available to purchase in the metaverse. NFTs are already incredibly popular in the digital arts space but they are also finding their way into many other trading areas within various virtual worlds of the metaverse. NFTs ensure that they are unique and they provide unique proof of ownership.

As an example, let's say you own a really cool limited-edition pair of your favorite brand of shoes. Wouldn't it be amazing to own a digital version of your much-loved pair of shoes in the metaverse? NFTs would allow you to have that, effectively giving you the option of creating a digital twin of some of your physical real-world assets.

Security and privacy

Security and privacy is another important defining quality of the role that blockchain plays in the metaverse. It is vital to ensure that users have a unique digital identity.

This enables both businesses and individuals to prove their identity at any time using blockchain-based identity certificates. These certificates allow users to participate in financial transactions in the metaverse after verification.

REMEMBER

The ability to be able to accurately authenticate a genuine user's unique identity helps to eradicate fraud or other types of illegal security breaches.

Payments and financial transactions

Payments and financial transactions are a hugely important part of the role that blockchain plays in the metaverse. For normal online transactions, a third-party payment processor (such as banks or payment gateways) is required.

However, peer-to-peer (known as P2P) transactions powered by cryptocurrencies would enable users in the metaverse to carry out transactions directly without any reliance whatsoever on third-party mediators. This new way of transacting in the metaverse — such as in virtual storefronts or within gaming — is quick, convenient, and usually at a much lower cost.

Getting Your Business Started in the Metaverse

Famous brand names such as Gucci, Adidas, and Samsung already own virtual stores in the metaverse and are conducting business in this new and exciting space. The metaverse is changing how business is being conducted both now and for the future, so let's explore how you can launch your own business or company into the metaverse.

TIP

The simple answer is that because the metaverse is in its infancy, there isn't a single choice or universal gateway to access the metaverse for your business needs — yet. There are several different types of metaverse that you could explore, and I recommend following these steps to discover which works best for your own business:

1. **Understand what the metaverse is and discover if this new way of doing business aligns with your core values and overall business model.** This chapter helps you get started! Businesses should also keep up to date on the everchanging metaverse developments, as well as topics such as Web3 (see the sidebar later in this chapter), VR wearables, and of course cryptocurrency. Signing up for metaverse related newsletters such as Time's Into The Metaverse (time.com) or AdAge's Metaverse Marketing Today (adage.com) helps keep you updated.

2. **Explore the different types of metaverse-compatible technologies that you could use to help you start to integrate the metaverse into your business.** These can include items such as VR headsets, extended reality wearables, smartphones, tablets, laptops, public blockchains, and crypto payment methods. These areas of technology are constantly evolving, so research and experimentation in this area is key! For example, use your favorite search engine to discover "how to integrate the metaverse into my business." Once you have researched your options and chosen your preferred method of metaverse integration, you could purchase the appropriate hardware or software to experiment with its usage to see if it could benefit your business goals.

3. **Think about and brainstorm how you could use the metaverse in your marketing campaigns to help you sell products or services to your customers.** Think about the different types of virtual experiences you might consider offering and understand what the benefits could be of doing so for your brand reputation, revenue, and customer loyalty. Be creative with your ideas and think outside the box. Perhaps you could offer some form of collectible such as an NFT to increase excitement and demand within your customers community. There are even virtual billboards where you could

consider placing advertisements, such as inside popular metaverse games like Roblox, or inside the 3D virtual world of Decentraland.

4. **Choose your metaverse platform.** There are many viable platforms but here is a list of some popular metaverse platforms for you to consider:

- Decentraland
- The Sandbox
- Roblox
- Axie Infinity
- Fortnite
- Horizon Worlds
- Virbela

Each of these platforms has its own distinctive and unique nuances so take the time to research which would best fit your business.

5. **Get ready to take the first step and join the metaverse!** Depending on the platform that you choose, this can be as easy as downloading some software and creating your avatar, or purchasing some hardware. Of course, you could always experience the metaverse yourself first before bringing it into your business. This is a great way for you to experiment with its capabilities and real-world potential before making any moves that could affect your business.

REMEMBER Regardless of the type of platform that you choose, you will need an avatar which you set up and create when you join a metaverse community. To get the fully immersive metaverse experience you will need a wearable device such as a VR headset.

Using Cryptocurrencies in the Metaverse

Just as there is no one Internet, there is also no one metaverse! There are many metaverse platforms. Some platforms accept certain types of cryptocurrencies as payment, and other platforms accept different types of cryptocurrencies as payment. The following sections look at how cryptocurrencies will interact with the metaverse.

REMEMBER Cryptocurrency is the fuel that powers the metaverse and ultimately, cryptocurrency will likely stand to benefit hugely from it.

How will crypto be used in the metaverse?

In essence, within the metaverse, crypto is becoming an invisible but integral part of the behind-the-scenes infrastructure. An infrastructure layer that facilitates payments and transactions. Cryptocurrency will make it easier to transfer money from inside and outside of metaverses in several ways.

Method 1: Payments

Just like any country with its own real-world currency, a key role of crypto in the metaverse will simply be about using crypto as "money" and as a payment method so that users can buy, sell, and trade digital products or services in virtual worlds.

REMEMBER

Crypto purchases in the metaverse will also have the advantage of being secure, private, and safe.

Method 2: Crypto coins and tokens

Remember that there is a crucial difference between cryptocurrency coins and cryptocurrency tokens: Cryptocurrency coins are essentially a digital version of money. A coin operates on its blockchain, acts as money, and can be mined. For example, Bitcoin is a coin because it runs on the Bitcoin blockchain.

However, cryptocurrency tokens are created as part of a platform that is built on an existing blockchain. So a crypto token represents what you actually own whereas a crypto coin signifies what you're able to earn.

Another important difference between coins and tokens is what they represent. Tokens can stand for assets whereas coins are simply digital versions of money. So if you wanted to, you could buy tokens with coins. For example, MANA is the crypto token used for transactions within the Decentraland metaverse and SAND is the token used within The Sandbox metaverse.

For more on coins and tokens, see Chapter 8.

Method 3: NFTs and digital assets

Cryptocurrencies will allow for NFTs to be bought and sold in the metaverse, as well as other digital assets. Metaverse projects ultimately require a medium of exchange or some form of payment mechanism to allow users to transact and buy or sell digital assets in the virtual world.

Shopping in the metaverse

The ability for people to be able to shop in the metaverse is certainly an exciting proposition and is filled with endless possibilities. Humans are naturally sociable and the act of shopping for many people is an enjoyable and interactive experience as well as an essential one! Even real-world retail has changed a lot in recent years and has become more focused on ensuring that the customer actually enjoys their shopping experience in a whole variety of different entertaining and engaging ways.

REMEMBER

From what is already known about the metaverse, shopping in the metaverse will likely become not only transactional but much more experience based. In an immersive virtual world environment such as the metaverse, people want to be entertained and inspired to make a purchase. Virtual worlds provide the perfect platform for shopping experiences to feel very special indeed.

Fashion brands are becoming increasingly keen to get involved in the metaverse as they recognize that the future of shopping and retail in general is starting to evolve into this exciting new space with almost unlimited possibilities.

Imagine wandering through different virtual stores with fashion brands offering 360-degree 3D virtual fitting rooms so that clothes could be tried on virtually before purchase. As the accuracy of this type of technology and service improves over time, this would be a win-win situation for customers and the fashion brands as it would lead to greater customer satisfaction as well as potentially reduce the volume of returns for the retailer.

As another example, imagine being able to purchase a new car after taking part in a highly realistic, adrenaline-filled virtual test drive. The metaverse could allow for a whole new way of shopping for things which would benefit from the "try before you buy" concept.

REMEMBER

Ultimately, shopping in the metaverse will be immersive and revolutionary. It will transform the way that we choose to buy many real-world items as well as the different types of virtual digital assets that are discussed earlier in this chapter.

Investing using the metaverse

There are lots of different ways to invest in the metaverse, such as investing in metaverse crypto, metaverse NFTs and real estate, and metaverse stocks. The following sections look at these popular options in more detail.

Investing in metaverse cryptos

Metaverse cryptocurrencies describe the native tokens of metaverse-based projects. Tokens such as these are often used for transactions and sometimes staking.

REMEMBER

As a general rule, each metaverse's native token can usually be used to purchase digital items directly from within the metaverse marketplace. As an example, users could buy Axie Infinity and use tokens to purchase extra "Axies" for use in their games, and in return, sellers would be rewarded in metaverse crypto which could be exchanged into other cryptocurrencies.

The most popular metaverse cryptocurrencies are available to purchase from crypto exchanges such as Coinbase and Binance as well as many others. For extra security, after purchase, you can transfer your metaverse-related crypto to a hardware wallet such as a Ledger or Trezor (see Chapter 7 for more on wallets). If you adopt the value-investing approach to investing, you could simply choose to buy low, hold, and then in the future sell at a higher price if your chosen crypto experiences good price appreciation over time.

Some of the top metaverse-related cryptocurrencies at the time of writing are:

>> Decentraland (MANA)

>> Sandbox (SAND)

>> Axie Infinity (AXS)

These types of cryptocurrencies can provide an easy way to invest in the metaverse because they are usually listed on the very best cryptocurrency exchanges. It also means that investors themselves don't actually need to be active within any given metaverse or virtual platform in order to still gain some exposure to its potential growth by investing in the tokens.

WARNING

Before making a decision to invest in metaverse cryptocurrencies, always perform thorough research so that you fully understand and believe in the future of what the particular cryptocurrency offers as a solution to the market it serves.

TIP

Using your everyday search engine may be your best strategy when researching the most recent metaverse cryptos. You can consider search terms such as "metaverse cryptocurrencies" or "top Metaverse cryptos 2023." Coinmarketcap is a fabulous cryptocurrency resource. It allows you to search for top cryptos in order of market cap as well as by specific categories: coinmarketcap.com/view/metaverse.

Investing in metaverse NFTs and real estate

NFTs and real estate represent another interesting and exciting way to invest in the metaverse. And it's no surprise that some top metaverse-related NFTs are available to purchase with the same crypto tokens discussed in the previous section.

Here are some of the top metaverse-related NFTs and real estate sites at the time of writing:

>> The Sandbox (SAND)

>> Decentraland (MANA)

>> Axie Infinity (AXS)

TIP

NFTs can provide "true" proven ownership of a virtual asset or in-game asset. One of the most famous metaverses is The Sandbox. The Sandbox is more than just a game. The Sandbox contains an enormous amount of NFTs within its ecosystem — hundreds of thousands, in fact! These NFTs include plots of virtual land, virtual buildings, and various attractions, as well as wearables for avatars. In fact, because The Sandbox is an incredibly creative platform, users have the tools to create almost anything they choose. This clever concept means that players are effectively constantly fueling the game's ever-growing economy.

The option to purchase NFTs which represent virtual plots of land in The Sandbox ecosystem has been of great interest to many business owners and investors. Once purchased, these plots of land can be fully customized to the user's unique and exact requirements. Some brands are even using their virtual plots of land to build communities and host virtual events. After purchase, these NFTs provide proof of ownership for the virtual land. Companies such as Gucci, Adidas, and Atari already own plots of land for virtual stores in The Sandbox.

A finite number of virtual plots of land are available, and these plots of land differ in price according to their size and location on The Sandbox NFT map. This is a great example of virtual real estate at its best. As more plots of land are sold, less plots of land will be available to buy, which will likely add to the scarcity value and increase the overall demand and price of the existing virtual real estate within The Sandbox map.

Investing in metaverse stocks

Subject to your individual risk tolerance and financial goals, investing in metaverse-related stocks could be a way of diversifying your stock portfolio and exposing it to this new industry.

TIP

If you think the metaverse is cool but you're still not ready to dive directly in it using the crypto market, consider investing in metaverse-related stocks instead.

Here are some of the top metaverse-related stocks at the time of writing:

>> Meta Platforms (META)

>> Nvidia (NVDA)

>> Microsoft (MSFT)

>> Roblox (RBLX)

>> Nike (NKE)

So how can these companies indirectly expose you to the metaverse? For example, Meta Platforms (previously Facebook) are heavily involved in VR (virtual reality) and the overall growth and expansion of metaverse concepts for both now and in the future. Nvidia would be another stock to consider as its chips are used to power many different metaverse projects. Over time, as the calling for metaverse-related technologies increases, Nvidia is well-placed to support and supply the necessary chips, providing further growth opportunities for the future of the company. Microsoft has already shown that it is developing its workplace metaverse inside Mesh for Microsoft Teams, its online collaboration platform; here avatars can be customized to reflect individual preferences as well as different workplace settings and drop in spaces. Nike has partnered with Roblox (Nikeland) to enhance its presence of virtual clothing and accessories in the metaverse.

Investing in metaverse-related stocks can be done through your chosen online stock broker. This can be a beginner-friendly way of gaining exposure in this space, even if you are a newcomer to stock investing and this particular market category. I explain the process of selecting a broker in Chapter 6.

REMEMBER

Confidence is the name of the game when it comes to profitable investing. The higher your confidence in the asset you're investing in, the higher your risk tolerance. That being said, you must be careful not to take more risks than you can financially afford. Flip to Chapter 3 for more on risk management.

TIP

Grab my risk management toolkit to easily see how much of your portfolio you can allocate to metaverse-related assets by attending this free Masterclass: investdiva.com/masterclass.

TECHNICAL
STUFF

EXPLORING WEB3

The original version of the web was known as Web 1.0. This was the Internet as we knew it from the 1990s to early 2000s. Web 2.0 is the current version of the Internet that we all use today, also referred to as "the web," including all aspects of social media. Web3 (sometimes called Web 3.0) is simply a successive version of the web. It's the third generation of the World Wide Web and the third major evolution of the Internet.

Much of what is Web3 is currently being developed and is a work in progress. Its aim is to be decentralized and provide greater utility for users. Web3 is built on and linked to technologies such as blockchain instead of being centralized on servers which are typically owned by corporations or individuals.

There is often some confusion and misunderstanding between the terms "metaverse" and "Web3" and it is easy to see why. They are absolutely related in several important ways but they also both describe different concepts.

Web3 will allow individual users to actually own and be fully in control of the systems and networks where applications run from and where data is stored. Users will also have voting rights over the types of regulations and rules in place. Web3 aims to create a more democratized Internet experience.

This is of course in complete contrast to Web 2.0. Web3 is also sometimes referred to as "the immersive web" and this is where our minds instantly make the connection to the concept and similarity of the metaverse which is all about immersive experiences.

The metaverse is primarily focused on virtual worlds where people can interact with each other as well as engage with different services and apps in a much more immersive way.

The term metaverse is also generally used in reference to any type of online spaces that create a virtual immersive environment and experience. Take Roblox, for example. Roblox offers businesses the opportunity to establish new branded worlds and these are also considered to be direct experiences of the metaverse.

Web3 and metaverse do share some important overlap in their use because blockchain is the underlying technology that is used to build Web3 and cryptocurrencies such as Bitcoin and Ethereum, and NFTs that are stored on blockchain, have direct implications for the way we use the metaverse for work and for play. When we want to decorate our avatar or buy or sell something in the metaverse, we will be using specific cryptocurrencies to do so.

Although Web3 and metaverse are different concepts, they are certainly related and they have the potential to support each other in powerful and extremely useful ways. As the technology in this space is ever evolving, it is important to regularly keep updated and perform thorough research when making decisions.

You can learn more about Web3 here: coinmarketcap.com/view/web3.

3
Alternatives to Cryptos

Understand how new cryptocurrencies are funded and how you can profit from getting involved in initial coin offerings (ICOs).

Dig into cryptocurrency mining and find out whether it's a better alternative for you than straight up buying and investing is.

Discover the truth about non-fungible tokens (NFTs) and how they can make or break your portfolio.

Discover how to get indirect exposure to the cryptocurrency and blockchain industries by investing in traditional assets such as stocks and exchange traded funds (ETFs).

Find out the basics of cryptocurrency futures and options.

See how cryptocurrencies are related to government-based currencies and the foreign exchange (forex) market.

IN THIS CHAPTER

» **Discovering the fundamentals of an initial coin offering (ICO)**

» **Getting invested in an ICO launch**

» **Going about an ICO launch of your own**

Chapter **12**

Getting Ahead of the Crowd: Investing in ICOs

CO is short for initial coin offering. In an age where ICOs aren't subject to many regulations, some would call them the easiest path to scams. And though a ton (and I mean a *ton!*) of ICO scams are out there, if you do your homework, you may be able to catch a few diamonds in the rough as well. In this chapter, I explain ICO basics and show how you can get involved.

Understanding the Basics of Initial Coin Offerings

Initial coin offerings are something like fundraising for a new start-up, except that your new idea revolves around a new cryptocurrency rather than a business idea or product. You're trying to raise "money" in the form of other, already established cryptocurrencies such as Bitcoin and Ethereum. In other words, an ICO is crowdfunding, using other cryptocurrencies, for a new cryptocurrency that's (hopefully) connected to an awesome product. The following sections provide the basics on ICOs.

How an ICO works and how to start one

REMEMBER

Simply put, an ICO works exactly how start-up fundraising works. You come up with a cool idea for a cryptocurrency. The cryptocurrency may be used for an existing product, or perhaps you have an idea for a product that can work well with a brand-new crypto.

As an example, say a fashion website in New York City showcases display windows in real time. (Okay, this is actually my friend Jon Harari's website, WindowsWear — check out www.windowswear.com. I've been trying to pitch him the ICO idea, but he doesn't really understand how it can work for his business.) But for the sake of argument, say that Jon decides he wants to change his business strategy, make his website available to the masses, and let people shop on his app using WindowsWear's very own digital currency. Call this brand-new crypto WEAR Coin. But unless Jon is a millionaire who wants to spend all his money on this idea, he needs to raise money to make this new cryptocurrency a reality. He can go to a venture capitalist, a bank, or angel investors and ask for money. The problem with that approach is that he'll most likely have to give up part of his ownership of his company. So instead, he can listen to his friend Kiana and go for an ICO. (Remember, this is an example only! By the time you read this book, there may actually be a crypto coin with the WEAR symbol.)

REMEMBER

Here are the general steps to take to initiate an ICO (see the later section "So You Want to Start an ICO: Launching an ICO Yourself" for more information):

1. **Create a white paper.**

    A *white paper* is a detailed document explaining a business model and the reason a particular coin may really take off. The more use cases Jon has in his white paper for WEAR Coin to show it can actually become a popular and high-volume coin, the better.

2. **Add a tab to your website dedicated to ICO funding.**

    In this example, Jon puts a tab on his WindowsWear site dedicated to WEAR Coin ICO funding.

3. **Spread the word to your connections and ask for funding.**

4. **Sell a quantity of your crowdfunded coin in the form of *tokens*, which means digital assets.**

    Normally ICOs ask for Bitcoin or Ethereum in exchange for the tokens. But you can also accept *fiat* (traditional government-backed) currencies such as the U.S. dollar.

5. **Send the investors coin tokens.**

    In this example, Jon sends his investors WEAR Coin tokens.

If WEAR Coin really hits, starts getting used a lot, and is listed on a ton of crypto exchanges, the early investors can see a significant return on their investments.

WARNING

People who invest in ICOs normally don't have any guarantee that the new cryptocurrency will increase in value in the future. Some ICO investments have been incredibly profitable in the past, but future ICOs may not be. Unless you really trust the management, the company's dedication to success, and its knowledge of the business model and the industry, investing in an ICO is very much comparable to gambling. Flip to the later section "Investing in an ICO" for more details.

ICOs versus IPOs

A lot of people experience a bit of a confusion about the difference between initial coin offerings (ICOs) and initial public offerings (IPOs, which is the first time a company sells its stocks to the public). These concepts sound similar, and in many ways, they are similar. Here are the main differences:

>> **In theory, anyone can do an ICO.** At the time of writing, ICOs aren't regulated in many countries. That means literally anyone can launch an ICO. All you need is a white paper, a pretty website, and a ton of rich connections who are willing to give you money. By contrast, only established private companies that have been operating for a while are allowed to carry out IPOs. (See the nearby sidebar "Watching ICOs in the United States" for more information.)

>> **You don't even need to have a product to launch an ICO.** Most of the companies that are doing ICOs don't have anything concrete to present to the public; some of them have *proof-of-concept* (which demonstrates the idea is workable), and others have proof-of-stake. Starting an ICO is even easier than starting a crowdfunding for a proper start-up. For start-ups to get funded, they normally need something called *minimum viable product* (MVP), which is a product with enough features to satisfy the early investors and to generate feedback for future developments. In the ICO process, you can reduce the MVP to documents like white papers, partnerships, and media relations.

>> **ICOs are easier to invest in — until they're not.** The only thing you need to start investing in ICOs is access to the Internet. You don't need brokers to carry out your investment. At the time of writing, you can buy any tokens of any company in most countries. However, the list of countries that started adding regulations or banning ICOs altogether started to increase in 2018. In the United States, it's even more complicated because the ICO rules vary from state to state. At the time of writing in 2022, only a handful of ICOs projects were able to raise over a million dollars in investments.

WARNING

Many ICOs block investments from their country of residence because regulatory bodies consider ICO tokens to be securities. These strict regulations limit the ICO participation only to accredited investors and severely limit the investor pool, making it difficult to participate in ICOs. That being said, people have been found to use a virtual private network (VPN) to bypass the geo-blocking (geographical blocks), thus making it look like they're coming from an authorized country so they can invest anyway and creating a lot of legal issues.

TIP

You can view ICO regulations by country at www.bitcoinmarketjournal.com/ico-regulations.

» **ICOs don't grant you ownership of the project.** When you invest in an IPO, you technically become a partial owner of that company. That's why they call the investors shareholders. This designation doesn't really matter if all you're looking for is to sell the stock as its value rises. ICO investors may benefit in many ways in the future, but they have nothing to do with the company itself. All they're getting are a bunch of digital coins (tokens) that may or may not rise in value in the future.

WATCHING ICOs IN THE UNITED STATES

The Securities and Exchange Commission (SEC) is watching the ICO space in the United States very closely and shuts down most of the ICOs that it thinks pose a huge risk to the public investing. The presale option of the ICO can *only* be open to accredited investors (thus not the general public). The ICO for the public can be problematic if the token is considered a security by the SEC as opposed to a platform token (it's absolutely needed to run the platform). Most ICOs launching new cryptos of Ethereum, for example, can't make the case for a platform token (as there is no new platform that requires its own token), so they fall into the securities category.

Also, for U.S.-based companies launching ICOs, there is a lockout period for investors buying in the presale stages, usually 12 months, in which they can't trade the new crypto they invested in. This is done to prevent a pump-and-dump operation, and it's watched very closely by the SEC.

Companies launching ICOs also have to comply with the U.S. federal KYC and AML regulations, which include not accepting or sending cryptos to a large list of wallet addresses that are on the Financial Crimes Enforcement Network's blacklist as either money laundering operators or terrorism financing.

Investing in an ICO

REMEMBER

ICO investing involves a lot of risk. You shouldn't invest money you can't afford to lose in an ICO. If your risk tolerance is low, you can consider many alternative investment assets, as I overview in Chapter 3.

Note also that some ICOs aren't even meant to be investments. They're a tool you can use for a specific product. In the real estate sector, you can use the Propy token to buy properties internationally. Unikrn's CEO Rahul Sood noted in 2017 that "buying a token is buying a product that we're selling that can be used on the Unikrn platform. People should not be looking at this as an investment. If they are looking at this as an investment, they're making a mistake. Tokens are not investments."

But this is an investing chapter in an investing book, and perhaps you've decided to give it a try. Here are some tips on how you can go about it.

Finding ICO listings

You may find out about upcoming ICOs through word of mouth, at a financial event, or through an online ad. If you don't have any specific ICO in mind and just want to search for one from scratch, you can get help from ICO listing websites. But finding the right ICO listing website can also be a challenge because more than 100 of them are already out there, and more are popping up every day.

Here are some tips to keep in mind when searching for an ICO listing website:

>> Start out by comparing two or three ICO listing websites at a time. Are they all featuring the same ICOs on top? This strategy can help you figure out which website is giving you the verified ICO listing.

>> Make sure a site has features such as an ICO calendar, ICO rating, and ICO description.

>> Offering market statistics about the ICO, filters, and scam warning features is a plus.

TIP

At the end of the day, using your everyday search engine may be your best bet to find an ICO listing website. You can consider search terms like "ICO listings," "top ICOs 2023," or "best ICO listing websites."

Analyzing an ICO listing

After you pick your ICO listing website, you're now ready to evaluate and choose the upcoming ICOs you're interested in investing in. With hundreds of ICOs popping out every month, this step can be lengthy, but it's a crucial process. The steps to take when researching an ICO can be similar to those I talk about in Chapter 9 for selecting cryptocurrencies. The following sections give you some research points to keep in mind.

Who's behind the ICO?

The team of developers and management behind the ICO is the most important thing you need to find out about. Who are they? What are their credentials? The ICO website should give you background on the team; otherwise, I would move on to the next ICO listing that provides such crucial information readily on its website. Try to find the team members on LinkedIn to verify their backgrounds (or even existence). In addition, try finding ICOs' boards of advisors and financial backers. Are these people you can trust your money with? Are they dedicated to take their idea to the next step?

WARNING

I've been to many ICO pitching conferences where the team just kept on name-dropping — things like "the Prince of Dubai is investing millions in us" or other unverifiable blabs. In these cases, I normally run, not walk, away and never look back.

What's the cryptocurrency for?

You want to familiarize yourself with the idea behind the crypto as much as possible. Sure, anyone can start a cryptocurrency and list an ICO. The question is why these people have chosen to do so. What specific value does their token have that other cryptocurrencies already in existence don't offer? Who's their competition? How are they better than the competition? What type of technology are they using? Who is their target market, and how large is it?

WARNING

The idea behind the cryptocurrency is important, but beware of unrealistic promises. Scam projects often make bold claims about their products but have nothing new or disruptive in their technology. If someone claims a new cryptocurrency will replace Bitcoin, end world poverty within a year, fix global warming, or increase in value by 10,000 percent, you can add that project to your scam list.

Does the team have a prototype or a code?

WARNING

As I mention in the earlier section "ICOs versus IPOs," you don't necessarily have to have a prototype to launch an ICO. But those with a minimum viable product can show you that the team is serious about the idea and is able to hit future milestones. If a project has no working code whatsoever prior to an ICO, that's a major red flag.

Does the team have a blockchain?

The majority of ICOs don't have a blockchain (flip to Chapter 4 for an introduction to blockchain technology). The founders simply pitch the idea for the utility their tokens can provide. Personally, I prefer to search among those that are based on solid blockchain technology that solves a solid problem rather than those that are glorified apps that can be built without creating a brand-new cryptocurrency.

What's the plan to drive prices higher after the ICO?

The main reason you invest in an ICO is in speculation that its price will go higher in the future. That's why the team behind the ICO should provide you with a road map on how it's planning to do so. This part of the analysis can be similar to that of any already-trading cryptocurrency I talk about in Chapter 8. Here are some key features to watch out for:

>> The crypto has a high enough network volume.

>> The crypto is better than the competition.

>> The ICO gives investors an incentive to hold rather than quickly spend the tokens.

>> The new tokens will have sufficient liquidity.

>> The team is proactive in getting the token listed in multiple exchanges.

WARNING

Many teams seek to create their own exchanges in order to generate the liquidity and volume needed to take off. But I wouldn't view that as sufficient evidence for the token's future success. Getting listed on various exchanges can be tough, which is why it's an important indicator of the token's success down the road.

Does the team have a wide, supportive community?

You don't want to be a sheep who simply follows others, but reaching out to the ICO community can give you a sense about the token. How many supporters does a given ICO have on sources like Reddit, Twitter, and Facebook? Do the supporters appear to be robots, or are they real people and crypto enthusiasts? Beware of paid "community members" whose job is to say positive things about the ICO on social media. Also look for proper media coverage, press releases, and the team's presence on the social media.

Outlining the ICO investment process

When you've found your unicorn ICO, you normally need to have a legit cryptocurrency to invest in it, although sometimes ICOs accept fiat currencies as well. Most importantly, you also need to have a cryptocurrency wallet. Flip to Chapter 7 to identify different types of wallets that can work for you.

TIP

Most ICOs are built on the Ethereum blockchain. That's why in many cases you specifically need Ethereum cryptocurrency and an Ethereum wallet to invest in an ICO. See Chapter 8 for more about this crypto.

REMEMBER

Not all ICOs are created the same. Therefore, I can't show you the exact steps to take when buying into an ICO. Regardless, here are some general guidelines:

1. Make sure you check the official page of the ICO.

2. If the ICO requires you to pay by another crypto, such as Ethereum or Bitcoin, you must first acquire those coins on an exchange (see Chapter 6) and store them in your crypto wallet (see Chapter 7).

3. After completing your due diligence on the ICO's nature (see the earlier section "Analyzing an ICO listing"), register for the ICO based on its website's instructions.

4. Wait for the launch date and follow the instructions. This step normally consists of transferring your cryptocurrency assets from your crypto wallet to the ICO's public address. This step may also cost a transaction fee.

5. After the ICO is launched, the team sends the new tokens to your crypto wallet.

TIP

Because of the risky nature of ICOs and the difficulty in selecting the best ones, you may consider skipping the ICO and waiting until the token/cryptocurrency is launched before buying it. Though many ICOs see an immediate and rapid surge right after launch, more often than not they come crashing down shortly after. The crash doesn't necessarily mean that the token isn't worthy of holding. Historically, these types of price changes happen in the tech industry quite often, providing an excellent post-launch buying opportunity. When things settle down and more people have analyzed the new token, its price can move back up slowly, giving you an opportunity to invest at your own pace. An ICO is rarely too good to pass up it (although it does happen).

Holding your tokens after your purchase

The method you choose to monitor your ICO purchase highly depends on the reasons you bought in the first place. Although not all ICOs are investment vehicles, most teams behind ICOs prefer that you don't buy and dump their tokens after the

ICO, so they do whatever it takes to convince you to hold onto the tokens. And doing so may just pay off in the long run.

REMEMBER

If you invested in the ICO for capital gain purposes only, be prepared to hold onto your investment for a while. At first, your investment may turn negative with a loss, or it may consolidate at the same price with no real returns for a while. Often these periods of losses and consolidation are followed by a massive surge, which may give you the opportunity to take profit. Keep in mind that sometimes the big surges are the beginning of an uptrend (or more gains) in the market, so by selling too rapidly you may miss out on more profit. Other times, the surge can be a simple pump-and-dump. Therefore, you need to continuously monitor and conduct the Invest Diva Diamond Analysis (IDDA; see Chapter 9) to create the best exit strategy.

REMEMBER

If you make money on your ICO investment, you have to report it as capital gains. See Chapter 23 for more on taxes.

So You Want to Start an ICO: Launching an ICO Yourself

In 2017, everyone seemed to be launching an ICO. But after a number of scams, failed ICOs, and a general buzzkill in the cryptocurrency world, the hype around ICOs cooled down somewhat. By February 2018, 46 percent of the 2017 ICOs had failed, despite the fact that they had raised over $104 million. People realized that in order to be taken seriously and have long-term success, they must give it their all. At the end of the day, integrity wins. That's probably why by 2022, the ICO buzz had quieted down, and people became more interested in already-established projects instead of looking for the next best thing.

One key debate is whether ICOs will replace the traditional start-up fundraising process. After all, over 50 percent of start-ups also fail within the first five years, so the statistics aren't that far off when comparing ICOs to venture capital.

The following sections give you a few things to keep in mind before deciding to go the ICO route.

Understanding the challenges

Throughout this chapter I talk about how anyone can start an ICO (see the earlier section "How an ICO works and how to start one" for specifics). Launching a *successful* ICO, on the other hand, is a different story. Here are a few things you need right off the bat:

>> A minimum of $60,000 to launch an initial campaign

>> Six months to one year of a pre-public engagement phase

>> A "dream team" to join your project

>> A product that uses your token

>> A meaningful reason to integrate the digital token into your product

Taking a few steps before the launch

If you're A-OK with the challenges in the previous section and want to become the next ICO success story, here are some steps to get you started. Just a heads-up: These steps are overly simplified.

Create a product that needs an ICO

The only thing that can increase the demand for your token is having a real utility. If a decentralized token doesn't really impact the value of your product, then forget about it. People are becoming increasingly smart about ICO investments. To become one of the success stories in the field, you need to have a thorough understanding of your market and your target audience. Most importantly, you must know what people will be willing to give you their money for. You can run a survey on a site like SurveyMonkey or BitcoinTalk Forum (check out bitcointalk.org) to see the market reaction to your idea. Make sure you also find out about your competition in the space.

Get legal advice

Are ICOs legal in your country? Are you legally covered if things go wrong? ICOs are becoming more regulated. That's why you must do your due diligence to comply with all relevant laws and regulations in the field. You can find attorneys who are experienced with ICOs using your search engine or LinkedIn; search for terms like "ICO lawyers near me" or "ICO lawyers [enter your country]."

Create a token

This step is actually the easiest step of the process, especially if you're not planning on creating a blockchain from scratch. You can simply use platforms such as Ethereum and Waves. If you follow their instructions, it can literally take less than 20 minutes to issue your own token on Ethereum. Creating a token is outside the scope of this book, but you can see a detailed road map at `medium.com/bitfwd/how-to-issue-your-own-token-on-ethereum-in-less-than-20-minutes-ac1f8f022793`.

Write a white paper

As I explain earlier in this chapter, white papers are essential for analyzing an ICO or a cryptocurrency. So you can imagine that your investors are likely to demand a thorough, clear one before they give you their money. Search for white paper templates online, and make sure you're up-to-date with what investors are looking for.

Create a launch buzz

This step is also very similar to launching any new product or start-up. As a start-up owner myself, I've been studying launching techniques throughout my entrepreneurial journey, and I'm still learning. Launching an ICO has other additional marketing requirements unique to its nature, including the following:

>> Getting listed on hot ICO listing websites

>> Reaching out to ICO journalists and bloggers

>> Creating your own Reddit, Twitter, Facebook, and LinkedIn pages

>> Considering doing an *airdrop*, which means distributing your token for free to the masses to gain attention and media buzz

>> Considering a global road show and participating in well-attended blockchain events/conferences or partnering with an influencer

TIP

Creating a successful marketing campaign around your ICO is well beyond the scope of this book. So if you're not a natural marketer, make sure you hire the right marketing team to help you along the way! Hiring a great marketing team is yet another challenge that is well beyond the scope of this book, but you can start by searching on your favorite search engine, looking on LinkedIn, or attending local networking events you may find on `www.eventbrite.com`.

Get your token listed on exchanges

Creating your own exchange can certainly help boost your token's liquidity and volume, but you must be proactive in getting your token listed on as many exchanges as possible. Exchanges will potentially become the main place people will buy and sell your token, so getting it accepted on the strongest and most established ones is critical — and something that requires a heck of a lot of hustling, networking, and proving your coin is worth it. See Chapter 6 more about exchanges. If you do want to create your own exchange, companies such as Shift Markets (`www.shiftmarkets.com`) can help with that sort of thing.

Chapter 13

Cryptocurrency Mining

When I first heard of Bitcoin mining, I immediately imagined a hot guy with a ripped body, wearing a helmet with a flashlight on it, getting dirty inside a mountain. However, I soon learned cryptocurrency miners don't have to have any of these qualities. All you need is access to high-speed Internet and a high-end computer. In this chapter, I explore the basics of crypto mining.

REMEMBER

As I explain in Chapter 5, not all cryptocurrencies require mining. Bitcoin, the granddaddy of all coins, started the mining craze in 2009, setting up the concept of blockchain technology (see Chapter 4). However, many new coins out there can't be mined and use alternative methods to generate value which is also more energy efficient.

Understanding How Mining Works in a Nutshell

Bitcoin and other minable cryptocurrencies rely on miners to maintain their network. By solving math problems or guessing numbers like a puzzle (see Chapter 5) and providing consent on the validity of transactions, miners support the blockchain network, which will otherwise collapse. For their service to the network, miners are rewarded with newly created cryptocurrencies (such as Bitcoins) and transaction fees.

REMEMBER

To really understand mining, you first need to explore the world of blockchain technology in Chapter 4. Here's a quick overview: If you want to help update the *ledger* (transaction record) of a minable cryptocurrency like Bitcoin, all you need to do is to guess a random number that solves a math equation. Of course, you don't want to guess these numbers all by yourself. That's what computers are for! The more powerful your computer is, the more quickly you can solve these math problems and beat the mining crowd. The more you win the guessing game, the more cryptos you receive as a reward. If all the miners use a relatively similar type of computing power, the laws of probability dictate that the winner isn't likely to be the same miner every time. But if half of the miners have regular commercial computers while the other half use supercomputers, then the participation gets unfair to the favor of the super powerful computers. Some argue that those with supercomputers will win most of the time, if not all the time.

Cryptocurrency networks such as Bitcoin automatically change the difficulty of the math problems depending on how fast miners are solving them. This process is also known as adjusting the difficulty of the proof-of-work (PoW) that I talk about in Chapter 5. In the early days of Bitcoin, when the miners were just a tiny group of computer junkies, the proof-of-work was very easy to achieve. In fact, when Satoshi Nakamoto released Bitcoin, he/she/they/it intended it to be mined on computer CPUs. (The true identity of Satoshi is unknown, and I'm adding "it" because there are even discussions that Satoshi can be a government entity.) Satoshi wanted this distributed network to be mined by people distributed around the world using their laptops and personal computers. Back in the day, you were able to solve rather easy guessing games with a simple processor on your computer.

As the mining group got larger, so did the competition. After a bunch of hard-core computer gamers joined the network, they discovered the graphics cards for their gaming computers were much more suitable for mining. My husband was sure among those people. As a gaming geek, he had two high-end computers with Nvidia graphic cards sitting in his game room, collecting dust after we got married. (For obvious reasons, he had to trade his gaming time up for dating time.) When he saw my passion for cryptos, he had to jump in and turn on his computers to start mining. But because he joined the mining game rather late, mining Bitcoin wasn't turning out to be that profitable. That's why he turned to mining other minable cryptos. (I talk about finding the best cryptocurrencies to mine later in this chapter.)

REMEMBER

Mining isn't a get-rich-quick scheme. To mine effectively, you need access to pretty sophisticated equipment. First you need to do the math to see whether the initial investment required to set up your mining assets is going to be worth the cryptos you get in return. And even if you choose to mine cryptocurrencies instead of buying them, you're still betting on the fact that their value will increase in the future.

As Bitcoin became more popular, mining it became more popular, and therefore more difficult. To add to the challenge, some companies who saw the potential in Bitcoin value started massive data centers, called *mining farms*, with ranges of high-end computers whose jobs are only to mine Bitcoins. Figure 13-1 shows an example of a mining farm setup.

© John Wiley & Sons, Inc.

FIGURE 13-1:
High-end computers in a mining farm.

So next time you think about becoming a Bitcoin miner, keep in mind who you're going up against! But don't get disappointed. You do have a way to go about mining: mining pools, which I talk about later in this chapter.

Discovering What You Need to Mine

Before getting started with mining, you should set yourself up with a few mining toys. When you've got everything up and running, mining becomes rather easy because everything happens automatically. The only thing left to do is pay your electric bills at the end of each month.

REMEMBER

First things first — here's a brief to-do list to get you started:

>> **Get a crypto wallet (flip to Chapter 7 for details).**

>> **Make sure you have a strong Internet connection.**

>> **Set up your high-end computer in a cool location.** By *cool*, I literally mean "low temperature" and not "stylish."

» **Select the hardware to use based on the cryptocurrency you want to mine.** I explain more about this in the next two sections.

» **If you want to mine solo (not recommended), download the whole cryptocurrency's blockchain.** Be prepared; for mature cryptos, downloading the whole blockchain may take days.

» **Get a mining software package (flip to the later section on software for more).**

» **Join a mining pool.** I explain more later in this chapter.

» **Make sure your expenses aren't exceeding your rewards.** I explain more later in this chapter.

Before you begin: The mining profitability of different cryptos

Some tech junkies mine just for the heck of it, but at the end of the day, most people mine cryptos with profit in mind. But even if you fall in the former group, you may as well get a reward out of your efforts, eh? Mining profitability can change drastically based on cryptocurrency value, mining difficulty, electricity rates, and hardware prices at the time you're setting up your mining system. You can go to websites like www.coinwarz.com to see which cryptos are best to mine at a given time. As of December 2022, for example, that site indicates the most profitable cryptocurrency to mine is Verge (XVG), while Bitcoin is ranked number four, as you can see in Figure 13-2.

FIGURE 13-2: Snapshot of mining profitability list in December 2022.

© CoinWarz.com

REMEMBER

Even if mining isn't profitable at the moment, your cryptos can be worth a lot in the future if the coin value surges. By mining cryptos that have low profitability at the moment, you're taking an investment risk. For more on risk, flip to Chapter 3.

Mining hardware

Different types of cryptocurrencies may require different types of hardware for best mining results. For example, hardware (such as ASICs, which stands for application-specific integrated circuits) has been customized to optimize cryptocurrencies like Bitcoin and Bitcoin Cash. But for cryptocurrencies without dedicated hardware, such as Ethereum, Dogecoin, and Zcash, graphics processing units (GPUs) are good enough to process the transactions. Of course, GPUs are still slow at mining compared to mining farms. If you decide to mine Bitcoin with a GPU, for example, you may wait years before you can mine one Bitcoin! You can find GPUs at any store that sells computer hardware equipment.

As mining became more difficult, crafty coders started exploiting graphics cards because those provided more *hashing power*, which is the rate at which you mine (flip to Chapter 5 to explore hashing). They wrote mining software (in other words, developed mining algorithms) optimized for the processing power of GPUs to mine way more quickly than central processing units (CPUs). These types of graphics cards are faster, but they still use more electricity and generate a lot of heat. That's when miners decided to switch to something called an *application-specific integrated circuit*, or ASIC. The ASIC technology has made Bitcoin mining much faster while using less power. (You can search "where to buy ASIC miner" on your favorite search engine.)

REMEMBER

During crypto hype, mining equipment such as ASICs becomes incredibly expensive. At the beginning of 2018, for example, they were priced at over $9,000 due to high demand. But during the crypto crash of 2022, its price dropped to below $3,000. That's why you must consider your return on investment before getting yourself involved in mining; sometimes simply buying cryptocurrencies makes more sense than mining them does.

TIP

Cryptocurrency mining may make more sense to do in winter, both *crypto winter* (the periods of time when crypto prices drop, people are not as excited about the industry as they were during the hype seasons, and therefore the demand for crypto equipment is lower) and the actual season of winter. During crypto winters when no one is hyping up the industry, you may find your mining equipment at a lower price. It's also more beneficial to mine during the actual season of winter because mining generates so much heat in the hardware. You may be able to reduce the cost of your electricity bill by using nature as your computer's natural cooling system. Or using your computer as your home's heating system! Of course, the cost of the electricity used by mining computers far exceeds the cost of heating or cooling the house.

Mining software

Mining software handles the actual mining process. If you're a solo miner, the software connects your machine to the blockchain to become a mining node or a miner. If you mine with a pool (see the next section), the software connects you to the mining pool. The main job of the software is to deliver the mining hardware's work to the rest of the network and to receive completed work from the other miners on the network. It also shows statistics such as the speed of your miner and fan, your hash rate, and the temperature.

Again, you must search for the best software at the time you're ready to start. Here are some popular ones at the time of writing:

>> **Awesome Miner:** Awesome Miner's interface manages all your mining activity in one program. It runs on Windows, Linux, and cloud-based web on any other browser.

>> **CGminer:** CGminer is one of the oldest and most popular examples of Bitcoin mining software. You can use it for pools like Cryptominers to mine different altcoins. It supports ASICs and GPUs.

>> **EasyMiner:** One of the easiest and fasest mining softwares to set up. However, it's only suitable for less powerful CPUs and GPUs.

REMEMBER

These options are just examples and not recommendations. You can go about selecting the best software by reading online reviews about their features, reputations, and ease of use. This market is evolving, and navigating your way to find the best options may take time. Personally I rely heavily on a search engine to find a number of resources, and then I compare the results to choose the one I feel most comfortable with.

Mining pools

Mining pools definitely bring miners together, but luckily you don't have to get into your beach body shape to join one.

Simply put, a *mining pool* is a place where regular miners who don't have access to gigantic mining farms (described earlier in this chapter) come together and share their resources. When you join a mining pool, you're able to find solutions for the math problems faster than going about it solo. You're rewarded in proportion to the amount of work you provide.

WARNING

Mining pools are cool because they smooth out rewards and make them more predictable. Without a mining pool, you receive a mining payout only if you find a block on your own. That's why I don't recommend solo mining; your hardware's hash rate is very unlikely to be anywhere near enough to find a block on its own.

REMEMBER

To find a mining pool that's suitable for you, I recommend doing an online search at the time you're ready to jump in. That's because this market changes rapidly, and so do the infrastructure and the participants. Here are some features to compare when selecting the best mining pool for you:

>> **Minable cryptocurrency:** Make sure the pool is mining the cryptocurrency you've selected.

>> **Location:** Some pools don't have servers in all countries. Make sure the one you choose is available in your country.

>> **Reputation:** This factor is an important one. Don't get in the pool with nasty people.

>> **Fees:** Some pools have higher fees than others. Make sure you don't prioritize fee over reputation, though.

>> **Profit sharing:** Different pools have different rules for profit sharing. One thing to consider is how much of the coin you need to mine before the pool pays you out.

>> **Ease of use:** If you're not tech-savvy, this feature can be important to keep in mind.

A mining setup example

Figure 13-3 shows what my husband's mining setup looked like at the beginning of 2018 to mine Ethereum:

>> Two custom-made, high-end gaming computers from boutique PC builders (one from Maingear and the other from Falcon Northwest)

>> Two Nvidia GTX 1070 Tis in his first PC; two Nvidia Titan X Pascals in the second PC

>> Two Ledger Nano S hardware wallets

>> Ethermine.org pool to mine Ethereum

© John Wiley & Sons, Inc.

FIGURE 13-3:
High-end gaming
rigs that can be
used for mining.

Keep in mind that he already had these systems sitting in his game room, so he didn't really make much investment with mining in mind. He did invest in the hardware wallet, though. (Head to Chapter 7 for more on wallets.)

Making sure mining is worth your time

After you have all your tools together, you then need to set up and start mining. It can certainly be challenging to do so, and the dynamic of the mining community changes regularly, so you must make sure that you are up-to-date with recent changes and have acquired the latest tools for your mining adventure. You can always do so by researching the key elements I mention in the previous sections on your search engine.

TIP

If you're looking to mine Bitcoin, keep in mind that your profitability depends on many factors (such as your computing power, electricity costs, pool fees, and the Bitcoin's value at the time of mining), and chances are very high that you won't be profitable at all. You can check whether Bitcoin mining is going to profitable for you by using a Bitcoin mining calculator (check out www.investdiva.com/mining-calculator). Mining calculators take into account all the relevant costs you may be paying to mine and show you if mining a certain cryptocurrency is profitable for your situation. Simple mining calculators ask you questions about your hash rate, the pool fees, and your power usage, among others. Figure 13-4 shows you a sample mining calculator powered by CryptoRival. Once you hit the "Calculate" button, it shows you your gross earning per year, month, and day.

By doing the mining calculation ahead of time, you may realize that mining other cryptocurrencies may make more sense.

FIGURE 13-4:
Example of a
simple mining
calculator.

Chapter **14**

Investing in NFTs

Non-fungible tokens, or NFTs, are a type of cryptocurrency that is growing quickly. They have been in the news a lot lately because more and more people are using them. Even if you don't know exactly what they are, you have probably heard of them.

Non-fungible tokens are a new way for people to own unique items. This is done through a digital certificate that shows you are the owner of that unique thing. The value of an NFT comes from how much people want it and how rare it is. It can also be sold in the future.

REMEMBER

There are many different types of NFTs that give us the ability to effectively tokenize things such as:

>> Artwork

>> Collectibles

>> Gaming assets

>> Virtual fashion

>> Event tickets

>> Music and audio content

When it comes to investing in NFTs, there are many different things to think about. In this chapter, I explore some popular ways you can invest in NFTs or the technology that helps create them.

Understanding What an NFT Is

Let's take a deeper dive into understanding exactly what an NFT is and the reasons behind the huge amount of ever-increasing interest in them.

An NFT is a digital asset that can't be duplicated or changed. You can think of it as a digital equivalent of artwork from a private collection, where each individual piece is unique and worth a specific amount.

This means that NFTs turn digital works of art and other collectibles into unique, verifiable assets that are easy to buy and sell through a database called a blockchain. Flip to Chapter 4 for a deeper dive into blockchain technology.

TECHNICAL STUFF

NFTs are a type of cryptographic token that represents unique assets in both the real and digital worlds. They act as a verification of authenticity and ownership for items within blockchain networks.

In order to be non-fungible, NFTs must:

>> Not be interchangeable

>> Not be divisible

>> Not be able to be replicated

>> Be unique

>> Be *immutable* (permanent and unalterable)

NFTs contain unique information. This information is recorded in a smart contract on a blockchain. This makes each individual NFT unique. They can't be replaced or swapped with another token because no two NFTs are ever identical.

Cash, for example, is a type of asset that can be easily exchanged. This means that you can trade one banknote for another, as long as they have the same value. There is no difference to the holder between different banknotes.

By contrast, *non-fungible* means that the item is unique and cannot be replaced. For example, if you have a dollar bill that is signed by a celebrity or famous artist, it becomes unique and cannot be replaced.

Some people say that NFTs are similar to cryptocurrency. This is because the proof of their existence is recorded on a blockchain, and they can ultimately be bought and sold using cryptocurrency. There isn't necessarily a physical asset that links them to the real world, but this doesn't mean that they aren't valuable.

NFTs are different from cryptocurrencies because they are not interchangeable. This means that every NFT is unique and cannot be replaced with another one of the same value. For example, in the earlier example of a one-dollar bill, Bitcoin and Ethereum would be interchangeable because they are all the same value.

NFTs are a way of tracking ownership of unique digital or physical items. They use cryptography to make sure that the item is unique and can be verified.

Knowing How NFTs Work

NFTs are stored on a blockchain. They are unique assets that prove authenticity. The ownership of an NFT is established and recorded on a blockchain network. A blockchain is a collection of data blocks that are linked together and electronically stored, and you can read more in Chapter 4.

This chain of blocks creates a digital ledger. A *digital ledger* is a group of data that records any activity within the chain. The easiest way to think about it is like a bookkeeping system that records every transaction within the blockchain. A *blockchain ledger* is a digital record of all transactions that have ever taken place on the system. This provides a perfect, verifiable audit trail for all transactions.

Proof of ownership is an important part of NFTs. This is because it proves that you own the original and authentic copy of a digital file.

When someone buys or sells an NFT, the information about that transaction is stored on the blockchain. This makes it easy for everyone involved to see what happened during the transaction.

Each blockchain ledger is stored on many different servers all over the world. This means that anyone who uses the blockchain technology can see and check other people's entries. This makes sure that the data in a block is safe, secure, and cannot be changed.

WHICH BLOCKCHAINS SUPPORT NFTs?

TECHNICAL STUFF

Many different blockchains support NFTs. At the time of writing, Ethereum is the overall leader among other blockchain networks and NFTs were originally born on the Ethereum blockchain.

Ethereum is a blockchain platform that supports decentralized apps (known as dApps) and also smart contracts. Smart contracts are used to issue NFTs because they are able to authenticate and accurately verify ownership.

Due to its data structure, Ethereum is a highly secure network and the majority of NFT projects run on the Ethereum blockchain in the form of ERC-721 coins/tokens.

Although Ethereum is the leading blockchain in support of NFTs, there are also many others, such as Solana and Cardano.

NFTs are created on the blockchain. The blockchain is a decentralized network that is used by many cryptocurrencies. But it is worth mentioning that because different types of NFTs are created on specific blockchains, they must stay on that specific blockchain. This is so that proof and authenticity of ownership can always be verified. They can never leave the blockchain ecosystem in which they were created.

Investing in NFTs

One of the main reasons people invest in NFTs is that they may increase in value over time. For example, the CryptoPunk 1422 NFT was bought for $74 in 2017, but it was recently sold for $2 million (more on CryptoPunks later in this chapter!). This is just one example of how some NFTs can have a lot of potential for price appreciation.

REMEMBER

Although NFTs are seen in many different industries, most of the trading volume for NFTs is related to digital art, music, digital real estate, blockchain gaming items, and other popular collectibles.

Almost every industry has some kind of collectible. Collectibles are a popular hobby all over the world. NFTs are popular because we like to own things that we like and that might be unique or rare. With NFTs, we have the chance to collect digital assets instead of physical things.

Finding NFTs

If you want to invest in NFTs, there are a lot of different ways to do it. One way would be to look at an online marketplace where you can find different types of NFTs by type or category. You can then purchase them with the cryptocurrency you want.

Some NFT marketplaces have a set price for NFTs, while others let you bid for an NFT through an auction until someone wins it.

You may need to use a specific type of cryptocurrency to buy an NFT depending on the blockchain that it was created on. But don't worry, these marketplaces make it easy for you to buy NFTs when you're ready. Here are some popular marketplaces:

- Opensea (https://opensea.io)
- Rarible (rarible.com)
- Nifty Gateway (www.niftygateway.com)

Working out which NFTs to invest in

This is a difficult question to answer because it depends on a lot of factors. Some people would argue that you shouldn't necessarily consider an NFT as an investment at all because predicting the future value of an NFT is impossible and highly speculative.

For many people, the primary reason for buying the majority of relatively inexpensive NFTs is simply because you want to and to prove that you own a unique digital asset that is aligned with your particular interests.

If you're thinking of investing in NFTs, it's important to know about the top assets available. Some of the most well-known NFTs are considered to be *top tier*. These NFTs are highly collectible and in high demand, but there is a limited supply which makes them expensive to buy and invest in. Examples include CryptoPunks and Bored Ape Yacht Club:

- **CryptoPunks:** CryptoPunks was one of the first collections of NFTs to gain a large following from enthusiasts. It is considered to be a trendy project with 10,000 8-bit characters based around a punk theme. CryptoPunks are currently the most expensive and highly valued NFTs in the world.

>> **The Bored Ape Yacht Club:** If you have ever done a Google search for "NFT," you may have found The Bored Ape Yacht Club (BAYC). This club has 10,000 unique NFTs. Each NFT is an animated ape with a different design. Thanks to the interest of many high-profile names and celebrities such as Snoop Dogg and Eminem, the Bored Ape Yacht Club's NFTs quickly became seen as a status symbol. At the time of writing, the total sales have reached $1 billion. Owning a BAYC unlocks access to the exclusive BAYC community and a whole host of other community-based features and benefits. The combination of their distinctive designs and their worldwide appeal helps to validate their rarity and therefore their high value.

The price of top-tier NFTs (such as the ones mentioned here) can vary a lot depending on how much people want them and how the market is feeling. It's important to be clear about your own individual risk tolerance, as well as how much you're willing to risk, if you're thinking about investing in top-tier NFT projects. Flip to Chapter 3 to calculate your risk tolerance. These types of aspirational NFT investments are considered higher risk.

TIP

To find out if NFTs are suitable for your portfolio, you can download my free risk management toolkit by attending my most popular free Masterclass: `investdivapig.com/masterclass`.

WARNING

Before investing in NFTs, it is important to do a lot of research. This is because it can be difficult to understand how much each NFT is worth, and also because the price of NFTs can change a lot.

Investing in NFT-related cryptocurrencies

Another way to invest in the NFT industry is to buy cryptocurrencies that are related to NFTs. This option might be simpler than picking a specific NFT to invest in.

TIP

Looking at one of the leading cryptocurrency resources allows you to research specifically NFT cryptocurrencies by category. For example: `coinmarketcap.com/view/collectibles-nfts`.

Here are some of the top NFT related cryptocurrencies by market cap. Some of these are discussed in greater detail in Chapter 11:

>> Flow (FLOW)

>> ApeCoin (APE)

>> Chiliz (CHZ)

- » The Sandbox (SAND)

- » Decentraland (MANA)

Investing in NFT-related stocks

Investing in stocks related to NFTs could be another way for investors to consider gaining exposure to NFTs in a potentially less volatile market than investing directly in NFTs or NFT-related cryptocurrencies. There are actually quite a lot of stocks that have links to NFTs, so it would be worth performing a Google search when you are doing research in this area. Here are a few well known stocks that have strong links to NFTs:

- » eBay (EBAY)

- » Cloudflare (NET)

- » Funko Inc (FNKO)

- » Coinbase (COIN)

Customers on eBay are able to trade NFTs related to images, video, artwork, and other items. Cloudflare is a content delivery network (CDN) and DDoS mitigation company that ensures the security and reliability of various resources such as websites, APIs, and other applications. Cloudflare also has other services within its business, such as Cloudflare Stream, and that service supports NFTs. Funko designs and sells unique pop culture collectibles, accessories, and toys, as well as NFTs. And Coinbase allows you to shop NFTs at the best prices from various market places.

TIP

In my Invest Diva Premium Investing Group, we have a section about the most recent top NFT-related stocks. We tell you how risky each asset is so it is easy for you to make your investment decision. You can join for free: investdivapig.com.

Making and Selling Your Own NFTs

Making your own NFT is actually a lot more straightforward than you might think. You can make NFTs from almost anything unique as long as it can be stored digitally and holds value.

The first thing you need to do in order to make and sell an NFT is to *mint* your NFT (the process of creating a currency and NFTs on a blockchain). There will likely be some up-front costs involved because NFTs are ultimately powered by a block-chain (usually Ethereum) and using a blockchain carries a cost known as a *gas fee*. You will usually have to pay this fee in order to get your artwork tokenized.

TIP

Two of the leading platforms for NFT creation are OpenSea and Rarible. Both platforms allow users to upload their art and create NFT collections with ease without any technical blockchain knowledge required. If you are planning on selling a small quantity of NFTs for a high price, then Rarible might be a good choice. However, if you are looking to sell a lot of lower-priced NFTs within a collection, then OpenSea could be a great choice for you. For the purposes of this example, I focus on OpenSea.

Let's take a look at an overview of the steps involved in making and selling your own NFT:

1. **Create and design your NFT artwork.**
2. **Choose and set up a digital wallet.**
3. **Tokenize your artwork.**
4. **List your NFT on the marketplace.**

The following sections consider each of the preceding steps in turn.

Step 1: Create and design your NFT artwork

Let's assume that you already have a piece of art in mind that you would like to turn into an NFT. Perhaps a painting or a drawing. Most NFT art collections are purely simple digital illustrations. You could always look at other popular NFT collections to give you some inspiration.

TIP

A great starting point would be to familiarize yourself with popular NFT art soft-ware programs such as Adobe Photoshop, Blender, and Procreate. Spend some time creating your design and then save your file.

Step 2: Choose and set up a digital wallet

After you have created your NFT and saved its file, you need to choose and set up a digital wallet. There are a few different digital wallets that you could consider, but in this example I refer to the MetaMask digital wallet.

Follow the steps to download and set up your digital wallet at https://metamask. io. Make sure you remember to keep track of your *seed phrase* (a recovery phrase for your crypto wallet that includes a series of random words) in case you ever need to recover the wallet. This wallet can hold your NFTs and you will also be using it to pay blockchain gas fees later.

TECHNICAL STUFF

This digital wallet doesn't actually store your NFT. It stores what is known as your *private key* which you will need to authorize transactions. Cryptocurrencies and NFTs are kept on the blockchain with the digital wallet ID designating ownership.

Step 3: Tokenize your artwork

Next, it's time to tokenize your artwork (or any other assets of your choice)!

Head to OpenSea at `https://opensea.io` and click on the "Create" button. This will allow you to connect your MetaMask wallet with OpenSea and get the process started.

Next, OpenSea will ask you to create a name for your NFT and you will be prompted to upload your artwork file that you made in Step 1. Once uploaded, you will be able to assign certain properties and characteristics to your NFT to distinguish it from any others that you might be uploading to your collection.

Lastly, determine exactly how many copies of each item you would like and set the price, either as a fixed price or a timed auction.

TIP

Selling at a fixed price is easier than a timed auction, but with a timed auction, you have a chance of making more than you expected, depending on the demand! Briefly sum up the advantages and disadvantages of both fixed price and timed auction here.

Step 4: List your NFT on the marketplace

Here comes the exciting part! So that you can sell your NFT, you will need to enable OpenSea to sell items from your account. In order to do this, it requires a blockchain transaction, and this is where that gas fee comes in. Simply send some Ethereum (ETH) directly to your MetaMask and that's it!

This fee is only due to be paid the first time that you create a new NFT collection.

You have now given permission to OpenSea to sell your NFT or collection of NFTs, so anyone on their marketplace can now search, find, and purchase on the OpenSea marketplace.

TIP

Lots of other more cost-effective blockchains and cryptocurrencies exist but bear in mind that using them might lower your chances of selling because many collectors prefer to use Ethereum.

THE PROS AND CONS OF NFTs

NFTs are an absolutely fascinating subject! Let's take a quick look at some pros and cons of them:

Pros of NFTs

- NFTs give content creators and artists ownership over the unique digital assets that they create as well as the opportunity and potential for exciting new streams of income.

- NFTs are collectible and unique. The opportunity to collect something that is unique or extremely rare is an exciting proposition for many people.

- NFTs are immutable and because they are based on the blockchain they can never be deleted, duplicated, or altered in any way. It is important for NFTs to have authenticity, proven origin, and provenance. This will always be identifiable within the on-chain audit trail created by transactions.

Cons of NFTs

- NFTs are a highly speculative market. Deciphering value is incredibly challenging.

- It is difficult to know whether NFTs represent a long-term investment opportunity or whether they are just a passing fad. Time will tell. New trends are constantly entering the NFT market which although is exciting, it potentially raises concern over the unknown longevity of older and more established NFT projects and collections.

- Despite the technology behind NFTs being very secure, some exchanges and platforms are not always completely secure. Cyber security is of paramount importance as there have occasionally been reports of stolen NFTs after cyber security breaches.

Chapter **15**

Stocks and Exchange Traded Funds with Cryptocurrency Exposure

E
ven if you're not a hard-core fan of cryptocurrency investing, or still have cold feet before diving right in, getting some indirect exposure to the industry rather than diving directly headfirst into the market is always a good idea. In this chapter, I overview some methods to find stocks and exchange traded funds (ETFs) that can get you just the right amount of exposure to the crypto market while diversifying your portfolio in other fields as well.

WARNING

Stocks, ETFs, and all other investment assets carry a certain amount of risk. To create an investment portfolio that is unique to your financial situation and goals, make sure you calculate your risk tolerance by checking out Chapter 3. You can grab my risk management toolkit by attending my most popular free Masterclass: investdiva.com/masterclass.

TIP

To buy stocks and ETFs, you likely must open an account with a broker in your area, which is different from your cryptocurrency exchange or broker. While some brokers offer cryptocurrencies as well as stocks and ETFs, at the time of writing the number of such brokers is limited in the United States. You can get a free stock to get you started if you open an account with Robinhood: `share.robinhood.com/kianad1`. See Chapter 6 for more information on brokers and exchanges.

Looking for Stocks with Exposure to Cryptos

When I want to start the process of strategy development for any asset, I make sure I check all the points of the Invest Diva Diamond Analysis (IDDA), as I explain in Chapter 9. That includes analyzing the markets from fundamental, sentimental, and technical points of view and then adding my risk tolerance and portfolio diversity to the mix to achieve a perfect, personalized strategy that works for me. The same works for picking stocks. But if you're looking specifically for stocks with exposure to the cryptocurrency/blockchain industry, you need to do the analysis on both ends — the stock itself and its crypto side. The following sections cover how you can conduct the analysis on your own.

TIP

Investing is personal, just like personal finance is personal. What works for me may not work for you because we are likely in a different financial situation, and are not the same exact age with the same exact family situation and goals. Learning how to invest on your own is one of the most important skills you can acquire to serve you and your family for generations to come, without having to pay money managers (who may not even have your best interest at heart) a commission.

My mission is to help 100 million families take control of their financial future. Join the Invest Diva movement here: investdiva.com/masterclass.

Fundamentals

Blockchain and cryptocurrencies are related, but not all companies who are investing in blockchain technology have direct exposure to the cryptocurrency market. And even though the cryptocurrency market takes a hit every few years, major public companies continue their rapid investments in blockchain technology. In fact, when PricewaterhouseCoopers (PwC) surveyed 600 executives from 15 territories in August 2018, 84 percent of them indicated their companies were "actively involved" with blockchain technology. This number is rapidly growing year after year.

As I discuss in Chapter 4, blockchain is the underlying technology for cryptocurrencies such as Bitcoin and Ethereum. In 2022, companies that were reorganizing their structure to incorporate blockchain included IBM (stock symbol: IBM), Microsoft (stock symbol: MSFT), Oracle (stock symbol: ORCL), Intel (stock symbol: INTC), Walmart (stock symbol: WMT), Goldman Sachs (stock symbol: GS), Alibaba (stock symbol: BABA), Amazon (stock symbol: AMZN), Overstock (stock symbol: OSTK), Citigroup (stock symbol: C), and Samsung (stock symbol: SSNLF), to name a few. I can only imagine more big names will have jumped on the blockchain wagon by the time you have this book in your hands.

So in other words, just by purchasing the stocks of companies that are using the blockchain technology, you can get exposed to blockchain technology while also riding the upside of these companies' potential capital gains as well.

Enough about companies that are investing in blockchain! How about cryptocurrencies? How can you get indirect exposure to this byproduct of blockchain technology? You need to think outside the box. The following sections give you some points to search for before you select stocks with crypto exposure. (For more information on fundamental analysis, check out Chapter 9.)

TIP

Companies can get involved with the cryptocurrency market in so many ways. Make sure to stay on top of the news on websites such as cryptobriefing.com and www.coindesk.com to be in the know.

Crypto mining exposure

Some major cryptocurrencies are minable. And to be able to mine, you need high-end computers with sophisticated hardware, as I cover in Chapter 13. When cryptocurrency mining is at its peak, such companies' stock value also skyrockets. One example of this trend has been Advanced Micro Devices stock (AMD) since 2016. My Invest Diva students and I saw over 1,000 percent return over the two-year period that we held onto our AMD stocks since 2016. More specifically, we started buying AMD shares when it was $1.84 per share at the beginning of 2016 and sold throughout 2018 as it reached $25 and above. We bought back again as its price dropped and took profit as it reached above $150. We developed this strategy using my IDDA method that I introduce in Chapter 9. Of course, cryptocurrency mining was only one of the drivers behind AMD's price surge. But for sure, as more people got into cryptocurrency mining, the demand for AMD graphics processing units (GPUs) went higher, and so did AMD's share value.

TIP

Many other companies are now focusing on this area and may potentially do a better job than AMD in the future. Media websites such as www.guru3d.com and www.anandtech.com often track the latest tech news, so following them can give you an edge in knowing which companies can give you crypto mining exposure.

Crypto payment exposure

Another way to get indirect exposure to the cryptocurrency market through public companies is to go after those that accept altcoins as a payment method for their services. Some pioneers in this area include Overstock.com (stock symbol: OSTK) and Microsoft (stock symbol: MSFT) who started accepting crypto payments in 2017 and 2018.

At the time of writing organizations that accept Bitcoin as payment include Home Depot, Save the Children, Whole Foods, Virgin Airlines, and Wikipedia to name just a few. You can use your preferred search engine to get the most recent list by searching the phrase "companies that accept crypto payments."

WARNING

If crypto payment exposure is the *only* reason you're investing in these types of stocks, you must remember that their price volatility can be directly correlated to the cryptocurrency market itself and therefore may not give you the diversification you're looking for. For example, Overstock's OSTK shares saw massive gains after it started to accept Bitcoin at the end of 2017 and throughout the beginning of 2018. However, as the Bitcoin price crashed, so did OSTK's share price, as you can see in Figure 15-1.

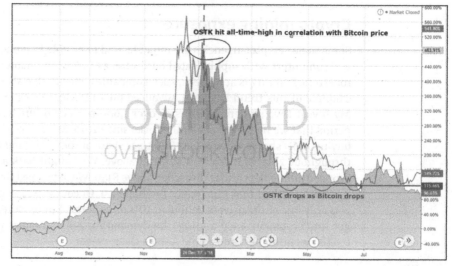

FIGURE 15-1: OSTK share prices throughout 2018 show a correlation to Bitcoin prices.

© tradingview.com

Crypto trading exposure

While the government authorities were trying to figure out regulations around cryptocurrencies, many public trading companies, brokers, and traditional exchanges got ahead of the crowd to offer cryptocurrency trading opportunities for the masses. For example, when Interactive Brokers Group (stock symbol: IBKR) announced on December 13, 2017, that it was allowing its customers to *short* Bitcoin (sell it in speculation that its value will drop), its stock price actually dropped. The reason for that may have been that at the time, Bitcoin's price was at its peak, and most people didn't like the idea of shorting Bitcoin. Of course, Bitcoin prices ended up falling a few months later, and IBKR saw a boost in its stock price value, as you can see in Figure 15-2. It then dropped again due to factors other than its Bitcoin exposure.

FIGURE 15-2:
The stock price of Interactive Brokers (IBKR) dropped on December 13 following the announcement of a Bitcoin speculation service.

© tradingview.com

WARNING

Speculative trading based on rumors and news can be very risky. When analyzing a stock from a fundamental point for a medium-to-long-term investment strategy, you must consider other factors, such as the company's management, services, industry outlook, financial statements, and financial ratios. See Chapter 19 for more on short-term trading strategies and Chapter 20 for more on long-term investing strategies.

Market sentiment factors

The second point of the IDDA (Invest Diva Diamond Analysis) focuses on market sentiment. As I indicate in Chapter 9, *market sentiment* is the general behavior and "feeling" of market participants toward a specific asset such as cryptos or stocks. When searching for stocks with crypto exposure, you must measure the market sentiment not only toward that stock but also toward the cryptocurrency industry. This approach gives you an idea about the direction you can take with your investment.

For a very simplified example, say all other IDDA points, including fundamental and technical analyses, are showing that you can expect the price of a given stock to go lower in the future. (The technical term for this move is a *bearish reversal* in a stock price.) But if you want to complete your IDDA analysis, you must also measure the market sentiment, using shorter time frames and indicators such as Ichimoku Kinko Hyo, which I talk about in Chapter 22.

TIP

Other market sentiment indicators include the following:

>> Moving average convergence divergence (MACD) (www.investdiva.com/investing-guide/macd)

>> Relative strength index (RSI) (www.investdiva.com/investing-guide/relative-strength-index-rsi)

>> Bollinger Bands (BOL) (www.investdiva.com/investing-guide/bollinger-bands-bol)

Other considerations

At the end of the day, if you're looking to create a well-diversified portfolio by getting indirect exposure to cryptocurrencies, you may want to avoid *double dipping* (investing in the same category/industry twice). Stocks with exposure to cryptos should only be a proportionate piece of your overall portfolio, as categorized by industry. If you're looking to get an idea of how much you'll make on your investment with the amount of risk you're taking, and how much you should value the company's stock price, you must analyze the industry properly from all points of the IDDA. Then you can focus on picking the best stock in that category.

REMEMBER

Here are some questions to ask before picking the top crypto related stocks for your portfolio:

>> Is the company working on any new developments in its technology?

>> What impact are potential breakthroughs likely to have?

>> Is the demand for the crypto-related services related to key economic variables? If so, which ones?

>> How much is the company planning to spend on crypto-related services? How is it planning to fund that spending?

>> Is the company rapidly employing and opening new crypto/blockchain-related jobs?

You can find the answers to these questions by researching the company's press releases and public reports. Your broker may also help you get your hands on the most recent developments. Of course, at Invest Diva, we also try to stay on top of all the developments, so make sure you subscribe free to my updates at investdiva.com/masterclass. Then you can move on to the next IDDA points, such as technical analysis (see Chapters 9 and 18) and risk management (as I explain in Chapter 3).

Considering Cryptocurrency and Blockchain ETFs

If you're having a hard time picking the right stock, then you may want to consider another option. One of the easiest ways to get exposure to a specific industry without having to pick the top assets in that category is trading an exchange-traded fund, or ETF.

An ETF is similar to a mutual fund in that they're both "baskets" of assets in the same category. But ETFs are becoming more popular for reasons such as the following:

>> They're more tax efficient than mutual funds.

>> They have lower trading expenses compared to those of mutual funds.

>> They're simpler/more flexible than mutual funds.

>> They're more accessible than mutual funds to an average investor.

REMEMBER

I personally prefer to invest in individual assets instead of investing in ETFs. That's because I like to have full control over my money, where it's invested, and how much allocation it has to different securities. ETFs are managed by someone else. While the risk may be higher, the rewards are equally higher. That's why I think it's a really good idea that we start teaching our children how to invest, and even prioritize financial literacy over getting a driver's license. The benefits children can gain from learning how to invest can make them literally millions of dollars over their lifetime.

TIP

If you start investing only $50 per month for your child the moment they're born, and they continue contributing over their lifetime, at an average 10 percent return per year, at age 65 your child will end up with $3,093,004.29. Together you have contributed only $39,000. This may not sound like much, especially in 65 years when we can't even imagine where inflation is going to be, but it's certainly better than $39,000. If you invest $500 per month, your child could hit million-dollar status at age 30.

We have come a long way in the blockchain-exposed ETFs sector since I wrote the first edition of this book. More funds have been created to give novice investors exposure to the blockchain world, arguably thanks to the hype and increased demand. Here's a list of ETFs that can give you exposure to blockchain technology as of October 2022:

>> **BLOK:** Full name: Amplify Transformational Data Sharing ETF. It was the first ever ETF focusing in blockchain technology that started in 2018. Its basket holds assets, including: a cloud-computing developer that holds a ton of Bitcoin in its balance sheet, MicroStrategy Inc. (stock symbol: MSTR); a bank that provides financial services to crypto businesses, Silvergate Capital Corp (stock symbol: SI); and the first online retailer that started accepting Bitcoin, Overstock.com (stock symbol: OSTK).

Other notable holdings include Walmart (stock symbol: WNT), BLOCK Inc (stock symbol: SQ), Meta (stock symbol: META), and Paypal (stock symbol: PYPL). You can more about this ETF and the rest of its holdings on their website: amplifyetfs.com/blok-holdings/learn.

>> **BITQ:** Full name: Bitwise Crypto Industry Innovators ETF. This tracks the performance of an Index called the Crypto Innovators 30 Index. This is similar to how the S&P 500 tracks the 500 largest companies listed on the stock exchange.

Bitwise Crypto Innovators 30 Index includes 30 stocks of companies that are deeply involved in everything crypto, from crypto-related financial services to mining equipment suppliers. Some of its top holdings include crypto exchange Coinbase Global Inc (stock symbol: COIN), Microstrategy Inc (stock symbol: MSTR), and Silvergate Capital Corp (stock symbol: SI). You can learn more about its holdings on its website: bitqetf.com.

>> **FDIG:** Full name: Fidelity Crypto Industry and Digital Payments ETF. Launched in April 2022, this ETF is a benchmark to the Fidelity Crypto Industry and Digital Payment Index that tracks the performance of global cryptocurrency, blockchain, and digital payment companies. Some of its notable holdings include the leading payment platform Block Inc (stock symbol: SQ), Coinbase Globale Inc (stock symbol: COIN), and Marathon Digital Holdings (stock symbol: MARA).

REMEMBER

Investing in ETFs makes the stock-analysis process a bit easier, but you still need a general understanding of the ETF's holding companies in order to be able to pick the one that best suits your portfolio. If various ETFs' holdings are widely different even in the same industry, you may want to consider investing in multiple ETFs, as long as their prices aren't correlated.

TIP

If you like to be in full control of your investments, get ideas of what to invest in by studying top ETFs and then invest in those assets on your own without having to pay a management fee. You can fully customize your investment strategy to your own risk tolerance and financial goals.

Chapter **16**

Cryptocurrency Futures and Options

Futures and options are two forms of a general financial instrument called *derivatives*. They derive their value from the price action of something else — traditionally, from financial assets like stocks, commodities, *fiat* (government-backed) currencies, and other market indexes. As the cryptocurrency market becomes more popular, different cryptocurrency derivatives have been popping up and are accessible to individual traders.

In this chapter, I first overview the basics of futures and options trading, and then I explore how they work in the crypto market.

At the time of writing, many regulations exist around such assets, so you can invest in them through a handful of brokers and exchanges around the world. In the United States, Bitcoin futures trading is available on a handful of brokers, exchanges, and Wall Street banks such as these:

» **Bank of America:** www.bankofamerica.com

» **Cboe:** cfe.cboe.com/cfe-products/xbt-cboe-bitcoin-futures

» **CME Group:** www.cmegroup.com/trading/bitcoin-futures.html

- **E*TRADE:** us.etrade.com/knowledge/education/events/trading-bitcoin-cboe-xbt-bitcoin-futures

- **Interactive Brokers:** www.interactivebrokers.com/en/home.php

- **TD Ameritrade:** www.tdameritrade.com/investment-products/futures-trading/bitcoin-futures.page

REMEMBER

In countries such as the United Kingdom, Japan, and Korea, you may be able to trade cryptocurrency options and futures on Deribit: www.deribit.com. However, at the time of writing, the company doesn't offer its services in the United States.

Focusing on the Fundamentals of Futures

Here's a hint: Futures have something to do with the future! For example, when you buy a sack of coffee from your local supermarket, you pay for it right then and there at the market price. But what if you think the price of coffee will go down in the future? You can't buy coffee now at its "future" price in your local market, but you sure can in the futures market. If you think the price of coffee per pound is going down from $5 to $4 by June of next year, you can create a futures contract to buy a certain amount of coffee at $4 next June.

In the following sections, I explain the features of commodity futures (the most common type) and discuss other types of financial futures.

Futures' features

Traditionally, futures are most popular among commodities such as grains, coffee, metals, wood, and meat. When you buy coffee in the futures market, you don't receive your coffee until a date in the future that you've agreed on with the seller. That's why your transaction isn't complete for some time. During this time, you own a highly liquid *futures contract* that you can hold or trade in the futures market.

No matter what you do with the contract, as long as it's outstanding, the seller has a legally binding obligation to deliver your coffee on that specified date in the future. You have a similar obligation to take the coffee delivery. No return policy!

Two of the most important futures trading features are *hedging* and *speculating*. In fact, the futures market can't exist and operate efficiently without either one. Another characteristic of futures is *margin trading*. Here's how they work:

>> **Futures hedging:** Traditionally, the hedgers are businesses that either produce a commodity or use it as an input to their production process.

As an investor, you can use hedging as a type of risk management to prevent losses and not necessarily to make capital gains. You can hedge one investment by making another investment to offset the risk of the first investment — it's something like investing in an insurance policy to offset the risk of something happening to you in the future.

>> **Futures speculating:** The speculators are quite the opposite of the hedgers. They trade futures simply to earn a profit on expected price swings. They have no inherent interest in the commodity or its financial future other that its price action.

For example, if you think the price of a commodity will increase in the future, you may be able to make a profit by purchasing the asset in a futures contract and selling it at a higher price later on. Regardless, the futures market depends on them because their trades help make the market more liquid.

>> **Margin trading:** You can take advantage of something called *leverage* when trading futures, just like in the foreign exchange or forex market (covered in Chapter 17).

The difference is that *all* futures contracts are traded on a margin basis. You can't opt out of this feature. When you buy a futures contract *on margin,* it means you need to put only a fraction of the total price in cash. When trading futures contracts, you usually need a margin of about 2 percent to 10 percent of the contract value. The good news is that you don't have to borrow money to finance the balance of the contract, which makes it less risky than how margin trading works in forex.

The margin deposit is simply a security or a guarantee to cover any losses that may occur. It is *not* a partial payment for your purchase.

REMEMBER

Financial futures

Although commodities make up for a big segment of the futures market, financial futures are another popular dimension of it. *Financial futures* use a different type of underlying asset than commodities do, and they offer a speculating vehicle for many markets such as forex, interest rates, and stock indexes. They have similar advantages to commodity future trading and have become a major hedging tool for institutions and individual traders alike.

One key difference is the way the price of each type of financial futures contract is quoted:

>> Currency futures in the United States are quoted in U.S. dollars per unit of the underlying foreign currency — for example, U.S. dollar per Canadian dollar or U.S. dollar per Japanese yen.

>> Interest rate futures contracts are priced as a percentage of the *par value* (face value) of the underlying debt instrument. For example, the par value of most Treasury-based interest rate futures is $100,000, and therefore each contract trades in whole-dollar bids of $1,000.

>> Stock index futures are quoted in terms of the actual underlying index. Such indexes include the S&P 500 and Nasdaq.

Just like commodities, financial futures can expose you to a ton of profit and loss. But you must thoroughly understand your investments as well as the risks involved in order to be a successful futures trader.

WARNING

Speculating each type of futures can be very a specialized task. If you don't know much about each industry, you may as well be gambling in Las Vegas.

Introducing the Basics of Options

Options help you enter a contract with someone else to buy or sell something of value. If you're the option buyer, you have the right to buy an underlying asset (such as coffee) within a given period of time at a price that was agreed upon at the time of the contract. If you're the seller, you must be ready to sell that underlying asset within the contract's instructions.

The following sections compare options to futures, describe types of options, and explain the risks.

Futures versus options

REMEMBER

Futures and options are very similar. They both involve the future delivery of something at a specific price. The big difference between a futures contract and an options contract comes down to the date of buying and selling.

Here are some important points to keep in mind:

>> When trading a futures contract, you must buy/sell on or before an agreed-upon date.

>> With options, you can buy/sell over a specified period of time.

>> Put and call options (see the next section) specify the price at which you can buy or sell.

>> Futures prices aren't spelled out on the contract. Instead, the price on a futures contract is established through the trades among traders on the exchange. This means the delivery price is set at whatever price the contract sells for.

Puts and calls

The two basic kinds of options are called puts and calls, which are basically a version of selling and buying:

>> With a *put,* you can sell an underlying security at a specific price over a period of time.

>> With a *call,* you get the right to buy that security at the agreed price within a certain period of time.

Why don't they just call it buying and selling and save trouble? One key benefit of using a different name is that you're forced to remember that with puts and calls, you get no ownership privileges and gain no interest or dividend income. All you get are gains and losses from the price movements of the underlying assets. Just like futures, you can take advantage of the leverage puts and calls offer.

TIP

Paul Mladjenovic, author of a number of *For Dummies* investing books, has a great education course on options investing. You can check it out at www.ravingcapitalist.com/home/ultra-investing-with-options.

Risks

WARNING

Options trading comes with a couple of notable risks:

>> One of the major risks with options puts and calls trading is that you can't make time your friend. Puts and calls have limited lives; the market may not have enough time to move favorably in your direction before the option

expires, and you may end up losing money right before the prices move to your advantage.

>> Another major risk is that you can lose 100 percent of your initial investment if the markets move a tiny bit in an unfavorable direction at a wrong time. Though with normal investing you can wait it out, puts and calls options are totally worthless when they expire.

Understanding Cryptocurrency Derivatives Trading

Derivatives trading may very well be the next big boom in the cryptocurrency market. In 2018, many financial organizations in the United States, such as Goldman Sachs and TD Ameritrade, started exploring cryptocurrency trading derivatives. By 2022, Nomura and JPMorgan joined their rivals and started giving their clients a way to access the crypto market.

By July 2022, crypto derivatives volumes surged to $3.12 trillion. At the time of writing, the derivatives market makes up 69 percent of total crypto volumes. This volume changes depending on the price of Bitcoin and the amount of hype circulating in the crypto markets. In other words, every time the crypto markets crash, the derivatives volume goes down with it.

But why are organizations jumping in crypto derivatives? The following sections give you the scoop.

The advantages of crypto derivatives trading

With crypto derivatives trading, you're betting on the price of specific coins (like Bitcoin or Ethereum) either on a future date or within a certain range of time. Derivatives trading may be more complex than simply buying and selling cryptocurrencies on an exchange, but a quick advantage is that you don't have to worry about storage security. If you're concerned about the risk of losing your crypto wallet or assets in a hacking attack, crypto derivatives have you covered. Because you don't actually own coins when trading options and futures, you don't have to worry about things like a crypto wallet, storage, and security (see Chapter 7 for an introduction to wallets).

The advantages of crypto derivatives for the industry

Even if you choose not to trade crypto derivatives, the existence of such trading options may be good for the crypto industry as a whole. Why?

>> First and foremost, crypto derivatives may be able to boost the liquidity and trading volume across digital assets other than Bitcoin, which makes them easier to trade. Higher liquidity helps traders buy and sell more quickly and avoid risk of sudden, massive movements in the price at the time they're placing their trading orders.

>> Another advantage of having regulated crypto derivative exchanges is that more people may become interested in the cryptocurrency market and put pressure on regulators to advance their views on the industry.

Trading resources

TIP

To stay up-to-date with the latest advancements in the crypto derivatives market, consider checking in regularly with financial news and cryptocurrency update providers such as those in the following list:

>> CoinDesk (www.coindesk.com)

>> Cointelegraph (cointelegraph.com)

>> Crypto Briefing (cryptobriefing.com)

>> Cryptonews.com (cryptonews.com)

>> Medium (medium.com/topic/cryptocurrency)

>> NewsBTC (newsbtc.com)

Chapter **17**

Dealing with the Dollar and Other Fiat Currencies

C alling typical currencies "fiat" isn't something I was used to before cryptocurrencies became a thing. I simply used to call them "currencies." If I wanted to get specific, I'd talk about "major currencies" like the U.S. dollar, the euro, and the Japanese yen, or "exotic currencies" such as the Mexican peso and the Iranian rial.

Currency trading, also known as the *foreign exchange market (forex)*, is the art of predicting the future value of fiat currencies against one another. Technically, a *fiat* currency is a legal tender that your local government supports through the central bank. The advent of cryptocurrencies has worried some fiat currency issuers (that is, central banks). Some believe that the cryptocurrencies may replace fiat currencies in the future. But for now, one of the ways to get your hands on cryptocurrencies is to exchange your fiat currencies for them. That's why understanding the basic movements in the world's fiat currencies may come in handy in your cryptocurrency investing endeavors.

In this chapter, I take a look at the U.S. dollar (USD) as the world's reserve currency along with other major currencies and their relationships with the cryptocurrency market. (I introduce trading cryptocurrencies versus fiat currencies in Chapter 10.)

Considering the World's Reserve Currency: The U.S. Dollar

If you live in the United States, your first cryptocurrency investment is likely an exchange between the U.S. dollar and a digital asset like Bitcoin. Bitcoin prices can be incredibly volatile, but you also must consider the fluctuations of the U.S. dollar, which may lead to a better or worse trading deal for you. For example, if the U.S. dollar is incredibly strong, you can buy more bits of Bitcoin with it. I explore some key factors that affect the value of the U.S. dollar in this section.

A LIFETIME FASCINATION WITH CURRENCY FLUCTUATIONS

As a child, I was fascinated by currency fluctuations. I always heard my parents worry about the value of our Iranian currency diminishing versus the U.S. dollar (USD). You see, after the Iranian revolution, most of my relatives, including my brother, left Iran for the United States in fear of the new government. In order for my brother to be able to go to school in the United States, my parents had to send him money from Iran, converting the ever-devaluing Iranian rial to the USD. The stronger the U.S. dollar got, the tougher it was for my parents to hit the $1,000 minimum per month to send to my brother. I always wondered who was behind all the currency fluctuations. I remember asking my dad when I was 10 years old, "Is there a guy in the government who decides the value of the USD every morning and announces it to the world?" My dad answered, "No, there are a whole lot of people behind the pricing, especially the central banks." I still didn't really get it then.

When I went to Japan to study electrical engineering, I started paying attention to currency fluctuations again. I was getting paid a scholarship in Japanese yen by the Japanese government. So I always wondered how my 20,000 yen per month would convert to the Iranian rial and the U.S. dollar if I were to exchange and save some of it in a foreign bank account.

I got into currency trading in 2008, when the stock market and the U.S. dollar crashed. In a bet against the U.S. dollar, I traded $10,000 worth of Japanese yen in September 2008 using a forex broker margin account. Within a month, my initial investment was doubled as the USD dropped like a rock. That was the most I had ever made in a month. Naturally, I decided to quit my electrical engineering career path, jump on a plane to the financial district on Wall Street in New York, and work in the currency trading industry.

Focusing on factors that affect the U.S. dollar

The U.S. dollar (USD) is one the most popular currencies globally. If you travel to any country in the world, that country likely accepts the U.S. dollar in return for its local currency. This clout gives the United States a great privilege. Many people simply pile up on U.S. dollars in their savings account. Often when the demand for USD goes higher, the dollar becomes even stronger. But when the U.S. economy takes a hit, or when the *Federal Reserve* (the United States's central bank, also called the *Fed*) makes pessimistic remarks about the future of the U.S. economy, the U.S. dollar is normally one of the first financial assets to go down.

Uncle Sam has been on watch because China's been ramping up to become a threat to the USD as the world's reserve currency. And now, Bitcoin enthusiasts think the USD and Chinese yuan won't stand a chance against cryptocurrencies in the future.

TIP

If you're buying cryptocurrencies by using the U.S. dollar, you get a better deal if the USD is strong. You can buy more units of a digital coin if its value is low against the USD.

REMEMBER

Many factors affect USD price action. Even though I've studied the U.S. dollar's market movements for over a decade now, I still can't say for sure where its price is headed next. However, by conducting the Invest Diva Diamond Analysis (IDDA; see Chapter 9), you can stack the odds in your favor. Market sentiment, crowd psychology, and supply and demand can all contribute to the strength and weakness of the U.S. dollar the same way they impact other financial assets. The fundamental points can be different, though. Some of the fundamental factors that impact the U.S. dollar value include the following:

>> **Interest rates:** The *interest rate* is the price those who borrow money pay. It refers to the percentage of the borrowed amount of money that the borrower pays to the lender. When the U.S. Federal Reserve increases interest rates or is expected to do so, the U.S. dollar often gets stronger versus other fiat currencies and cryptos alike. While all economic calendars on websites such as Bloomberg (www.bloomberg.com) or Yahoo! Finance

(`finance.yahoo.com`) track upcoming and previous interest rate decisions, you can also keep track of the changes directly on the Federal Reserve website in the United States: `www.federalreserve.gov/monetarypolicy/fomccalendars.htm`.

- » **Inflation:** *Inflation* is the reason why your grandmother paid less for a dozen eggs than you do. It refers to the general increase in the prices of goods and supplies. When inflation gets high, the Fed tries to control it by raising interest rates. Because of the way inflation affects interest rates, an increase in inflation usually has a positive impact on the USD. Inflation data is measured by something called the Consumer Price Index (CPI), which is also tracked on most economic calendars. In the United States, you can also track inflation on the Bureau of Labor Statistics website: `www.bls.gov/schedule/news_release/cpi.htm`.

- » **Gross domestic product (GDP):** *Gross domestic product* reflects a country's yearly production and revenue. The U.S. dollar grows stronger when the GDP is high. To get direct access to GDP data, you can check out the Bureau of Economic Analysis website: `www.bea.gov`.

- » **Unemployment rate:** The U.S. unemployment rate in particular is a huge forex gossip topic. A decline in the unemployment rate means that the economy is doing well and more jobs have been created, which results in a stronger dollar in the United States. You can find the unemployment rate announcement schedules for the United States here: `www.bls.gov/schedule/news_release/empsit.htm`.

- » **Nonfarm payrolls (NFP):** The *nonfarm payrolls* figure shows the total number of paid U.S. workers in every business, excluding employees of places like farms, private households, and general government. An expanding nonfarm payroll is a good indication that the economy is growing and therefore can lead to a stronger USD. You can find the event schedule and data here: `www.bls.gov/schedule/news_release/empsit.htm`.

Looking at Bitcoin versus the U.S. dollar

REMEMBER

Even the biggest Bitcoin enthusiasts don't believe Bitcoin can replace the U.S. dollar anytime soon, if ever. Bitcoin must overcome way too many hurdles before it can claim to be the world's reserve currency. Plus, even though Bitcoin is the celebrity of all cryptocurrencies, other, "better" versions of Bitcoin may climb up the digital currency ladder and replace Bitcoin even before it can replace the USD. A few more reasons why Bitcoin likely won't ever replace the USD include the following:

>> Unknown miners all over the world pose a major security threat. We don't know where some of those massive mining farms are located and how they are planning to spend their Bitcoins.

>> In cryptocurrencies like Bitcoin that can be mined, a group of miners hypothetically can get together to control over 50 percent of the network, preventing the normal transaction process and possibly leading to security issues and hacking.

>> There is a very limited supply of coins ever to be created (21 million coins).

>> Forty percent of the world's Bitcoins are held by 1,000 people, so the financial inequality has already begun, putting the power in the hands of a small portion of the world's population. This doesn't sit well with one of the main reasons for blockchain technology (see Chapter 4) and the idea of cryptocurrencies, which is to fix the financial inequality issue around the globe.

>> There is a lack of security, as I talk about in Chapters 3 and 7.

One of the main differences between Bitcoin and the U.S. dollar is price fluctuations. As you can see in Figure 17-1, even when Bitcoin (BTC) was considered to have calmed down in the period between June and September 2018, its price action was way crazier than that of the U.S. Dollar Index, DXY. The DXY measures the value of the USD relative to a basket of foreign currencies. This relative stability gives the USD an edge in terms of security.

FIGURE 17-1:
U.S. Dollar Index (DXY) price action compared to BTC/USD.

© tradingview.com

Even though the forex market is known for its price volatility and unpredictable nature, Bitcoin certainly beats the USD at its own game.

REMEMBER

While the mainstream media usually follows only Bitcoin, other cryptocurrencies such as Ethereum (ETH), Litecoin (LTC), and Bitcoin Cash (BCH) can also be traded versus the U.S. dollar on cryptocurrency exchanges such as Coinbase (`www.coinbase.com/join/59d39a7610351d00d40189f0`). However, at least at the time of writing, the majority of other cryptocurrencies, even some of the famous ones like Ripple (XRP) and Stellar Lumens (XLM), can only be traded versus other cryptocurrencies on exchanges such as Binance (`www.binance.com/?ref=18381915`), as they aren't available on exchanges that support the U.S. dollar. On the other hand, if you're only speculating on cryptocurrency price actions, you may be able to track other cryptocurrencies' values versus the U.S. dollar on websites like the following:

>> **AVATrade:** `www.avatrade.com/?tag=87597&tag2=~profile_default`

>> **eToro:** `partners.etoro.com/A75956_TClick.aspx`

Examining the Euro and Other Major Currencies

REMEMBER

You can technically trade any country's currency in the forex market, but seven specific currencies are the most popular. Investors call these currencies the *majors*. They're popular not only because they're more accessible worldwide but also because their movements are more predictable. Moreover, their countries' economies are considered more stable (although this can be debatable). And importantly, transaction fees for trading them are lower compared with other, less popular currencies. Here's the list of majors:

>> Euro (EUR)

>> British pound (GBP)

>> Swiss franc (CHF)

>> Japanese yen (JPY)

>> Canadian dollar (CAD, also known as the loonie)

>> Australian dollar (AUD, also known as the Aussie dollar)

>> New Zealand dollar (NZD, also known as the Kiwi dollar)

TECHNICAL
STUFF

When you trade the majors against the U.S. dollar, they're called the *major currency pairs*.

I explain a bit more about each currency in the following sections. I compare the general forex market versus the cryptocurrency market later in this chapter.

The euro and the British pound

The euro is a shared currency among 19 out of the 27 members of the European Union. If the U.S. dollar is the king of the forex market, the euro is queen; it's the second most traded currency in the world after the USD.

The British pound is that black sheep in the family that didn't get on with the euro after the United Kingdom became a member of the eurozone. The British pound was more valuable than the euro, and the UK government didn't want to give it up. Other countries had to give up their national currencies in favor of the more powerful euro. But having a stand-alone currency may be considered a lucky move because when the United Kingdom voted in 2016 to leave the eurozone (in an act called *Brexit*), the separation became a tad less complicated because the currencies were already separate.

TIP

Though the long-term view of the EUR and GBP remains unclear, some of my medium-term strategies have worked out in making my students and me richer. For example, I traded the GBP/JPY pair (the British pound versus the Japanese yen) multiple times, as you can see in Figure 17-2. I used a combination of technical analysis, fundamental analysis, and sentimental analysis to develop these trading strategies based on IDDA, which I introduce in Chapter 9. While due to the change in my personal risk tolerance I no longer trade forex, I teach about the principles of forex trading in my Make Your Money Work For You PowerCourse. You can learn more about it here: investdiva.com/masterclass.

Safe havens: The Swiss franc and the Japanese yen

The Japanese yen and the Swiss franc are some forex traders' go-to currencies when the U.S. dollar and euro are doing poorly and getting weaker in value. Historically they're often called *safe havens*. I saw this effect firsthand in 2008 when the USD's value was dropping and JPY became one the biggest winners, allowing me to double my first-ever forex trade within a month (check out the sidebar in this chapter for details). The Japanese yen is considered more of a safety zone than the Swiss franc, especially because of a sudden move by the Swiss National Bank (SNB) in 2015 that shocked the financial markets and therefore created a ton of volatility in the CHF on January 15, 2015.

© tradingview.com

FIGURE 17-2:
Trading GBP/JPY between key support and resistance levels of 144.85 and 147.50.

REMEMBER

Safe havens often change depending on the overall state of the global economy. For example, in the most recent global economic turmoil, the USD has gained uncharted strength versus the GBP, EUR, and even JPY. The only traditionally safe-haven currency able to keep up with the USD has been the Swiss franc (CHF).

TECHNICAL STUFF

January 15, 2015, was a dark day in the forex community. Many traders, including myself, had parked our bets on the Swiss franc, thinking the Swiss are too neutral to do anything sudden and outrageous to endanger our investments. Boy, were we wrong! On that day, out of nowhere the Swiss National Bank made a change in its currency valuation policy that resulted in a sudden 30 percent increase in the franc's value against the euro. That also meant that my bullish position on the USD/CHF got in trouble. But I was actually lucky, considering I only lost a trade. Many companies actually went bankrupt because of this! You can read about the Swiss franc history and the day that's now remembered as Black Thursday here: www.investdiva.com/investing-guide/swiss-franc-trading-history-future.

The Aussie, Kiwi, and Canadian dollars

Forex traders consider the Australian dollar, New Zealand dollar, and Canadian dollar *commodity currencies*. The reason is that they're highly correlated to commodity price fluctuations, among other things. For example, Australia has a lot of natural resources like iron, gold, and aluminum. It also has large farms and a ton of cows that produce milk and other dairy products. Australia's economy depends on these commodities, and that's why the Australian currency, the AUD, often takes cues from commodity prices and the state of imports and exports in the country.

TIP

Being China's trading buddy, Australia's economy is also correlated to changes in the Chinese economy. For example, if the Chinese economy is doing poorly or getting hit by tariffs from the United States, then the Australian dollar gets weaker. Like its Aussie neighbor, New Zealand is also big on agriculture, so the Kiwi can be impacted by things like the price of grains and dairy products. The Canadian dollar, on the other hand, is often viewed as highly correlated to oil prices. In other words, if the price of oil plummets, then you can expect the Canadian dollar to go down with it. Keep in mind, though, that these correlations aren't absolute, and sometimes other factors such as geopolitical risk events can take over price action.

Comparing the Forex Market and the Crypto Market

People rarely view Bitcoin and other cryptocurrencies as currencies when they invest in them. Most investors and market participants alike treat cryptos like securities such as common stocks. But the fact of the matter is that to buy any cryptocurrency, you have to trade it versus another currency — fiat or crypto — as I explain in Chapter 10. Because of this need, many forex brokers have started offering cryptocurrency services to their forex trading crowd. (Flip to Chapter 6 to explore how you can trade cryptos by using a forex broker.) The following sections spell out some similarities and differences between the forex and the crypto markets.

REMEMBER

Despite a few similarities, comparing forex with cryptocurrencies is like comparing apples and oranges. They're two different financial instruments and require a different type of approach when you're developing investment strategies around them.

The similarities

One of the key similarities between forex and cryptocurrency trading is that they both carry a huge amount of risk. If you choose to trade cryptocurrencies on a short-term basis versus other digital or fiat currencies, you may need to study their price actions by using the technical analysis methods I introduce in Chapter 18. However, as the cryptocurrency market becomes more mainstream, you can expect its movement to become more predictable.

The crazy amount of day-to-day volatility can also be viewed as a similarity. Day traders may benefit from the price fluctuations in both markets. In most cases, liquidity is high enough for major cryptocurrencies and forex pairs to make it easy for trading orders to go through pretty easily.

The differences

Now this point is a lot easier to write about! Here are some of the main differences between the forex and cryptocurrency markets:

WARNING

>> **Size:** The forex market is by far the largest market in the world, and no crypto, no matter how large its market cap is, comes even close to forex. To give you an idea, the forex market has a daily trading volume of around $5 trillion USD. The cryptocurrency market, on the other hand, has a daily volume close to that of the New York Stock Exchange at around $50 billion USD. It's not bad, but forex is the clear winner. (Chapter 8 has more on cryptos and market cap.)

The fact that the forex market is ultra large doesn't mean you can make more profit in it. If anything, the daily fluctuations make it riskier and harder to predict.

>> **Variety:** You can choose from a ton of cryptocurrencies, but only seven major fiat currencies are actively traded. This range makes the *choosing* part easier for forex traders, while you have to analyze hundreds of cryptos to find yourself a catch. Head to the earlier section "Examining the Euro and Other Major Currencies" for more on the most popular fiat options.

>> **Purpose:** Forex is more suitable for day traders. Although short-term trading isn't exactly my cup of tea, most forex traders get in and out of positions a lot more quickly than any other types of investors. By contrast, most crypto investors hold on to their assets for longer period of times.

>> **Money supply:** Money supply is perhaps the key difference between forex and crypto. A country's central bank plays a massive role in determining its major currency's future. But Bitcoin and other cryptocurrencies are products of the blockchain industry; they aren't regulated by a central bank. So the fundamental analysis I talk about in Chapter 9 is entirely different for forex and cryptocurrencies.

Resources for forex trading

Forex was my first love. I made my first trade in forex, wrote my first book about forex, and named my first company Forex Diva. With that, I like to think I'm pretty resourceful when it comes to forex.

TIP

Here are some quick tips to get you started in forex trading if you're planning to mix things up a little bit with the crypto world:

>> **Forex brokers:** Finding a forex broker that suits your needs is no easy task. You must make sure the broker is safe to carry your investments, complies with your local financial guidelines, has enough money supply and liquidity to execute your trading orders fast, and has reasonable fees for its services, among other things.

I explain all about forex brokers and the steps you need to take in choosing one in my education courses, but here's a place you may be able to find the right one for you: `forestparkfx.com/?id=UU1UckhZSVN3OW1WNnNuNHIxaHlqUT09`.

WARNING

>> **Your forex account:** Though many brokers offer you an option to start with as little as $50, keep in mind that in order for you to really make profit in the forext market, you must have at least $10,000 of disposable money in your account, as well as superior knowledge about how the market works. Otherwise, you're just gambling and likely to lose your initial investment within months, if not days.

>> **Economic calendar:** To know what's going on in the forex market, you must follow the economic calendars of the countries whose currencies you're about to trade.

Many websites offer the forex economic calendar for free, such as the following:

- `www.forexfactory.com`
- `www.investing.com/economic-calendar`
- `www.fxstreet.com/economic-calendar`

>> **Forex news:** Besides the economic data, other factors — such as geopolitical tensions, supply and demand of commodities like oil and gold, and speeches by important political figures in a country — influence currency fluctuations.

You can find out about these news items on websites such as these:

- `www.dailyfx.com`
- `www.fxstreet.com`
- `www.reuters.com/finance/currencies`

WARNING

Forex news outlets often create false hype around the market, which leads to emotional trading decisions. Make sure you don't fall in the trap of clickbait headlines like "The Number One Currency You Should Be Trading Right Now."

>> **Education:** Okay, now I have to toot my own horn. My *Forex Coffee Break* education course has won a bunch of awards and is known as one of the easiest and most fun ways to learn all about forex. This service is now a part of my even cooler *Make Your Money Work For You PowerCourse*, where I dive deep into financial literacy and the power of exposing your portfolio to other online financial markets. You can learn more about this program here: investdiva.com/masterclass.

>> **Strategies:** Before becoming a mom (back when I had a ton more time on my hands!) I used to trade forex as a part of my portfolio. Some of my students still trade forex using the IDDA technique I introduce in Chapter 9. If you have the time and the high risk tolerance that's required for forex trading, you can consider applying the IDDA to develop forex trading strategies.

4

Essential Crypto Strategies and Tactics

Find out whether technical analysis is a good technique for developing an investment strategy or nothing more than voodoo.

Explore the differences between short-term trading and long-term investing, and decide which is the right route for you.

Dig into different investment strategy development methods, and incorporate your risk tolerance into your plan for minimizing losses and maximizing gains.

Get introduced to Ichimoku and Fibonacci techniques, and find out how you can use them to enhance your investment strategy.

Make sure you're not getting burned by taxes.

Chapter **18**

Using Technical Analysis

S ome people believe that the financial markets, crypto or otherwise, are just another form of legalized gambling. They believe that the markets move randomly and have no connection to market psychology or to the fundamentals, such as the state of the economy or the people behind blockchain technology.

I'm not one of those people. Over years of observing and investing in many different markets, I (along with many other fellow investors) have come to see history repeating itself (or if not repeating, rhyming with itself) in the markets over and over again. The markets move as a result of a combination of the three top points of the Invest Diva Diamond Analysis (IDDA), which I showcase in Chapter 9:

» Fundamental analysis

» Market sentiment analysis

» Technical analysis

Flip to Chapter 9 for basics of fundamental and market sentiment analysis in the cryptocurrency market. In this chapter, I show you how technical analysis can help you identify the best buy and sell price levels, whether you're a long-term investor or an active trader.

TIP

Many cryptocurrency exchanges and brokers offer charting services to make it easier for you to trade directly from their platform. Some of these charts are sophisticated, and some aren't. Personally, I like using TradingView (www.tradingview.com) for all my technical analysis, from foreign exchange (forex) to stocks and cryptocurrencies. You can use its free service for almost all assets, or you can choose to upgrade to its paid services to access charts without ads and to get some other perks.

Beginning with the Basics of Technical Analysis

In short, *technical analysis* is the art of studying the history of an asset's price action to predict its future. The reason it often works is the result of a bunch of factors, including the following:

>> **Investor behavior:** Research in behavioral finance shows that investors make decisions based on a number of psychological biases that repeat themselves.

>> **Crowd psychology:** Many market participants use the same technical analysis methods, therefore strengthening the key price levels.

When the price movement patterns repeat themselves, investors who spot them early can get an edge in their strategy development and get better-than-average returns. Even though the cryptocurrency market is relatively new, the patterns are already forming in short- and medium-term time frames. The following sections give you basics on chart types, time frames, and psychological factors.

WARNING

Past performance doesn't guarantee future results. Technical analysis helps only stacking the odds in your favor and doesn't guarantee profit. Therefore, you must conduct proper risk management, as I discuss in Chapter 3.

REMEMBER

Technical analysis is a skill that needs a lot of practice. I try my best to explain all my moves here, but imagine what would happen if you decided to take on skiing as a new sport and committed to becoming a professional skier (fun fact: I'm a ski fanatic!). So you pick up a book called something like *Ultimate Skiing* and read it word by word from beginning to end. Filled with confidence, you go to the nearest mountain and ask where the most difficult Double Black Diamond route is. You go all the way to the top, reminding yourself of all the techniques you read in the book. You get off the gondola, put your skis on for the very first time, and . . . Well, you might be able to guess what happens if you go on top of the mountain for the first time after just reading a book about skiing. You need a coach to hold your hand, show you the way, and give you feedback as you put your knowledge into practice. The same goes for cryptocurrency technical analysis.

I hold my students' hands and show them how to become investing and technical analysis pros in my *Make Your Money Work for You PowerCourse*. Learn more about it at investdiva.com/masterclass.

The chart art

So you want to get down and dirty with the historical price movements of your favorite cryptocurrency? As technical as this type of analysis sounds, you often find yourself using the creative side of your brain when you do it; the chart is your canvas. You can use different types of charts to plot the behavior of any cryptocurrency's price against other currencies, *fiat* (government backed) or not. Technical analysts love charts because they can visually track an otherwise number-oriented activity. Charts have evolved in the past decades as an increasing number of investors have used them to develop their strategies across different markets, including the stock, foreign exchange (forex), and cryptocurrency markets.

Some charts are simple and track only the price at the end of a session. Other charts are more complex and track every price movement during the session. Some of the most popular charts include these:

>> **Line charts:** Line charts display only the closing prices of the market. That means for any given time period, you can know only what the crypto's price is at the *end* of that time period and not what adventures and movements it's had *during* that time period. A line is drawn from one closing price to the next closing price, and you can see the general movement of a currency pair over a period of time. Figure 18-1 shows an example, featuring Bitcoin versus the U.S. dollar (BTC/USD) over a one-day time frame.

FIGURE 18-1:
Line chart of
BTC/USD over
one day.

© *tradingview.com*

- » **Bar charts:** No, this option isn't a list of the local drinking establishments! At any given time frame, a *bar chart* shows you the opening market price, the price action during that time frame, and the closing price, as you can see in Figure 18-2. The little horizontal line to the *left* shows the price at which the market opened. The little horizontal line to the *right* is the closing point of the time period. Watch this fun video where I explain about bar charts: investdiva. com/bar-charts.

- » **Candlestick charts:** *Candlestick charts* look like bar charts, but the area between the open and close prices is colored to show you the general movement of the market during that time period. If the market generally moved up during the time period (known as *bullish* market sentiment), the area is normally colored green. If the market goes down (*bearish* market sentiment), the area is normally colored red. Of course, you can choose any colors you like; I normally like to use green for a bullish market movement and purple for a bearish market movement, as you can see in Figure 18-3. A candlestick chart also shows the low and high price of the asset during the time period.

TECHNICAL STUFF

This type of chart is my favorite not only because it's the most visually appealing but also because it was developed by a Japanese rice trader. I lived in Japan for seven years, so I love anything that has Japanese roots or sounds Japanese, like Bitcoin's anonymous founder(s)! Even though no one really knows who started Bitcoin, the anonymous founder(s) at least pretended to be a Japanese guy named Satoshi Nakamoto. Regardless of the fact that there is no proof for this, the smallest unit of Bitcoin is called a Satoshi, and I get a kick out of it whenever I hear it.

© *John Wiley & Sons, Inc.*

FIGURE 18-2: Bullish and bearish bars.

FIGURE 18-3:
Candlesticks showing the general market movement in a chart.

HIGH
CLOSE
OPEN
LOW

Prices generally went up

HIGH
OPEN
CLOSE
LOW

Prices generally went down

© *John Wiley & Sons, Inc.*

The time factor

Depending on the type of investor you are, you can choose different time frames to conduct technical analysis. For example, if you're a day trader and want to take advantage of the crypto markets' fluctuations, you can study the market prices in the past 30 minutes, hour, or four hours. On the other hand, if you're a long-term investor and want to let the markets find their way toward your buy/sell limit orders, then you can analyze the price actions in the past days or months to find repetitive patterns and key psychological price levels. (*Hint:* That's how I develop my own strategies.)

All types of charts can be used in different time frames. A one-hour line chart shows you the closing price at the end of every hour. A daily candlestick chart shows you the open, close, low, and high prices during one-day periods as well as the general market movement over a longer time frame, as you can see in Figure 18-4. That figure shows Ethereum's price action versus the U.S. dollar (ETH/USD) plotted on a daily candlestick chart.

The psychology factor: Trends

As you study market movements, you may start finding patterns and prices that keep showing their faces on the chart. A lot of this repetition has to do with market psychology and the crowd's general feeling about the cryptocurrency.

One of the most eye-catching formations on a chart is a trend. A trend on a chart has nothing to do with trends on Twitter or in the fashion world, but the idea behind it is similar. When you notice that a cryptocurrency's price keeps going up on a chart, that movement means the market participants are feeling good about the crypto. They keep buying it and therefore pushing its price higher. You may even say that the crypto is trending.

© tradingview.com

FIGURE 18-4:
Daily candlestick chart of ETH/USD.

REMEMBER

You may have heard the famous investing phrase "the trend is your friend." If you spot the trend early enough, you may be able to take advantage of the rising prices and make some money. Same goes for when the crypto's price is moving down, or is on a *downtrend*. If you spot a downtrend early enough, you may be able to either sell your cryptocurrency or set a limit order (see Chapters 19 and 20) to buy more at a lower price.

Spotting the Key Levels

The whole point of technical analysis is to identify the best prices at which to buy and sell. Ideally you want to buy at the lowest price the cryptocurrency can drop to in the foreseeable future. And you want to hold on to it and sell at the highest price it can reach within your preferred time frame. In well-established markets with a ton of historical data, you can identify these prices by spotting key price levels that have created some sort of restriction for the market movements in the past. In the following sections, I break down some of these important levels.

Support levels

REMEMBER

A *support level* is a barrier that helps hold the prices at the lows and provides a psychological hurdle for the price to drop lower. It's always below the current market price on your chart. Market participants who spot the support generally wait at that level to buy the cryptocurrency. One of the popular ways to spot a support level is to study the cryptocurrency's past performance on the chart. If a price level keeps "supporting" the cryptocurrency's value from dropping lower, you can mark it as a support level.

As you can see in Figure 18-5, one of Bitcoin's key support levels is around $15,500, and another at around $3,500 Bitcoin's price tested around the $3,500 psychological level multiple times in 2019 and 2020. But each time, the support level prevented Bitcoin from dropping lower. In 2022, Bitcoin's price dropped to as low as $15,500 but bounced back up, creating a new support level. At the time of writing, Bitcoin's price still hasn't been able to break below this psychological level. If it does, the doors could be open for the price to drop to the next support level at $3,500.

© tradingview.com

FIGURE 18-5:
Bitcoin's key
support levels at
around $15,500
and $3,500.

REMEMBER

Notice I say "around." Support levels aren't always a concrete number. Even though most news outlets say things like "Bitcoin dropped below the $15,500 psychological level," key supports are often a zone rather than a round number.

TIP

The support level becomes stronger the more it's tested. But after strong support is broken, the market sentiment runs a good chance of shifting to bearish and starting to drop lower toward the next support levels. For example, in 2018, a $6,000 support level was broken. This led to Bitcoin's price dropping to the next support level at around $3,500 before the next bubble started in 2020 and pushed Bitcoin's price to over $68,000. (See Chapter 3 for more on the risks of bubbles.)

Resistance levels

REMEMBER

Resistance is a barrier that resists the prices from going higher. It must be above the current price on your chart, and you can use it as a point to sell your crypto assets. You can identify a resistance level with your naked eye by looking for *peaks* on the chart. Every peak can be considered a resistance level as long as it's above the current market value.

Check out Figure 18-6 for some of Bitcoin's key resistance levels in 2021 and 2022 at around $65,000, $59,000, and $47,000, respectively.

© tradingview.com

FIGURE 18-6:
Bitcoin's key resistance levels in 2021 and 2022.

TIP

I personally prefer to use Fibonacci retracement levels to identify support and resistance levels. By applying Fibonacci to a past trend, you can immediately see a number of support and resistance levels without having to apply them one by one on your own. Of course, Fibonacci levels aren't always completely accurate, and you may need to play around with your application a bit to get it right. Check out Chapter 22 to see how.

Trends and channels

Earlier in this chapter, I explain how trends can be formed based on market psychology. Some trends are very easy to spot. For example, the period between July and December 2017 was a period of an extreme *uptrend* in Bitcoin and many other cryptocurrencies when the prices just kept going up. Of course, this strong uptrend caught the attention of many people, investor or not, which led to the crypto bubble that came down crashing in 2018. But spotting trends isn't always as easy.

Drawing trend lines is an art. And just as with any other type of art, everyone has a unique opinion on them. Here are two basic methods to draw an uptrend and a downtrend:

>> To draw an uptrend line, when you've casually identified a bullish momentum on the chart, simply click on the trend line instrument on your trading platform and connect two or more major valleys (bottoms), as shown in Figure 18-7.

>> To draw a downtrend, connect two or more major peaks (tops).

© John Wiley & Sons, Inc.

FIGURE 18-7:
How to draw
uptrends and
downtrends.

If the trend lines are above the current price, you can also consider them *angled* resistance levels. If the line is below the current price, you can use it as a support level.

TIP

Check out this fun, short video where I explain the art of drawing trend lines: investdiva.com/the-art-of-drawing-trend-lines.

Now what if the market is moving between two parallel support and resistance levels? Technical chartists call this formation a *channel*. You can use lengthy channels for short-term trading strategies that I talk about in Chapter 19. For example, a common strategy is buying at the lower band of the channel and selling at the upper band. Figure 18-8 shows basic channels you can identify on your chart.

FIGURE 18-8:
Basic forms of
channels.

© John Wiley & Sons, Inc.

When the trend is no longer your friend

Unfortunately, trends never continue forever. All good things must come to an end. What goes up must come down. And many other clichés. Identifying the exact time a trend ends is one of the hardest jobs of technical analysts. Oftentimes, the market just teases the crowd with a sudden but short-lived change of direction. Many investors panic. But then the price gets back on track with the long-term trend.

TIP

Though key support and resistance levels can help you predict when a trend may end, you must back up your discoveries with fundamental and market sentiment analysis, as I explore in Chapter 9.

Picking Out Patterns on a Chart

Technical analysts are constantly looking for ways to identify key support and resistance levels. This job is no easy task, but chart formations can help you with your observations. Becoming an expert technical chartist can take time, and many analysts go through years of studying for certifications such as the Charted Market Technician (CMT). But for now, here's the gist of some important chart patterns.

Bullish reversal patterns

When a *bullish reversal* formation is confirmed, it normally indicates that the trend of the market price will reverse from a downtrend into an uptrend. It reverses the market into a bullish position. Some well-known bullish reversal chart patterns (shown in Figure 18-9) include the *double bottom* (when the price tests a key support level twice, creating two valley shapes at the support level), *the head and shoulders bottom* (when the price tests approximately the same support level three times), and the *saucer bottom* (when the price gradually reaches a key support level and gradually moves up, forming a shape of a bowl).

Double Bottom   **Head and Shoulders Bottom**   **Saucer Bottom**

© *John Wiley & Sons, Inc.*

FIGURE 18-9:
Examples of bullish reversal chart patterns.

A popular trading strategy that uses bullish reversal patterns is to buy when you identify the pattern at its so-called *neckline* (which is a key resistance level) and sell at the next key resistance levels.

TIP

Bearish reversal patterns

As its name suggests, a *bearish reversal* formation is the exact opposite of a bullish one (see the preceding section). With a bearish reversal, the prices normally hit a resistance during an uptrend and can't go any higher. Therefore, they're forced to reverse into a bear market. Some famous bearish reversal patterns (shown in Figure 18-10) include the *double top* (a formation of two mountain-like shapes on the chart as the price tests a key resistance level), the *head and shoulders* (when the price tests approximately the same resistance level three times, but the second time it goes a bit higher, making it look like a peaking head), and the *saucer top* (when the price gradually reaches a key resistance level and then gradually moves back down).

FIGURE 18-10: Examples of bearish reversal chart patterns.

Double Top   Head and Shoulders   Saucer Top

© John Wiley & Sons, Inc.

TIP

Some typical strategies using bearish reversals include the following:

>> Take profit of assets you've been holding after you identify the pattern.

>> Short-sell at the neckline and take profit at the next support levels.

Smoothing Charts Out with Moving Averages

If you find price charts and all the information they contain too complicated, you're not alone! Likeminded investors and chartists often turn to tools categorized as moving averages (MAs) to identify those trends more easily.

By definition, a *moving average* is a mathematical procedure that records the average value of a series of prices over time. You have a ton of ways to calculate moving averages and use them based on your trading needs. Some are basic, and some are more sophisticated. Personally, I like to mix and match MAs with technical chart patterns and, of course, Fibonacci retracement levels. The following sections have more on MAs; flip to Chapter 22 for details on Fibonacci retracement levels.

WARNING

You may have gotten used to the idea that trading signals and indicators are often just full of it. The cryptocurrency market often acts in an arbitrary fashion, ignoring all the supposed rules. That's why you should never rely on only one method of analysis and should *always* confirm your decisions with other tools and points of the Invest Diva Diamond Analysis (IDDA) in Chapter 9. On top of that, you should never invest money you can't afford to lose.

Basic moving averages

On your trading chart, you can find basic moving averages (MAs) that smooth out the prices ranging from 10 to 200 time periods. For example, if you look at a daily chart, you can select a short-term moving average that calculates a series of 15 data points. This figure is called a *15-day moving average*, or a *fast MA*. If you want to see a longer-term average movement, you can use a longer period, such as 200 days, and call it a *slow MA*.

REMEMBER

Longer-term moving averages do a better job at picking up the major trends. On the other hand, shorter-term MAs are more sensitive to recent price actions. Technical analysts often use a combination of MAs and study their positioning versus one another.

Sophisticated moving averages

Geeky technical analysts like me often take their MA practice to the next level, using more complex combinations of moving averages to understand the market sentiment better. Here are some of the most widely used sophisticated MAs:

>> **Moving average convergence divergence (MACD):** MACD is an indicator that shows the difference between a short-term moving average and a long-term moving average. Click here for more information: www. investdiva.com/investing-guide/macd.

>> **Bollinger Bands:** Created by Mr. Bollinger in the 1980s, this indicator includes two bands above and below the market price. Click here for more information: www.investdiva.com/investing-guide/bollinger-bands-bol.

>> **Relative strength index (RSI):** RSI is a momentum indicator, or oscillator, that measures the relative internal strength of the cryptocurrency's price

against itself. Click here for more information: `www.investdiva.com/`
`investing-guide/relative-strength-index-rsi`.

» **Ichimoku Kinko Hyo:** This option is my personal favorite; it consists of five different MAs all on top of each other. It gives you all you need to know all at once (hence its name, which means "a glance at the chart in balance"). Head to Chapter 22 for more details.

IN THIS CHAPTER

» **Using different time frames in short-term trading**

» **Exploring short-term crypto strategies**

» **Managing the risks involved with short-term trading**

Chapter **19**

Short-Term Trading Strategies

L et me set this straight: I'm not a big fan of short-term trading. It's a personality thing. Some traders thrive on the thrill of short-term trading adventures, or *speculative trading*. I sweat on speculations. I prefer to invest long-term, sit back, relax, have nights of peaceful sleep, and let the markets do their thing. (You can discover some long-term investing strategies in Chapter 20.)

That being said, I have many students who ask me for short-term strategies. And being the awesome coach that I am, I deliver. In this chapter, I go through some methods I use to develop short-term strategies that have worked for my students in the past. Although the basics of short-term trading are similar across different assets, crypto trading requires you to consider some additional steps to stack the odds in your favor.

Distinguishing Three Short-Term Time Frames

Short-term trading can also be called aggressive trading. Why? Because you're taking more risk in the hope of making more profit. As I discuss in Chapter 3, investment of any kind requires a constant balancing and trade-off between risk and return. To earn more return, you must take more risk. When aiming to make money in the short term, you must be prepared to lose your investment (and maybe even more!) in that time frame as well, especially in a volatile market like cryptocurrencies.

Short-term trading can be divided into different categories within itself based on how quickly you realize the profits — hours, days, or weeks. Generally speaking, the shorter the trading time frame, the higher the risk involved with that trade. The following sections spell out the three most common short-term trading time frames for cryptocurrencies.

Profiting within hours

If you've ever wondered what a day trader does, this is it! *Day trading* is one form of aggressive short-term trading. You aim to buy and sell cryptos within a day and take profit before you go to bed. In traditional markets like the stock market, a trading day often ends at 4:30 p.m. local time. But the cryptocurrency market runs 24/7, so you can define your day-trading hours to fit your schedule. Pretty neat, right? With this great power comes great responsibility, though. You don't want to lose your shirt and get your spouse angry at you.

Here are a few questions to ask yourself to determine whether day trading is indeed the right crypto route for you:

>> Do you have the time to dedicate to day trading? If you have a full-time job and can't stick to your screen all day, day trading probably isn't right for you. Make sure you don't use your company time for trading! Not only you can get fired, but you also won't be able to dedicate the required time and energy to trading either. Double the trouble.

>> Do you have sufficient risk tolerance for day trading? Check out Chapter 3 for more on risk management, and attend this free Masterclass to get my risk management toolkit: investdiva.com/masterclass.

>> Even if you can financially afford to potentially lose money day trading, are you willing to do so? Do you have the stomach to see your portfolio go up and down on a daily basis? If not, perhaps day trading isn't right for you.

If you've made up your mind that day trading is the right crypto route for you, the following sections share some tips to keep in mind before getting started.

Define crypto trading sessions

Because cryptocurrencies are traded internationally without borders, one way you can define a trading day is to go by the trading sessions in financial capitals of the world like New York, Tokyo, the *eurozone* (made up of the European countries whose official currency is the euro), and Australia. Figure 19-1 shows these sessions. This method follows similar trading sessions as in the foreign exchange (forex) market.

© John Wiley & Sons, Inc.

FIGURE 19-1: Cryptocurrency trading sessions based on international time zones.

Sydney Market Open	Tokyo Market Open	London Market Open	New York Market Open
Trading Day 5 PM (EST) ↓ Next Day 2 AM (EST)	Trading Day 7 PM (EST) ↓ Next Day 4 AM (EST)	3 AM (EST) ↓ 12 PM (EST)	8 AM (EST) ↓ 5 PM (EST)

TIP

Some sessions may provide better trading opportunities if the cryptocurrency you're planning to trade has higher volume or volatility in that time frame. For example, a cryptocurrency based in China, such as NEO, may see more trading volume during the Asian session.

Know that day trading cryptos is different from day trading other assets

When day trading traditional financial assets such as stocks or forex, you can follow already established fundamental market-movers such as a company's upcoming earnings report or a country's interest rate decision. The cryptocurrency market, for the most part, doesn't have a developed risk-event calendar. That's why conducting fundamental analysis (see Chapter 9) to develop a day-trading strategy is way harder for cryptos.

Set a time aside

REMEMBER

Depending on your personal schedule, you may want to consider scheduling a specific time of the day to focus on your trades. The idea of being able to trade around the clock is pretty cool in theory. You can just get on your trading app during a sleepless night and start trading. But this flexibility can backfire when you start losing sleep over it. Remaining alert during day trading, or night trading for that matter, is very important because you need to develop strategies, identify trading opportunities, and manage your risk multiple times throughout the trading session. For many people, having a concrete discipline pays off.

Start small

Day trading involves a lot of risk. So until you get the hang of it, start with a small amount and gradually increase your capital as you gain experience. Some brokers even let you start trading with a minimum of $50.

WARNING

If you start trading small, make sure you aren't using margin or leverage to increase your trading power. Leverage is one of those incredibly risky tools that's projected as an opportunity. It lets you manage a bigger account with a small initial investment by borrowing the rest from your broker. If you're trying to test the waters by starting small, using leverage will defeat that purpose.

Don't take too much risk

According to Investopedia, most successful day traders don't stake much of their account — 2 percent of it, max — with each trade. If you have a $10,000 trading account and are willing to risk 1 percent of your capital on each trade, your maximum loss per trade is $100. So you must make sure you have that money set aside for potential losses, and that you aren't taking more risk than you can afford.

Secure your crypto wallet

One major problem with day trading cryptocurrencies is securing your crypto wallet. As I explain in Chapter 7, the least secure cryptocurrency wallets are online wallets. Because you're going to need your capital handy throughout the trading day, you may have no choice but to leave your assets on your exchange's online wallet, which can expose you to risk of hacking.

TIP

One way to enhance your security here is to not actually buy and sell cryptocurrencies but rather to speculate the price action and crypto market movements by using brokers who facilitate such services, as I discuss in Chapter 6.

Stay away from scalping

WARNING

Scalping is the shortest-term trading strategy some individual traders choose. It basically means jumping in and out of trades frequently, sometimes in a matter of seconds. If you're paying commission fees for every trade, not only are you exposing yourself to a ton of market risk when scalping, but you can also get burned out by the fees before you make any profit. Individual traders rarely make any profit scalping. Now, if you're part of an enterprise that has access to discount commission fees and huge trading accounts, the story may be different.

Profiting within days

If you want to trade short term but don't want to stick to your computer all the time, this time frame may be the right one for you. In traditional trading, traders who hold their positions overnight are categorized as *swing traders*. The most common trading strategy for swing traders is *range trading*, where instead of riding up a trend, you look for a crypto whose price has been bouncing up and down within two prices. The idea is to buy at the bottom of the range and sell at the top, as you can see in Figure 19-2. If you're using a broker who facilitates short-selling services, you can also go the other direction.

FIGURE 19-2:
A simplified range-trading strategy.

© John Wiley & Sons, Inc.

Of course, in real life the ranges aren't as neat and pretty as what you see in the example I put together for Figure 19-2. To identify a range, you must be proficient in technical analysis. A number of technical chart patterns (see Chapter 18) and indicators can help you identify a range. For more on technical analysis, check out my Masterclass at investdiva.com/masterclass.

REMEMBER

If you choose swing trading rather than day trading, one downside is that you may not be able to get an optimized tax rate that's created for day traders in some countries. In fact, swing trading is in the gray area for taxation because if you hold your positions for more than a year (long-term investing; see Chapter 20), you also get an optimized tax rate. For more on tax optimizations, flip to Chapter 23.

TIP

If you're trading the cryptocurrency market movements without actually buying them, make sure you aren't paying a ton of commission fees for holding your positions overnight. Consult with your broker before developing your swing-trading strategy.

Profiting within weeks

This time frame falls into the category of *position trading* in traditional markets. Still shorter than a long-term investing strategy but longer than day trading, this type of short-term trading can be considered the least risky form of short-term trading. But it's still risky. (Flip to Chapter 3 to read more about risks involved in trading cryptocurrencies.)

For this type of trade, you can identify a market trend and ride it up or down until the price hits a resistance or a support. As I explain in Chapter 18, a *resistance* level is a psychological market barrier that prevents the price from going higher. A *support* level is the opposite: a price at which the market has difficulty "breaking below."

WARNING

To hold your positions for weeks, you need to keep your crypto assets in your exchange's online wallet, which may expose you to additional security risk (as I explain in Chapter 7). You may be better off utilizing a broker that provides price-speculation services for this type of trading strategy so you don't have to own the cryptocurrencies.

One popular position-trading strategy involves the following steps, as you can also see in Figure 19-3:

» Identify a trend (using technical analysis).

» Wait for a pullback.

» Buy at the pullback within the uptrend.

» Take profit (sell) at a resistance.

TIP

In my Premium Investing Group, our Invest Diva coaches often provide position-trading strategies for members by using the Ichimoku Kinko Hyo + Fibonacci combo technique. See Chapter 22 for more about this technique.

FIGURE 19-3:
Buying at the
pullback in an
uptrend market,
taking profit
at resistance.

SELL

Pullback

Uptrend

BUY

© John Wiley & Sons, Inc.

Trying Short-Term Analysis Methods

You can't become a successful short-term trader just by reading the news. Short-term trading is an art that combines active risk management with a great understanding of crowd psychology and price actions that goes beyond the scope of this book. Also, the cryptocurrency market isn't as established as other markets, so trading the lesser-known cryptos on a short-term basis can be even riskier. You can compare that to trading penny stocks or gambling, which are almost sure ways to lose money.

Regardless, the following sections present some analysis methods that professional traders with large accounts and a high risk tolerance can use.

WARNING

According to Medium.com, day trading the cryptocurrency market has brought some investors profits between 1 and 2 percent, while on other values they *lose* money. For most, day trading the crypto market has been a zero-sum game.

Deciphering chart patterns

You can use the majority of the chart patterns I talk about in Chapter 18 for short-term trading as well as medium- and long-term trading strategies (covered in Chapter 20). All you need to do is to set your chart view to a shorter time frame. I normally check with three different time frames when developing a trading strategy. If I'm analyzing the markets for more rapid profit-taking, I look at three short time frames. For example, if you're looking to profit within hours, you can analyze the price action on these three time frames:

>> 30-minute chart (to get a sense of the market sentiment)

>> Hourly chart

>> Four-hour chart (to get an understanding of the bigger picture)

If you see different forms of bullish reversal chart patterns (see Chapter 18) across all three time frames, you may have a higher probability of a new uptrend starting, which can lead you to a successful bullish trading strategy. The following sections show an example of the Bitcoin/U.S. dollar (BTC/USD) crypto/fiat pair on September 5, 2018.

TIP

I use tradingview.com for charting as they provide many technical analysis tools and customizable charts.

A 30-minute chart

You're looking at the 30-minute chart, and at 9:30 a.m., you suddenly see a massive drop that brings Bitcoin's price down from approximately $7,380 to $7,111, as you can see in Figure 19-4. This formation is called a *bearish engulfing candlestick pattern* among technical analysts. Is this the beginning of a new downtrend?

FIGURE 19-4:
BTC/USD
30-minute chart
on September 5,
2018.

© tradingview.com

An hourly chart

By switching from the 30-minute chart (see the preceding section) to the hourly chart, you notice the same drop (shown in Figure 19-5). But because now you can see the bigger picture, you discover that this drop was after a period of uptrend in the market, which may be a signal of a pullback during an uptrend. But how low can the pair go?

FIGURE 19-5: BTC/USD hourly chart on September 5, 2018.

© tradingview.com

A four-hour chart

By switching from the hourly chart (see the preceding section) to the four-hour chart, you notice that the bearish engulfing pattern is formed in a much longer uptrend that has been moving up since the middle of August. By observing the four-hour chart, you can pinpoint the key support levels, shown at $6,890 and $6,720, that the price can pull back toward within this newly established bearish market sentiment. In Figure 19-6, I've used the Fibonacci retracement levels to identify the key price levels with higher accuracy. Flip to Chapter 22 for more on Fibonacci.

Following the technical analysis guidelines, you can expect a bit of a correction after this sudden drop, followed by more drops to key support levels on the four-hour chart. With this, a potential trading idea may be to sell at correction or at market price and then to take profit at one or two support levels.

FIGURE 19-6:
BTC/USD
four-hour chart
on September 5,
2018.

© tradingview.com

After sudden drops in the markets, sometimes the market corrects itself before dropping more. Often, it corrects itself to key *pivot levels* (a level that's considered trend-changing if the price breaks below or above it), which in this case is the 23 percent Fibonacci retracement level at $7,090. The reward for waiting for a correction is that you may be able to take more profit short-selling at a higher price. The risk with it is that the market may not correct itself, and you may miss out. Personally, if I think the market is really going to shift into a bearish senti-ment, I sell some at market price and set a sell *limit order* at the key pivot level just in case the market corrects itself before further drops. This way, you can distribute your risk. A sell limit order is a type of trading order you can set on your broker's platform, which enables you to sell your assets at a specific price in the future.

For a short-term profit-taking, I consider setting buy limit orders at both key support levels at 38 percent and 50 percent Fibonacci retracement levels. In this example, I aim to take partial profit at around $6,890, and then exit the trade completely at $6,720. Again, this approach may limit my gains if the market con-tinues to drop, but it also limits my risk if the price doesn't fall as low as the second key support, so it gives me a proportionate risk-reward ratio. Figure 19-7 shows how the market actually performed.

The BTC/USD price did correct a little bit, but it didn't go as high as the 23 percent Fibonacci retracement level. So if you had only waited for a correc-tion to sell, you would've missed out on the trading opportunity. The market did drop to both key support levels at 38 percent and 50 percent Fibonacci retracement levels. So if you had sold at market price, you would've taken profit at both key support levels. On the other hand, the price continued to drop beyond the 50 percent Fibonacci retracement level, so that may represent a missed opportunity to maximize your returns.

FIGURE 19-7:
BTC/USD
four-hour chart
strategy
performance.

© tradingview.com

REMEMBER

However, in my opinion, it's always better to be safe than sorry. That's why I always recommend that my students avoid being greedy when it comes to strategy developments.

Using indicators

Another popular technical analysis method is to use indicators such as the relative strength index (RSI), Bollinger Bands (BOL), and Ichimoku Kinko Hyo (ICH). I call such indicators elements of a beauty kit. By adding them to your chart, you make it more beautiful and accent the important features just as you would by putting on makeup on your face!

Indicators are mathematical tools, developed over the years by technical analysts, that can help you predict the future price actions in the market. You can use these indicators in addition to chart patterns to get a higher analysis accuracy. But in short-term trading, some traders use only one or two indicators without paying attention to chart patterns. In fact, you can create a whole trading strategy by using only one indicator in short-term trading. Flip to Chapter 18 for more on indicators. To find out more about my signature Ichimoku-Fibonacci combo strategy, check out Chapter 22 and my book, *Ichimoku Secrets* (CreateSpace Independent Publishing Platform, 2016).

Avoiding illegal pump-and-dump stuff

As a cryptocurrency trader, you need to be aware of what can happen among illegal group activities that manipulate the markets, take profit, and leave others shirtless. A *pump-and-dump* scheme happens when a group of people or an influential individual manipulates the market prices in its own favor.

For example, in an unlikely illegal act, a highly influential person named Joe goes on TV and says, "I think Bitcoin is going to reach $60,000 tomorrow," while he already has an established buy and sell strategy to trade a ton of Bitcoin. The moment his speculation hits the news, everyone else who's watching TV gets excited and start buying Bitcoin based on this suggestion. The hype helps Bitcoin's price go up and Joe's strategy to go through. But before the rest of the market can catch up, Joe sells (dumps) his Bitcoins, taking a ton of profit but sending Bitcoin's price crashing down.

Managing Short-Term Trading Risk

Managing your risk when short-term trading can be quite different from that of medium- and long-term investing. To avoid a major account meltdown trading short term, you must balance your risk and return more actively. Some short-term traders like using a stop-loss order is one method to consider.

A *stop-loss* order is a price at which you tell your broker to "stop your losses" and get you out of your position. For example, say you think Bitcoin is going to go up from $6,000 to $6,100 in the next hour, so you enter a buy position. But instead, Bitcoin starts dropping below $6,000, putting you in a losing position. To avoid losing too much money, you can set a stop-loss order at $5,950. You can set a risk-reward ratio at any number that makes sense to your risk tolerance.

I famously don't use stop-losses when investing long-term. In fact, I believe stop-losses are a scam promoted by brokers. Why? Because it gives you a false feeling of safety while 90 percent of traders end up losing all their money to the stop-loss. Guess who makes money when you lose? The broker.

WARNING

In medium to long-term trading, using a stop-loss can be riskier than not using it, especially if you're not a full-time trader. Make sure you have a complete understanding of your trading objectives and risk tolerance before using a stop-loss in crypto trading.

TIP

One easy way to calculate your risk-reward ratio is to divide your estimated net profit (the reward) by the price of the maximum risk you're willing to take. For example, if you want to have a 1:2 risk-reward ratio, that means you're willing to make double the amount of what you're willing to risk. But before you understand how much risk you can take, you must calculate your risk tolerance, which I discuss in Chapter 3.

Chapter **20**

Long-Term Investing Strategies

D o you know how long the first Bitcoin investors waited to see any type of return? Around seven years. Some Bitcoin miners and early investors actually forgot about their crypto assets and had to go on a treasure hunt to find their Bitcoin wallets during the 2017 bubble.

The point is that just like many other markets, time and patience can be your best friends. But you still need to have a plan based on your risk tolerance and financial goals in order to profit long term. In this chapter, I go over the basics of long-term investing in cryptocurrencies.

Time Is on Your Side: Getting Started with Long-Term Investing

When I talk about long-term investment strategies, I'm basically treating cryptocurrencies as assets. And just like any other type of financial investment, you need to create a portfolio that goes along with your risk tolerance and financial goals. To do so, you can begin by examining the criteria for constructing your crypto portfolio (such as risk management, discussed in Chapter 3) and then use them to develop a plan for allocating different types of crypto assets in the various categories I explore in Chapter 8.

In the following sections, I dig into a couple of things to keep in mind when getting started with your portfolio management.

Your personal goals and current situation

REMEMBER

You should consider a wide variety of issues when managing your portfolio long term. Factors like risk and return are some of the obvious ones that I cover in Chapter 3. But when it comes to long-term investment in risky assets like cryptocurrencies, you need to take it a step further. Here are some questions you should answer:

>> What's your income size now, and where can it go in the future?

>> Are you likely to change your job in the future? Is your current job secure?

>> What's your marital status now? Do you have any children? Where do you see yourself on this front in five years?

>> What's your investment experience?

>> Do you have any other investments in assets such as equities or real estate? How diversified is your overall portfolio?

These questions may sound cliché, and you may already have the answers in your head. But investing long term is a logical process, and actually writing down the most basic elements of your personal goals and characteristics always pays off. When you've assessed your own financial situation and goals, you can have a better understanding of how to move forward with your crypto portfolio. Your needs may even determine the avenue you choose.

For example, if you're retired and your income depends on your portfolio, long-term cryptocurrency investing may not be suitable for you. You may want to consider a lower-risk, current-income-oriented approach. If you're young and willing to take the risk in the hope of getting high returns, you may even consider the short-term trading strategies I cover in Chapter 19. Personally, as a mom and the owner of a multi-million dollar business (Invest Diva), I allocated 15 percent of my portfolio to cryptocurrencies in 2017 and gradually increased it as the markets fell. By the 2022 market crash, I increased my crypto allocation to 25 percent of my overall investment portfolio. For my parents, on the other hand,

I chose a different approach. They're retired and need current income to survive. That's why I recommended that they allocate only 5 percent of their savings to cryptocurrencies in 2018 with the goal of capital gains in the next few years. We sold half of their crypto as the markets gained in 2021. I'm repeating this process for them at the time of writing this book.

REMEMBER

To sum it up, build your portfolio around your needs depending on the following variables:

>> Your current income

>> Your age

>> The size of your family

>> Your risk preferences

TIP

For more on risk management and calculating your risk tolerance, check out Chapter 3 and my most popular free Masterclass: investdiva.com/masterclass.

Your portfolio's objectives

REMEMBER

Assessing your personal goals and life situation brings you one step closer to creating your own portfolio (see the preceding section). When creating a long-term portfolio, you generally want to consider these objectives:

>> **Generating current income:** These investments can generate a regular payment, which can be at odds with high capital appreciations.

>> **Preserving capital:** This low-risk, conservative investment strategy generates moderate returns.

>> **Growing capital:** Focusing on capital growth requires you to increase your risk tolerance and reduce your need for a current-income-based investment strategy.

>> **Reducing taxes:** If you're in a high tax bracket, you may consider a portfolio that generates capital gains. If you're in a lower tax bracket, you have lower incentive to defer taxes and earn high investment returns, so a portfolio with higher-current-income assets may be suitable for you.

>> **Managing risk:** You should always consider the risk-return trade-off in all investment decisions.

TIME AND CRYPTOS: THE FAMOUS PIZZAS

To truly understand the significance of time in holding your assets, consider this true story. On May 22, 2010, a Bitcoin miner named Laszlo Hanyecz spent 10,000 Bitcoins to buy (hold your breath) two large pizzas from Papa John's. At the time, the 10,000 Bitcoins were worth about $30. This transaction is widely believed to be the first time anyone used Bitcoins to buy something tangible. He even posted about his purchase on a popular Bitcoin forum at the time, Bitcoin Talk, as you can see here: `bitcointalk.org/index.php?topic=137.0`.

On May 22, 2022, 12 years later, and even though Bitcoin's price had already dropped from the all-time high levels of above $68,000, the amount he paid in Bitcoin for the two pizzas was the equivalent of $300 million. That's about $150 million per pie. Now May 22 is known as Bitcoin Pizza Day.

What's the moral of this story? Every time you get impatient with your long-term crypto investments, remember poor Laszlo kicking himself on Bitcoin Pizza Day, knowing he could've been a millionaire had he just sat on his Bitcoins for a few years instead of getting the instant gratification those two pizzas brought him.

They get tied together with your personal goals and other investments. For example, current income and capital preservation are good objectives for someone with a low risk tolerance who has a conservative personality. If you have medium risk tolerance and don't need to depend on your investment for current income as much, you can select capital growth as your portfolio objective. In many countries, including the United States, taxes also play a major role in your investment goals. For example, if you're in a high tax bracket, focusing on capital gains may be a better option for you because you can defer taxes. Last but not least, you should consider your risk-return trade-off in all your investment decisions, whether long term or not.

Creating Long-Term Strategies

Any type of investment can be summed up in four words: Buy low, sell high. But of course no one can get it perfectly right every time. With cryptocurrencies in particular, the market is still testing out new psychological levels, so predicting the highs and lows can be that much more difficult. The following sections introduce some methods I've been using to expand my long-term cryptocurrency portfolio.

Observing psychological levels

If you were to take a guess, who do you think moves the prices of assets in the markets up and down? It's the market participants. It's us. And the bigger our trading position and our influence, the bigger the impact on the markets.

As time goes by, key psychological support and resistance levels start to develop in online financial markets. The same has now happened for most major cryptocurrencies. Of course, the older the crypto, the more historical data we have to study. I've found Fibonacci retracement levels (see Chapter 22) very helpful in identifying key psychological levels even in the newer cryptocurrencies. In my Premium Investing Group (PIG), my students and I are often blown away by how many times Fibonacci predicts the key psychological levels.

The reason psychological levels are already appearing in the crypto market may be that many crypto investors are using traditional technical analysis methods (see Chapter 18) for their cryptocurrency investment strategies. With that, you can expect the crypto crowd psychology to form similar chart patterns to those of other markets, such as equities and the foreign exchange market (forex), in longer time frames like weekly and monthly charts. Crowd psychology is the constant battle between the sellers (the bears) and the buyers (the bulls) in the market that leads to price movements in an asset. Psychological levels are those that the prices have difficulty breaking, due to the strength or weakness of the bears and bulls in the market.

TIP

You can find a great deal about investing crowd psychology in plain (and funny) videos in my *Forex Coffee Break* portion of our signature *Make Your Money Work For You PowerCourse*. You can learn more about it by attending my Masterclass: invest-diva.com/masterclass.

After you identify the psychological levels, you can use them to develop different types of strategies based on your current portfolio, your risk tolerance, and your financial goals. Here are some examples:

>> Buy at a key support level and sell at a key resistance level.

>> Buy at current market price and sell at a key resistance level.

>> Wait for a pullback when the price reaches a key resistance level and buy lower. Then sell at the next key resistance level.

>> Buy at a key support level and hold long term.

You can use the techniques in Chapters 18 and 22 to identify such support and resistance levels for your investment strategy.

Selling when you reach your goal

A cryptocurrency's price may continue going higher after it reaches a key resistance level. But how long do you wait? Which resistance level do you choose? Does using resistance levels even make sense for your financial goals? One realistic way to approach your investment strategy is to sell when you've reached your investment goal. (You can use a sell limit order, which I talk about later in this chapter, to do this.) The key here is that you shouldn't look back and regret your decision after you've made the sale, even if the price continues going up after you sell. You achieved your goal, so instead of regreting, consider patting yourself on the shoulder and celebrating your win!

REMEMBER

Markets may continue to go up after you sell. Don't let your emotions take over your logical decision to sell. If you need the money and have already achieved your investment goal, you have no reason to regret an early sale. If anything, you can always get back in the market with a brand-new investment strategy.

Keeping tax consequences in mind

TIP

Tax laws change all the time, and they vary in different countries. However, in most cases taxes affect nearly all investment actions. As of 2022, in the United States a maximum of $3,000 of capital losses in excess of capital gains can be written off against other income in any one year. If you have a loss position in an investment and have concluded that selling it is wise, the best time to sell is when you have a capital gain against which you can apply the loss.

Before starting to invest, you must understand the basics of taxes in your country. Flip to Chapter 23 for an overview of how you should consider taxes before making investment decisions.

Considering Limit and Stop-Loss Orders

Cryptocurrency exchanges and brokers alike allow you to use various types of orders to buy and sell altcoins. Most active traders use *market orders* to buy or sell at the best available price, but long-term investors can use other types of orders such as limit orders and stop-loss orders.

TIP

Long-term investors can also use market orders in abnormal circumstances if they need to make a quick investment decision. Market orders are normally filled quickly at a price close to the current market price.

WARNING

Using market orders can sometimes involve risks, especially in volatile markets such as cryptocurrencies. Sometimes the price of cryptocurrencies drops or skyrockets in a matter of seconds. If you happen to use a market order on those occasions, you may get blindsided by the actual price at which your order is executed. That's why using a limit order is always safer than using market orders.

Limit orders

A *limit order* is a type of transaction order that allows you to buy or sell at your preferred price. For example, if the current Bitcoin market price is at $15,748, you can set a *buy limit order* to buy at $15,000 or even below that level if you think the price has the potential to drop.

Then you can set a *sell limit order* to take profit when you reach your investment goal, say at $16,000. I love using limit orders because they allow me to go about my life without worrying about prices too much while the markets do their usual movements.

REMEMBER

Always double-check your limit orders before putting them through. Make sure your buy limit order isn't above the current market price and your sell limit order isn't below the current market price. Traditional brokers often send you a warning if you make a mistake in setting limit orders, but at the time of writing, most crypto exchanges don't offer such courtesies. Personally, I've been the victim of setting a careless buy limit order that was way above the current market price, and it immediately went through without a warning from my exchange.

Just like in other markets, cryptocurrency limit orders have different options for how long they stay in effect. The most common types are good 'til canceled and fill-or-kill:

>> A *good 'til canceled* (GTC) order normally stays in effect for six months. If it's not executed within that time frame, your broker/exchange may cancel it. If you still want to keep the position in effect, you may need to renew it after six months.

>> A *fill-or-kill* order is canceled if it's not immediately executed. Therefore, it may be a better fit for short-term trading strategies (like those in Chapter 19).

Other types of limit orders offered by your trading platform may include *good 'til time* (your order stays in effect until a specific time you select) and *immediate or cancel* (your order is canceled if it's not immediately fulfilled by your broker). You can set more than one limit order for your cryptocurrencies. You can also choose to buy fractions of a cryptocurrency, especially when those like Bitcoin are so expensive. For example, in one account, I've set a buy limit order for Bitcoin versus U.S. dollar (BTC/USD) to purchase 0.4 Bitcoins when the price reaches $6,000. On the order form, I've also added a good 'til canceled buy limit order to buy 0.2 Bitcoins at $5,851. By having multiple limit orders, I eliminate the risk of missing out and avoid going all in at one price.

Stop-loss orders

You can use *stop-loss orders* to limit the downside loss exposure of your crypto investment. Stop-losses are basically a form of limit orders (see the preceding section), where you ask your broker to close your position and take losses at a specific price. I'm not a big fan of stop-losses. In fact, as years go by, I grow more and more against stop-losses. I believe stop-losses are the biggest trick of all times which helps the brokers make more money.

But for some investors, cutting the losses short in case of a rapid decline in the market may make sense. Just like limit orders, stop-loss orders have different types like good 'til canceled.

WARNING

Volatile markets such as cryptocurrencies normally bounce back up from the lows as rapidly as they fall. That's why by using a stop-loss order, you may end up getting out of your position prematurely and miss out on potential gains. If you're looking to use a stop-loss order, you must analyze the market carefully and choose an appropriate level for your stop-loss. To get the latest cryptocurrency investment strategies and buy/sell limit order ideas, consider joining Invest Diva's Premium Investing Group (PIG) for free at investdivapig.com.

Chapter **21**

Minimizing Losses and Maximizing Gains

Depending on whether you're a short-term trader or long-term investor, you can manage your portfolio either actively or passively. If you're a long-term investor (see Chapter 20), you may find yourself managing your portfolio passively by buying and holding a well-diversified portfolio over a set amount of time. If you're a short-term trader, you can use the tools I present in Chapter 19 to manage and obtain your desired objectives in a more active way.

I'm a big fan of long-term value investing, but that doesn't mean I'm against active portfolio management. In fact, I've seen over and over again that you can get better returns, whether they're long term or short term, by actively managing your portfolio. Now, by *active*, I don't mean sticking to your screen all the time and covertly checking your investment apps throughout the day during conversations and meetings. This chapter explains some management strategies that can help you find a sweet balance to do it all and still maintain an outside life.

Keeping the Losses Down

A phenomenon called *loss aversion* occurs in behavioral finance when investors keep the losing assets in their portfolios while actively selling the "winners." This tendency is why going against the crowd is one way to curtail your losses. In the following sections, I explain some techniques you can use to keep your crypto investing losses down.

Measuring returns

Managing your cryptocurrency investments can be challenging because your assets may be scattered over different exchanges and cryptocurrency wallets. Additionally, you may have purchased some altcoins by using Bitcoin, some others by using the U.S. dollar (USD), and more by using cryptos such as Ethereum or Litecoin. That's why I recommend you keep a log of your investments and ink any changes you make to your portfolio. Here are the three steps in determining your portfolio returns:

» Measuring the amount you've invested

» Measuring capital gains, which is the profit you make through buying and selling cryptos

» Measuring income, which is the payment you get by holding some cryptos (if applicable)

To calculate the amount invested, you can create a list similar to the one in Figure 21-1. The table shows numbers of coins, buying date, cost (both total and per coin), and current value.

My Crypto Portfolio as of September 1, 2018

Coin	Full name	Number of coins	Date bought	Total cost (including commission) (USD)	Cost per coin (USD)	Current price per coin (USD)
BTC	Bitcoin	0.5	6/29/2018	2,965	5,900	7,155
ETH	Ethereum	8	8/14/2018	2,250	275	293
XLM	Stellar Lumens	200	8/07/2018	44	0.200	0.2257
EOS	EOS	50	8/16/2018	225	4.45	6.55

© John Wiley & Sons, Inc.

FIGURE 21-1:
An example of a cryptocurrency investment log.

TIP

Now, because you may be purchasing different coins by using either *fiat* (government-backed) currencies, such as the U.S. dollar, or other cryptocurrencies, you may need to convert your investment value to one type of currency to keep it simple and easier to track. In Figure 21-1, I converted all my purchasing value to the U.S. dollar (USD). Another way to track your investment is to create separate logs depending how you purchased your altcoins. For example, you can have a separate log for your investments with BTC and another one for those you purchased with USD.

You can create such logs on a monthly, quarterly, or annual basis depending on your investing time frame. For example, if you're a short-term trader, you may need a monthly log. If you're a medium-to-long-term investor, you can use quarterly and annual logs. You can normally find the return on your investment calculated by your brokerage or exchange services (see Chapter 6 for more on brokerages and exchanges).

WARNING

Many crypto enthusiasts have given up measuring returns against fiat currencies like the USD altogether. If you believe Bitcoin is king and Ethereum is queen, you may end up buying most of your altcoins by using the king and queen anyway. Converting your crypto purchase to its USD value can be time-consuming. Also, most of the time you can't cash out in fiat currencies on your exchange anyway. USD, Bitcoin, and Ethereum all have fluctuations of their own versus other currencies, so a conversion may give you a false gain or loss impression. By converting to USD, it may look like you've gained profit on your initial investment, while in reality you may be in a losing position versus Bitcoin.

TIP

If you purchased your coins on an exchange by using another cryptocurrency such as Bitcoin, you can find the relevant USD value by searching your coin and the date you purchased it on websites such as tradingview.com. Many exchanges and brokers also offer charting services.

To measure your capital gains and income, you can simply check your account information with your broker and exchange. With cryptocurrency exchanges, your capital gain information is normally under tabs labeled "Wallet" or "Funds." Most exchanges provide the estimated value of your whole account either in Bitcoin or USD. If you have more than one account, you can add up these estimated numbers in your investment log and monitor them on a regular basis.

Monitoring exchange fees

To buy and sell cryptocurrencies, you need services like crypto exchanges and brokers. These companies mainly make money through transaction fees, as I discuss in Chapter 6. Although I don't recommend choosing an exchange based only on low fees, sometimes fees can become an important decision-making factor, especially for active traders. The fees can get even larger if you're looking to convert a fiat currency to a cryptocurrency like Bitcoin and then send it to another exchange to buy another cryptocurrency by using Bitcoin, and so on. Fees can be the biggest downside to short-term trading strategies for cryptocurrencies.

TIP

Here are some tips for keeping your exchange fees minimal while keeping your investment secure:

>> Buy your lump-sum major cryptos on more secure exchanges, which may have higher transaction fees. For example, when I need Bitcoin and Ethereum to trade other cryptocurrencies, I buy a large amount of both on an exchange with higher fees that allows using the U.S. dollar.

>> For active trading, choose exchanges that offer lower rates for your specific cryptocurrency pair, but make sure to periodically store your profit on a hardware wallet (see Chapter 7 for more on wallets).

>> Consider active trading with the exchange's native cryptocurrency. It may have a lower transaction fee than trading other cross-cryptos. For example, the Binance exchange offers cheaper trading options for its cryptocurrency, Binance Coin (BNB).

>> Always include the transaction fee when calculating your profit to be on top of your game. For example, if you buy 1 Ethereum coin for $200 but you pay $1.50 in transaction fees, you have spent $201.50 for your investment. While this amount doesn't make a great impact for long-term investments, active traders can feel the accumulative fees over time.

Understanding the art of getting out

I normally like to stay true to two of Warren Buffett's most famous investing rules:

1. Never lose money.

2. Never forget rule number one.

But no matter how thoroughly you conduct your analysis, at times you may find that getting out of a bad investment is better than holding onto it. The following sections give a few of my general strategies when it comes to getting out of an investment. Check out Chapter 9 for information on my Invest Diva Diamond Analysis (IDDA) system.

Don't be greedy

REMEMBER

If you're using one of the technical chart patterns I present in Chapters 18 and 22, always set your profit taking limit order at the price level that's consistent with the technique. You may get a feeling that the market will continue going up after your profit target (PT) is triggered, and you may be tempted to readjust your PT prematurely. Sometimes the market will continue to rise. Sometimes it won't. Personally, I prefer to be safe rather than sorry, so I refrain from readjusting the PT orders way too often (unless I have a valid fundamental reason to do so besides just gut feeling).

Take partial profits

I simply love this rule and swear by it! You can call me a hoarder, but I can never let go of all my coins (or any other assets, for that matter) all at once. I set up strategic, partial profit taking prices depending on my (or my students') investment goals and let the markets handle the rest.

For example, if I buy ten Ethereum coins (ETH) at $200 and I'm looking to take partial profit at key levels, I may sell two of my Ethereum coins at $470, sell two more at $591, and keep the rest long term. This way, I gain some profit along the way but don't let go of all my coins, so I still feel happy when the Ethereum price continues going up after I sell. Of course, calculating those key levels needs thorough analysis.

TIP

I dive deep into different types of investment strategies and partial profit taking in my award-winning *Make Your Money Work For You PowerCourse*. Learn more here: investdiva.com/masterclass.

Let go of bad investments

Every once in a while, you find yourself holding onto a coin that's just not worth it. With worthy long-term investments, I tend to buy more coins as the price drops, but sometimes the cryptocurrency, its community, and its management simply don't have a future. This point is when reexamining your fundamental analysis (see Chapter 9) becomes important. When it becomes evident that this coin just ain't gonna bounce back, you may as well just bite the bullet and get out before your losses get bigger. If you're too scared to do so, you can always take losses in parts, using the partial profit method I talk about in the preceding section.

REMEMBER

By letting go of your bad investments and taking losses, you may receive tax credits you can use to offset the taxes you must pay on your capital gains. Flip to Chapter 23 for more on taxes.

Letting the Profits Rise

I have to deal with two emotions when the markets start to rise. One is regretting not buying more when the prices were down. The other is the temptation to sell and take profit before reaching my carefully analyzed profit target limit order. What I need to keep reminding myself (and my students and fellow investors alike) is that emotions rarely lead to maximizing profit. At the end of the day, discipline is what makes your bank. The following sections detail some tricks I use to avoid emotional investing.

Buying at the bottom

Being able to purchase at the lowest price every time you invest is highly unlikely. But studying the market psychology and historical price patterns can help you get close. One of my go-to technical analysis tools to identify the bottom is the Ichimoku-Fibonacci combo.

As I explain in Chapter 22 and in my book *Ichimoku Secrets* (CreateSpace Independent Publishing Platform, 2016), you can use the Ichimoku-Fibonacci combination to gauge crowd psychology and identify key support and resistance levels. (*Support* is a price level where the market has difficulty breaking below; *resistance* is a price level where the market has difficulty breaking above.)

For longer-term investing, I generally use the daily chart for Ichimoku analysis. As you can see in Figure 21-2, after the price of Ethereum (ETH) dropped below $3,000 on April 27, 2022, it also broke below the daily Ichimoku cloud. Following the Ichimoku Kinko Hyo's guidelines, I had an indication that the price of ETH might drop further toward key Fibonacci retracement and support levels at around $2,512, $1,977, and $1,301. By conducting this analysis, I was able to set a buy limit order at these levels ahead of time and aim to purchase at lower prices instead of buying immediately. This way you can maximize your profit and lower your net purchasing price.

TIP

If you're dealing with new cryptocurrecnies, you wouldn't be able to find enough historical data to rely on. In those cases, sometimes the price continues to drop below the all-time-low levels, creating new lows. If you're confident enough in the fundamentals of the cryptocurrency, the new lows can give you an opportunity to buy more at lower prices. You can use Fibonacci's extended levels to identify new lows. To use these levels, you must first identify a trend where the price went either up or down for an extended period of time recently. Then drag the Fibonacci tool on your charting platform from the top to the bottom of the trend (if it's a downtrend) and from bottom to the top (if it's an uptrend). By doing so, the Fibonacci levels magically appear on your chart.

Break below the Ichimoku Cloud

50% Fibonacci Retracement Level

38% Fibonacci Retracement Level

23% Fibonacci Retracement Level

FIGURE 21-2:
Using the Ichimoku-Fibonacci combo to identify bottoms.

© tradingview.com

Knowing that patience is a profitable virtue

"Patience is a profitable virtue" is my main mantra in all the education courses at Invest Diva! My students say repeating this mantra has changed the way they invest and has increased their profit returns by a fair bit. Whenever I feel the adrenaline rushing through my head from looking at a chart, I take a step back. I change the time frame and look at the big picture. I do more fundamental research. If all five points of the IDDA (see Chapter 9) aren't aligned, I simply log off my trading account and go about my day. Getting nervous is very easy when the markets take a dip and you've invested a bunch of money in an asset. Being patient can often be the ultimate path to making tangible returns.

Identifying the peaks

"Buy low and sell high" is the name of the game! Again, you've got to be either Nostradamus or Lucky Luke to take profit at the highest price every time you invest. But if you use historical data and technical chart patterns, you can stack the odds in your favor. For active trading and medium-term investing in the cryptocurrency market, I still find the Ichimoku-Fibonacci combo pretty useful, as I explain in Chapter 22. Other tools include technical chart patterns and key psychological resistance levels.

Using Ripple's XRP as an example, in September 2018 I identified a double bottom chart pattern in the process of formation on the daily chart, as you can see in Figure 21-3. A *double bottom* is a popular formation on charts, where the price has difficulty breaking below a support level twice, forming two valley-shaped bottoms. When confirmed, it can be interpreted as a bullish reversal pattern, meaning that the prices may start going up.

© tradingview.com

FIGURE 21-3:
A double bottom chart pattern forming on XRP/ USD daily chart.

Following the double bottom chart pattern guidelines (see Chapter 18), medium-term investors can expect the market to take profit when the price has moved up from the neckline ($0.3666 in Figure 21-3) the same distance from the bottom to the neckline, or the next available Fibonacci retracement levels (0.4273 and 0.5314). To be safe, I normally recommend taking partial profits at each level to distribute risk.

As you can see in Figure 21-4, on September 21, XRP reached both levels and then some before dropping back down. A medium-term investor would've taken profit at these levels, while a long-term investor would've stayed in his or her position.

For long-term investors, timing the profit taking can be a bit more challenging. The crypto market is an exciting new investment opportunity that a majority of people are just discovering. Just like with the dot-com bubble, the hype can lead to extreme volatility. You saw the results of the hype in 2017 when Bitcoin price surged over 1,000 percent and Ripple's XRP gained a whopping 36,018 percent. I personally know investors who sold right at the peak and became millionaires and others who bought at the peak and had to sit on their losses until the next surge. In this case, most investors who were able to sell at the peak are those who went against the hype and against the majority of the crowd.

© tradingview.com

FIGURE 21-4:
A double bottom chart pattern confirms, and XRP reaches profit target levels.

WARNING

Technical chart patterns such as double bottoms, indicators such as Ichimoku, and going against the crowd don't guarantee optimal results. These items are simply tools that increase the probability of identifying the best price to buy and sell. At the end of the day, you must conduct thorough risk management that applies to your personal financial goals and risk tolerance, as I discuss in Chapter 3.

Finding peaks and bottoms with a few trading tools

TIP

Here are some cheat sheets of the trading tools I use to identify peaks and bottoms:

>> **Bearish reversal chart patterns:** These patterns form on the chart during a period of surging prices and indicate that the market sentiment and price action may turn bearish and start dropping. Find out more at www.investdiva.com/investing-guide/bearish-reversal-patterns-list1.

>> **Bullish reversal chart patterns:** These patterns form during a downtrend and indicate the prices may start to turn bullish and rise. Check out www.investdiva.com/investing-guide/bullish-reversal-patterns-list.

>> **Ichimoku Kinko Hyo:** This Japanese indicator consists of five different moving averages, helping you get a better view of the current market sentiment and predict the future price action. See www.investdiva.com/investing-guide/ichimoku-kinko-hyo-explained.

IN THIS CHAPTER

» **Familiarizing yourself with Ichimoku Kinko Hyo**

» **Applying Fibonacci retracement levels in technical analysis**

» **Putting the Ichimoku and Fibonacci methods together**

Chapter **22**

Using Ichimoku and Fibonacci Techniques

n Chapter 18, I talk about how you can use technical analysis to develop crypto-currency trading and investing strategies. Though a ton of moving averages and chart patterns can help you with your strategy, one of my favorite techniques is combining Ichimoku Kinko Hyo and Fibonacci retracement levels. In this chapter, I overview the basics of these two technical indicators and show you how you can use them for trades.

TIP

Advanced Ichimoku-Fibonacci methods are beyond the scope of this publication; you can discover more about them in my book *Ichimoku Secrets* (CreateSpace Independent Publishing Platform, 2016).

Getting a Handle on Ichimoku Kinko Hyo

Its name may sound intimidating, but let me reassure you that Ichimoku Kinko Hyo is here to make your technical analysis easier, not harder! It's a Japanese phrase that roughly translates to "one-piece balanced table." In cryptocurrency investing, Ichimoku Kinko Hyo allows you to find out everything you need to know about the price action in "one glance": Ichimoku.

REMEMBER

The Ichimoku indicator is most suitable for shorter-term traders (for example, if you're looking to apply the "buy low, sell high" strategy within a day, a few days, a few weeks, or even a few months). If you're a long-term value investor, you can still use Ichimoku for certain buy signals, especially if the asset is volatile. For growth assets that don't go up and down a lot, we use other methods of individual chart pattern analysis (such as trend analysis and identifying key psychological levels detailed in Chapter 18).

The components of Ichimoku Kinko Hyo

REMEMBER

This indicator consists of several different moving averages (MAs). Each of these MAs serves a specific purpose, and their positioning versus each other and the price can help you understand the current market sentiment and predict its future direction. Here are some of the components you see when you add the Ichimoku Kinko Hyo (ICH) to your chart:

>> The Ichimoku cloud (Japanese name: Kumo)

>> The base line (Japanese name: Kijun)

>> The turn line (Japanese name: Tenkan)

>> The delay span (Japanese name: Chiko)

Your charting provider may use different colors for each of these components, but in Figure 22-1 I use a thick pink line for Kijun, a thick blue line for Tenkan, and a thin green line for Chiko. The Ichimoku cloud is actually the space between two other moving averages, Senkou (leading) span A and B. Depending on the direction of the cloud, this space is normally colored green for bullish and red for bearish market sentiment. (A *bullish* market sentiment means the price is expected to rise. A *bearish* market sentiment is when the prices drop.)

Name	Kumo	Kijun	Tenkan	Chiko
Meaning	Cloud	Base	Turn	Delayed
Image				

FIGURE 22-1:
Ichimoku Kinko
Hyo components.

© John Wiley & Sons, Inc.

TIP

If you're looking for an easy charting service that helps you with technical analysis including Ichimoku and Fibonacci, I recommend TradingView (www.tradingview.com), which I personally use as well. You can use this charting service for almost any asset, including cryptocurrencies, foreign exchange (forex), and stocks.

Figure 22-2 shows the Ichimoku Kinko Hyo components in action on a chart that displays the price action of Ripple (XRP) versus Bitcoin (BTC) on a four-hour (or 240-minute) basis. That means each of the candlesticks (see Chapter 18) shows the price movements of XRP versus BTC in four hours. The Ichimoku components dance around the prices, crossing above and below the price action depending on the calculations. You can take these movements as indications about the future price direction.

FIGURE 22-2:
Ichimoku Kinko
Hyo applied to
the XRP/BTC
four-hour chart.

© *tradingview.com*

Ichimoku interpretations

You can use the Ichimoku components' positioning against each other as well as versus the price to predict where the price may go next. The following sections present some basic interpretations of Ichimoku Kinko Hyo.

REMEMBER

Past performance is never an indication of future results. Therefore, all these indications are merely an addition to your thorough research on your investments; you shouldn't treat them as guaranteed strategies. For technical analysis, you must study other chart patterns (see Chapter 18) to further strengthen your Ichimoku strategy. Additionally, always conduct all points of the Invest Diva Diamond Analysis (IDDA; see Chapter 9) before making a final investment decision.

Buy signals

If you identify one or more of the following signals on a chart, chances are that the price may continue higher and therefore it's a good time to buy:

>> If the price is moving above the Ichimoku cloud, this movement may indicate a bullish momentum in the market and is therefore a buy signal.

>> When the Chiko (delayed) line moves above the cloud, it can be considered a buy signal.

>> When the Tenkan (turn) line crosses above the Kijun (base) line, that crossing may indicate a shift in the market sentiment from bearish to bullish and therefore be a buy signal.

Sell signals

The following represent sell signals:

>> When the price moves below the Ichimoku cloud

>> When the Chiko (delayed) line crosses below the cloud

>> When the Tenkan (turn) line crosses below the Kijun (base) line

Other common interpretations

Besides pure buy and sell indications, Ichimoku Kinko Hyo can also help you iden-tify support and resistance layers as well as provide a general understanding of market conditions. Here are some of the interpretations:

>> As long as the five lines are parallel, the trend will continue in that direction.

>> When the prices are inside the Ichimoku cloud, that means that the market is in the process of consolidating, which isn't a good time to buy or sell.

>> You can use the lower band of the prevailing cloud as a layer of support, which is a level that the price has difficulty breaking below.

>> You can use the upper band of the prevailing cloud as a layer of resistance, which is a price that the market has difficulty breaking above.

TIP

You can use Ichimoku as an entry level for both buy and sell positions. You can also combine two or more of the interpretations to adjust your strategy based on your risk tolerance.

Introducing Fibonacci Retracement Levels

Using Ichimoku Kinko Hyo all by itself gives you just a partial view of the markets and doesn't help you with an exit strategy. (Head to the earlier section "Getting a Handle on Ichimoku Kinko Hyo" for more on that indicator.) The next step is to identify key support and resistance levels that the market may have difficulty moving below (in case of a support level) and above (in case of a resistance level). You can search for support and resistance levels in many ways. My favorite is to use Fibonacci retracement levels.

Some background on Fibonacci

Fibonacci is the nickname for Italian mathematician Leonardo Pisano Bigollo, who some refer to as the most talented Western mathematician of the Middle Ages. Some of his most famous contributions to science include introducing the positional decimal numeral system, also known as the Hindu-Arabic numeral system, to the Western world and popularizing the Fibonacci sequence.

Mathematically, the *Fibonacci sequence* is the series of numbers where each number in the sequence is sum of the two numbers before it. So if you add the numbers 0 and 1, the result is 1, and you add that digit to the sequence. Then add up 1 and 1 and add the result, 2, to the sequence. Now add 1 and 2 — you get the idea. You can continue this way forever: 0, 1, 1, 2, 3, 5, 8, 13, 21, 34, 55, 89, 144, and so on!

REMEMBER

The Fibonacci sequence has applications in technical analysis, but the sequence itself isn't exactly what you use. The *Fibonacci retracement levels* you use in technical analysis are a result of calculating the alternate ratio between the numbers in the sequence. By applying the ratios to an uptrend or a downtrend, you can identify support and resistance levels easily.

TECHNICAL STUFF

Here's how the ratios are calculated: After the first few numbers, if you divide any of the numbers by the succeeding number, you get approximately 0.618. For example, 34 divided by 55 rounds to 0.618. If you calculate the ratio between alternate numbers, you get 0.382. The ratio between every third succeeding number is 0.235. The sequence used in technical analysis consists of these ratios: 0.78, 0.618, 0.5, 0.382, and 0.236.

How to insert Fibonacci retracement levels into your chart

The good news is that you don't have to do any math calculations at all! All you have to do is to find the Fibonacci tool on your charting service and apply it to the price action. Here are the specific steps you need to take:

1. **Find a trend in the prices.**

   It can be an uptrend or a downtrend. Flip to Chapter 18 for an introduction to trends.

2. **Find the Fibonacci retracement tool on your chart and click on it.**

3. **Click to apply the Fibonacci tool to the bottom of the trend (if it's an uptrend) or to the top of the trend (if it's a downtrend).**

4. **Drag the Fibonacci tool to the other end of the trend and then click again to drop the Fibonacci retracement levels on the chart.**

   The Fibonacci retracement levels appear. Figure 22-3 shows an example.

Figure 22-3 shows the price action of Stellar Lumens (XLM) versus Bitcoin (BTC) in a four-hour chart. The bottom of the trend for the XLM/BTC pair is at 0.00003309, and the top of the trend is at 0.00003901. By dragging the Fibonacci tool from the bottom to the top, you can see the Fibonacci retracement levels marked as 0.78, 0.618, 0.5, 0.382, and 0.236.

FIGURE 22-3:
Fibonacci retracement levels applied to an uptrend on the XLM/BTC chart.

© *tradingview.com*

Combining Ichimoku and Fibonacci Techniques

When you've got your eyes used to having Ichimoku and Fibonacci indicators on your charts separately (see the preceding sections), you can apply both of them to the chart and let the fun begin. Seeing so many lines on the chart may give you a headache at the beginning, but after a while you may even think that a chart without Ichimoku and Fibonacci is totally naked.

REMEMBER

Sometimes you have so many options to choose from when selecting a trend (up or down) for Fibonacci. More often than not, most trends give you the same Fibonacci retracement levels. The key Fibonacci resistance and support levels also often coincide with Ichimoku layers of support and resistance because Fibonacci is working to show you the key psychological levels that remain true across the board. This specifically is the beauty and magic of Fibonacci.

REMEMBER

You can use Ichimoku and Fibonacci in a number of ways to assist you with your technical analysis. I recommend that you use other technical analysis methods and chart patterns (see Chapter 18) as well to confirm your analysis. For example, you can use Ichimoku to spot a buy or sell signal, and then use Fibonacci levels to determine the price at which you can take profit.

Here's an example: You discover a double bottom bullish reversal chart pattern on a daily chart. (A *double bottom* pattern is a bullish reversal chart pattern that consists of two valleys at a key support level on the chart; turn to Chapter 18 to see examples.) You apply Ichimoku to the chart and notice an Ichimoku buy signal (as I describe earlier in this chapter). This discovery is a perfect opportunity to identify an entry point based on the double bottom chart pattern and the Ichimoku signal.

But where do you go from there, and where do you take profit? This point is when you can use Fibonacci. Depending on your risk tolerance (see Chapter 3), you can select a Fibonacci retracement level as your profit target and create a limit order through your broker account to sell at that level. (A *limit order* is a direction you put through your broker to buy or sell an asset at a specific price.)

Figure 22-4 shows a case study on the XLM/BTC four-hour chart where I've identified an Ichimoku-based bearish signal after the price broke below the Ichimoku cloud at 0.00003579.

Based on the Ichimoku strategy, you can create a *sell* limit order either at the lower band of the Ichimoku cloud (0.00003579) or a bit higher at the 0.5 Fibonacci retracement level of 0.00003605.

© tradingview.com

FIGURE 22-4:
Using Ichimoku and Fibonacci to create a bearish trading strategy.

For profit taking, you can consider the 0.786 Fibonacci level at 0.00003435. For traders who like using stop-losses, you can use the 0.382 Fibonacci level or higher, depending on your risk tolerance. (For simplicity, I'm not mentioning other bearish signals that you can find on this chart.) A *stop-loss* is an order you can put through your broker to get you out of a losing trade before the losses get out of hand; flip to Chapter 19 for more info.

WARNING

The preceding case study is conducted on the four-hour chart, which is considered short-term and thus carries a high level of risk. If you're looking for more conservative investment strategies, consider using the daily and monthly time frames. I discuss the various time frames in Chapter 18.

TIP

If you're looking for a fun, done-with-you community to help you with your Ichimoku or Fibonacci analysis, helping you create the perfect investment strategy based on your risk tolerance and financial goals, why not check out Invest Diva's Premium Investing Group (PIG) and claim your 30-day free access here: investdivapig.com.

Chapter **23**

Taxes and Cryptocurrencies

B efore the 2017 crypto hype, many people who got into cryptocurrencies (whether through mining or investing) probably didn't even think about its tax implications. But as cryptocurrency investing becomes more mainstream, its taxation guidelines have taken center stage, and governments around the world are playing catch up with people who hold, trade, or use cryptocurrencies, ensuring they pay their fair share of taxes. In this chapter, I review the basics of cryptocurrency taxation.

WARNING

Keep in mind that these guidelines are based on the U.S. tax laws as of 2022. Crypto taxes are constantly changing. By the time you read this book, things might have changed. It is critically important that you stay on top of your country's crypto tax code, and consult with a professional before tax day to stay safe.

Distinguishing Three Types of Crypto Taxes

The tax setup for cryptos is a big area of enforcement for the U.S. Internal Revenue Service (IRS) at the time of writing. The IRS — alongside the FBI — tracks and traces cryptocurrencies such as Bitcoin as part of their criminal investigations, opening the doors for many people to be targeted for an audit or compliance verifications.

The good news is, if you're already familiar with capital gain taxations in other financial instruments (such as stocks), you can treat your crypto investing activities in a similar manner. That means you pay capital gain taxes on your cryptocurrency investments. In this case, you don't have any tax obligations until you sell your coins for a profit. But what if you got your coins by mining? Or what if your employer pays you in cryptocurrencies?

You're likely to get taxed when being exposed to cryptocurrencies if you are:

>> Selling cryptocurrencies for a fiat currency (such as the U.S. dollar)

>> Trading one cryptocurrency for another

>> Using cryptocurrency to buy goods or services

REMEMBER

Buying cryptocurrency is not a taxable event.

To make it simple, I've divided crypto taxation obligations into three likely scenarios in the following sections.

Income taxes

If you've invested in all the expensive equipment I talk about in Chapter 13 and are getting crypto mining rewards as a result, then your crypto is considered taxable income. According to Turbotax.intuit, your crypto mining income can be reported on Form 1099-NEC at the fair market value of the cryptocurrency the day you received it.

TIP

This could mean if you mine cryptocurrencies when their price is lower, you not only will pay less taxes, but you also can enjoy the potential future upside as the value of your crypto asset goes up.

TECHNICAL STUFF

Personally, I was offered to get paid in Bitcoin when I started to report for NewsBTC back in 2016. You know how much I regretted not accepting that offer in 2017 when Bitcoin value surged to $20,000? A lot! But of course, if I had taken it, I would've had to pay the income tax on the Bitcoins I received; if I'd then chosen to trade my Bitcoins for the U.S. dollar (USD) at the 2017 peak, I also would've been subject to capital gain taxes on the profit I made on my transaction. I talk about capital gain taxes in the next section.

If you receive mining or income rewards in crypto worth over $400 in one year, you must report it to the IRS. If you've set up a mining operation at your home, you can report your mining income as self-employment income on Schedule C of your tax return. Personally, though, I've set up my mining activity through my Invest Diva business, which helps me get a more generous tax policy when my net income is high. I talk about minimizing your crypto income tax later in this chapter.

REMEMBER

Always make sure to keep a record of your mining activity and financial statements in case you get audited by the IRS. Also, if you're filing as a business entity, make sure to consult with a tax professional to discover the best options for your particular scenario. Don't worry — you can claim the accountant fees on your business!

REMEMBER

Even as a crypto miner and a business owner, you must understand the basics of cryptocurrency investing. If you sell or trade your cryptocurrencies for other altcoins or any products, then you must pay capital gain taxes as I discuss in the next two sections (depending on whether they're long term or short term). Your mining activity profits often rely on the market value of the cryptocurrency as well as the amount of tax you'll be paying on them. To identify the best cryptocurrencies to mine, actively conduct the Invest Diva Diamond Analysis (IDDA) technique I introduce in Chapter 9, and swap to better cryptocurrencies if your mining strategy isn't making sense anymore. One point of IDDA is capital analysis, which includes your tax considerations.

Long-term capital gain taxes

In Chapter 2, I point to capital gains as one of the main reasons people invest in cryptocurrencies. That's how the IRS categorizes cryptocurrencies as well. Just like owning stocks and real estate, you must pay capital gain taxes after you sell your crypto assets for a profit. If you take a loss, you can lower your tax bill. Now, if you hold your crypto assets for over a year, you often get a better tax rate. This rate is called a *long-term capital gain tax.*

TIP

You can calculate your capital gains by doing simple math on the amount you gained or lost after you purchased your cryptos. For example, if you buy one Bitcoin for $5,000 and sell it for $10,000, then you've made $5,000 in capital gains minus the amount you pay for transaction fees.

Short-term capital gain taxes

A *short-term capital gain tax* is very similar to the mining and crypto income tax I mention earlier in this chapter. If you sell or trade your cryptos regularly and hold them less than a year, then your profit or losses may be categorized as income, which often has less favorable tax implications. Even if you don't officially cash out your cryptos, you may still be subject to short-term taxes if you use the cryptocurrency to purchase stuff, whether it's tangible products or other cryptocurrencies.

REMEMBER

Active traders who make a few trades every now and then are subject to different tax laws than day traders who trade cryptos for a living. I discuss the difference in the later section "Reducing your trading tax."

INTRODUCING SOME CRYPTO TAX EXPERTS

The crypto investing market is a fairly new industry, and therefore many traditional tax folks may not have the necessary knowledge to help you with the best crypto tax decisions. Doing a search within my LinkedIn connections, I found some U.S.-based crypto tax experts who may be able to help you out:

- **Camuso CPA:** Camuso CPA is a CPA firm that works with investors, businesses, and individuals nationwide and is a market leader in cryptocurrency tax advisory. In fact, Camuso CPA is the first CPA firm in the country to accept cryptocurrency payments in return for professional services. The firm caters to clients from Camuso CPA's network of investors, miners, and small businesses along with taxpayers who need help dealing with Bitcoin and other cryptocurrencies. My point of contact here is the firm's founder, Patrick Camuso. You can reach him through the firm's website: www.CamusoCPA.com.

- **Crypto Tax Girl:** My point of contact here is Laura Walter, a certified public accountant specializing in cryptocurrency tax. Her mission is to bring tax clarity to those who currently hold crypto, those who have held crypto in the past, or those who are looking to acquire crypto in the future. You can check her out here: cryptotaxgirl.com.

Minimizing Your Crypto Taxes

Whether you've earned your crypto as income or have seen capital gains on your assets, the following sections show you some ways to cut the amount you owe the IRS.

Lowering your mining income tax

In the United States, you may get a better tax rate if you create a company or a business entity around your mining activities instead of mining as a self-employed individual. By doing so, you can take advantage of the tax breaks business owners get for paying for business-related stuff and get a better tax rate than individuals. Got that high-end computer to mine Bitcoin? Claim it on your business and lower your taxable income. Got your computer set up with mining equipment like the ASICs and expensive GPUs that I talk about in Chapter 13? Paying a ton on electricity when mining? Congrats, you can get a tax break on the rewards you got paid through mining.

TIP

That is, of course, if your coins are actually worth something. Even at a personal level, your mining operation can be very profitable, but it also can cost you a ton — way more than its rewards, especially if the crypto market isn't doing very well at the time. At the time of writing, if your overall net income is more than $60,000, filing as an S corporation, or an LLC that's taxed like an S corporation, may help you. Consult a tax professional for guidance.

REMEMBER

You can claim your expenses on your business only if the LLC, C corporation, or S corporation was created prior to earning the income from mining. Anything earned prior to the company formation won't be able to be included under the company for tax purposes.

Reducing your trading tax

Do you consider yourself a day trader? Then you may be eligible to pay way less in taxes than occasional traders. But first you must pass the IRS day-trading test by being able to answer "yes" to these three questions:

>> Do you aim to make profit from the daily price changes in the crypto market instead of holding your positions long term or even overnight?

>> Do you spend most of your day trading instead of having a full-time day job?

>> Do you have a substantial and regular trading pattern and make a ton of trades on a daily basis?

If you do qualify as a day trader, you may be able to claim your rewards as a self-employed individual. This designation means you can deduct all your trading-related expenses on Schedule C like any other sole proprietor.

TIP

According to finance.zacks.com, your corporation will be taxed based on your profits and losses whether or not it's a one-owner corporation. You can also use the money you make from day trading to pay for your insurance, healthcare, and employee benefits, if you have any.

WARNING

Tracking your short-term crypto trading activities can be incredibly confusing. The industry has a ton of volatility and market fluctuation, and an exploding number of tradable cryptos are available to you 24/7. These situations make monitoring your resources manually almost impossible. Later in this chapter, I introduce some tracking resources you can use for your trading activities.

Bringing down your capital gain taxes

If you can't qualify as a day trader (see the preceding section), your best bet to reduce your crypto capital gain taxes is to be a long-term investor. That means holding your assets for over a year. Don't sell, trade, or buy anything with your cryptocurrencies within a year of your purchase.

As I mention earlier in this chapter, capital gain taxes on investments held for more than one year (long term) can be much lower than capital gain taxes on investments held for less than one year (short term). In 2022, long-term capital gains are taxed at 0 percent, 15 percent, or 20 percent, depending on your tax bracket. If you're in the high-income tax bracket, for example, your capital gains tax rate may be 20 percent. You can find out more about tax brackets here: www.irs.gov/newsroom/irs-provides-tax-inflation-adjustments-for-tax-year-2022.

REMEMBER

Trading one cryptocurrency for another may put you at risk of paying more taxes. To purchase certain cryptocurrencies at specific crypto exchanges, you have no choice but to convert your cryptos for one another in a shorter time frame, but if you make a huge profit on the initial crypto, you no longer fall into the category of long-term investor. Talk to a tax professional to ensure that you're paying the correct rate.

Checking the rate of your state

In the United States, different states have different state tax laws, and some states have better rates than others for specific groups of people or certain industries. Some states like Florida are considered a "retirement haven" because you don't have to pay individual income and death tax, and you'll also get a ton of asset protection and property tax benefits. When it comes to cryptocurrency investors, certain states like Wyoming have great tax incentives for crypto companies and investors because cryptocurrencies are exempted from property taxation altogether. In 2018, Wyoming became the first state to define cryptocurrencies as an entirely new asset class. Wyoming officials labeled it as the "utility token bill" and passed it into law in March 2018; it was designed to exempt specific cryptocurrencies from state money transmission laws.

TIP

As cryptocurrencies become more popular, you can expect more states to create such laws to incentivize businesses and individuals to bring their crypto talents and money there. That's why it's important that you're in the know with the latest developments in the industry. Websites such as coindesk.com can help you get such information in a timely manner.

Evaluating Taxable Income from Crypto Transactions

REMEMBER

At the end of the day, reporting your crypto income and capital gains is on you. You must keep track of all your taxable events, which means every time you sell or trade your crypto assets for other stuff. At the time of writing, the IRS doesn't require third-party reporting for cryptocurrencies (meaning the entities you buy the cryptos from don't have to report the sales), which makes the tracking and reporting more complicated.

Here are some tips and points to keep in mind when you're evaluating your crypto activities.

Tracking your crypto activity

TIP

The crypto market is expanding, and more monitoring resources are becoming available for traders, investors, and miners alike. Here are a few resources you can check out:

>> **CoinTracker (www.cointracker.io/?i=eALc60xcyXpD):** CoinTracker automatically syncs your crypto transactions with a growing list of exchanges such as Coinbase, Kraken, KuCoin, and more to generate tax forms. It also has an online support team.

>> **CoinTracking (`cointracking.info?ref=I248132`):** CoinTracking analyzes your investment activity and generates a tax report based on your profit and losses.

>> **CryptoTrader.tax (`cryptotrader.tax?fp_ref=behp6`):** This website connects you to a growing list of exchanges such as Coinbase, Binance, Bittrex, and more, and helps you calculate your crypto taxes in a few minutes. It has great online customer support that answers your questions immediately.

Handling crypto forks

In Chapter 5, I talk about how you can get free coins when a cryptocurrency is *forked* (where a portion of a crypto's community decides to create its own version of the currency).

Of course, nothing is completely free, and you're likely required to pay taxes on the additional cryptos you receive through the fork. For example, if you own Ethereum and it undergoes a hard fork that pays you an equal amount of the new cryptocurrency in addition to your original Ethereum assets, you must pay ordinary taxes on the new free coins as opposed to long-term capital gain tax. You pay these taxes based on the U.S. dollar value of the new cryptocurrency the day you receive it.

REMEMBER

The IRS still offers little guidance regarding hard forks and taxation. Make sure you consult with a tax professional and stay ahead of the game by tracking all your crypto records using professional websites such as `cryptotrader.tax?fp_ref=behp6`.

Reporting international crypto investments

The cryptocurrency market and its rules are constantly evolving. That's why you must remain up to date about all your crypto transactions. But even if you invest in cryptocurrencies outside the United States, you must report the activity to the IRS.

REMEMBER

At the time of writing, you don't have to report your cryptocurrency on your Foreign Bank Account Report (FBAR). This guideline is based on a 2014 IRS statement that said, "The Financial Crimes Enforcement Network, which issues regulatory guidance pertaining to Reports of Foreign Bank and Financial Accounts (FBARs), is not requiring that digital (or virtual) currency accounts be reported on an FBAR at this time but may consider requiring such accounts to be reported in the future." Make sure you keep up to date with the IRS crypto regulations because they're subject to change every year; consult a tax professional. Also keep in mind that not having to report your cryptos on your FBAR doesn't mean you can hide your foreign cryptocurrency activities from the IRS.

WARNING

It bears repeating: You're responsible for knowing the tax ramifications of your crypto activity. The IRS has been going after cryptocurrency investments inside and outside the United States. It even forced Coinbase to turn over its customer records in 2017 and in 2022. So people who simply didn't know about the crypto tax implications got into trouble alongside those who were trying to hide their crypto investments.

5

The Part of Tens

Get an overview of what to consider before getting started in the world of cryptocurrencies.

Discover the best things you can do when you're sitting on losses.

Read about ways you can turn obstacles into opportunities when investing in cryptocurrencies.

» Discovering things you may need along the way

Chapter 24

Ten Considerations Before Getting Started with Cryptocurrencies

A re you ready to try cryptocurrency investing? In this chapter, I highlight some of the most important things to think about before starting your crypto investing journey, many of which I explain in detail in earlier chapters.

Don't Get Too Excited

REMEMBER

Starting to explore a whole new world is always exciting. Starting early can also sometimes get you ahead of the crowd. However, just like any type of investment avenue, cryptocurrency investing requires discipline, risk management, and a whole lot of patience. You shouldn't treat crypto investing as a get-rich-quick scheme. Even though your hopes may be up, as we've seen in the many ups and downs in the crypto market in the past decade, the likelihood of seeing such gains in such a short amount of time again is pretty low.

The reason is simple: The crypto market is driven by a whole lot of hype and FOMO. Investors are becoming more educated about the whole market, making more calculated investment decisions. So should you!

Measure Your Risk Tolerance

REMEMBER

Is crypto investing right for you? How much of your money should you invest in this market? Can you stomach high volatility? Do you have the patience to wait out potential storms? You can find the answer to all these questions by measuring your risk tolerance. This essential first step to any type of investment includes both your willingness to risk and your ability to risk. Flip to Chapter 3 for an explanation of different risk types and resources on measuring your risk tolerance.

Protect Your Crypto Wallet

A *crypto wallet* is where you store your digital assets like Bitcoin; you have to have one before you buy a cryptocurrency. So many different types of wallets are available, some of which come from the cryptocurrency exchanges that sell you the cryptos. But those aren't the most secure types of wallets, and they've often been the victims of hacking attacks that resulted in the loss of cryptos. Chapter 7 details different methods you can use to protect your cryptocurrency wallet before you start investing.

Find the Best Crypto Exchange/ Broker for You

Some of the most popular places to get your hands on cryptocurrencies are exchanges and brokers. Some of these marketplaces offer only a few cryptocurrencies, and some carry a wide range. Some have higher transaction fees. Some have better customer service. Some have a better security reputation. With some, you can exchange your *fiat* currency (which is the local currency of your country, such as the U.S. dollar) for cryptocurrencies. With others, you must already have a cryptocurrency, such as Bitcoin, and exchange it for other digital assets, such as Binance exchange's coin (BNB) or Ethereum (ETH).

To find the best crypto exchange or broker, you must go through all these options and see which one fits your crypto needs most. In Chapter 6, I give a more thorough overview of different types of cryptocurrency exchanges and brokers out there.

REMEMBER

Sometimes, you're better off using multiple exchanges for different purposes. Personally, I use two!

Determine Whether You Should Invest Short Term or Long Term

The time frame you invest in depends on your risk tolerance, your financial goals, your current financial situation, and the amount of time you have on your hands. For example, if you have a full-time job that requires most of your attention, you don't want to worry about short-term management of your crypto portfolio, or any other asset for that matter. You want to focus your energy on your main job (so you don't get fired) and manage your investment portfolio every few weeks or so to stay on top of things. Investing long term also requires less risk-taking.

TIP

In Chapter 3, I walk you through calculating your risk tolerance. In Chapters 19 and 20, I explore more about short-term and long-term investing. You can also check out my *Make Your Money Work for You PowerCourse* by attending this free online Masterclass: investdiva.com/masterclass.

Start Small

If you're just testing the waters and don't have a solid financial plan, don't dump a whole chunk of money into the market. Start with a few hundred dollars, or whatever you can afford, and slowly grow your portfolio. Also, don't use your money to invest in only one type of crypto. If you're new to investing in anything, don't allocate all your investment funds to cryptos, either. Diversification is key until you find your sweet spot, especially for new investors.

Personally, my biggest chunk of monthly investments typically goes into myself to learn new skills. The second chunk goes into my scaling my business. Having a business is super-important when building wealth, especially because it gives you access to many tax-break techniques that are unavailable to normal people with a regular job. The third chunk goes into online financial markets such as stocks and cryptocurrencies.

REMEMBER

Unless they get super-lucky, most millionaires don't become wealthy just by investing in the online financial markets. There are many avenues to build wealth. In my most popular five-day *Build More Wealth* challenge, I unveil the five steps I used to go from zero to over a $5 million net worth in 10 years:

1. **Step 1: Breaking the wealth mindset you were likely handed down by your parents and society so you are open to receiving more wealth.**

2. **Step 2: Increasing your income by becoming a business owner.**

3. **Step 3: Investing your increased income and make your money have babies!**

4. **Step 4: Increasing your impact and influence.**

5. **Step 5: Building a Wealth Ecosystem where your money makes more money, and the money your money makes also makes more money, to build generational wealth.**

Join the challenge here: buildmorewealth.com!

Follow the Cause

TIP

Many cryptocurrencies are based on blockchain applications that aim to solve a specific problem in the world or in society (see Chapter 4 for the scoop on blockchain technology). Blockchain applications can provide a solution to almost any problem that's close to your heart, from banking the under-banked to preventing voter fraud to helping out farmers. By investing in the cryptocurrency of a blockchain application whose cause appeals to you, you support that cause in achieving its goals faster. This sense of accomplishment can make investing more meaningful and more fun for you.

Focusing on causes also helps when you're picking cryptocurrencies out of the hundreds of options available. I talk about different crypto categories in Chapter 8.

Mull Over Mining

Mining is the backbone of many cryptocurrencies like Bitcoin. *Mining* cryptocurrencies refers to solving complex math equations to guess random numbers by using powerful computers; successfully solving the problems earns you a reward in cryptos. Mining is normally considered very expensive because you have to invest in expensive computer gadgets and use up a lot of electricity while you run your computer for mining. But sometimes, especially depending on the cryptocurrency's value, mining may make sense. For example, if your electricity bill for mining is going to be lower than the cost of actually buying that cryptocurrency, you may want to consider mining instead.

Head to Chapter 13 for more on mining, its terminology, and the stuff you need to buy to do it. You can check out mining profitability by using mining calculators like the ones at investdiva.com/mining-calculator.

Look into Investing in Other Assets First

If you've never invested in anything, you may find the whole cryptocurrency industry a bit overwhelming. Educating yourself about developing investment strategies while also learning about a financial sector you've never had any personal experience with can be difficult. In this case, you may consider starting by investing in things you know, like the stocks of a company you're already familiar with. After you become comfortable investing in things you know, you can then expand your portfolio to new vehicles like cryptocurrencies. See Chapter 2 for details on different types of assets.

Get a Support Group

Most people trade alone on their computers or smartphones. That can soon become a very lonely activity, especially if none of your friends are into it. It might become even more dangerous if you're getting all your investing information from Twitter and news media that are fighting for your attention through clickbaits. When the markets are going against you, you can get frustrated, and when the markets are doing well, you may get overwhelmed, not knowing when to get out.

Though I explore strategy development methods to identify the best entry and exit points in this book, it always helps to have people who are in the same boat as you. Many cryptocurrencies have channels on the Telegram app or their very own rooms on websites like Reddit and Discord, where you can share information and commiserate with other crypto investors.

Unfortunately, as crypto gains popularity these public domains are flooded with bots, scammers, and impersonators. If you ever feel lonely or overwhelmed or simply want to join one of the most authentic investing groups ever, consider joining the Invest Diva Movement. You can discover how you can join us by attending the free Masterclass detailed earlier in this chapter.

IN THIS CHAPTER

» **Reconsidering your investment approach or amount**

» **Surveying what's going on behind the scenes**

Chapter **25**

Ten Possible Moves When Your Crypto Portfolio Is Down

Whether you're a short-term trader or a long-term investor, at times you find your crypto portfolio in the red zone with one or more of your holdings moving against you. Before you know it, you can find yourself in a FUD situation (crypto talk for fear, uncertainty, and doubt), which can become incredibly frustrating and can contribute to your making an emotional decision rather than executing a well-thought-out strategy. This chapter covers ten potential next steps when the market isn't on your side.

Do Nothing

In most cases, patience is a profitable virtue. If you got into a specific position after doing a thorough analysis from all points of the Invest Diva Diamond Analysis, or IDDA (see Chapter 9), chances are the current dip in the market is temporary. If you give it time, you may find yourself in positive territory again. Even the toughest markets find their way back up again if you wait long enough.

Of course, the cryptocurrency market is very new and not all crypto assets have shown enough evidence to prove that it follows the sentiment of other markets like the stock market. However, because most investors categorize cryptos as a capital gain asset just like stocks, many of the older cryptocurrencies such as Bitcoin and Ethereum have started following a market psychology similar to traditional assets. *Capital gain assets* are those you invest in expecting a gain in their value to give you a positive return. Of course, waiting for a long time may not be suitable for all traders and investors.

REMEMBER

Depending on where you are in your life and what your financial goals are, you may be able to take advantage of making time your best investing friend. If you're on a ten-year plan to reach a financial goal — buying a house, for example — you shouldn't worry about the minor ups and downs in the markets.

Reevaluate Your Risk Tolerance

As I discuss in Chapter 3, measuring your risk tolerance is the very first step you need to take when you start investing in anything. But as life goes on, circumstances change in ways that may impact your risk tolerance. A down period for your portfolio may be a good time to reassess your risk tolerance to identify the best thing to do next.

For example, if you now have a higher risk tolerance than you did when you entered a position, you may consider adding to your losing position as I discuss later in this chapter. But if your financial situation has impacted your risk tolerance in a negative way and you don't have much time in your hands, you may consider cutting losses (also described later).

REMEMBER

The bottom line, however, is never make a rash decision based only on emotions and the *feeling* that your risk tolerance is high or low. By carefully calculating your tolerance, you may get a surprise to the contrary.

Look at the Big Picture

You can evaluate the bigger picture from both technical and fundamental viewpoints:

>> On the technical side (see Chapter 18), you may get a better idea of where the market is going by switching to longer-term time frames. For example,

the market may be on a very long-term uptrend, where the price has been going up for quite some time. In that case, the current dip may be a healthy correction, which can even be a good point to buy more of your crypto asset.

» On the fundamental side, you need to go back to the basic reasons you chose to invest in a specific cryptocurrency — things like the cause, the management and community, the technology, and everything else that can contribute to the long-term growth of the cryptocurrency's valuation. Flip to Chapter 9 for more on fundamental analysis.

Research the Fundamental Reasons the Crypto Is Down

When evaluating the big picture as I discuss in the preceding section, you may find that a core fundamental problem is driving the devaluation of your crypto asset. Perhaps the cryptocurrency is no longer backed by giant financial corporations, has gotten involved in a scam, or is running out of money and therefore not able to invest in its technology. You can use your favorite search engine to look into the fundamental details of any specific cryptocurrency. Simply search the crypto's name online and go through the most recent search results under the "News" category. If the fundamentals have changed for the worse and are the reason the value is down, you may need to reevaluate your position and potentially cut losses.

TIP

As a crypto enthusiast, I recommend that you keep up to date with the most recent crypto news anyway by following websites such as cryptobriefing.com, www.coindesk.com, and www.newsbtc.com.

Consider Hedging

Hedging is a common investment practice to manage risk. By *hedging*, you basically go against your current position or industry to offset the risk it involves. I talk about hedging in derivatives like options and futures in Chapter 16, but you can also hedge by diversification (described in the following two sections) as well as by going against your current position. For example, if you've bought Bitcoin versus another cryptocurrency like Ethereum and Bitcoin's price is dropping, you can consider selling Bitcoin in a different trade and take advantage of the current downtrend.

TIP

Positional hedging is especially useful when you're trading cryptocurrencies on brokerages that allow short selling. For more on hedging strategies, consider joining Invest Diva's premium group (find out more here: investdiva.com/masterclass).

Diversify within Crypto Assets

Adding other crypto assets that are exposed to a different type of risk than your losing cryptocurrency is another form of hedging (see the preceding section) that may help you balance out your portfolio. Identifying such cryptocurrencies can be very difficult, though, because at least at the time of this writing, most crypto assets are exposed to similar types of risk. See Chapter 3 to find out more about risk and Chapter 9 to identify top performing cryptos.

Diversify across Other Financial Assets

This is the good old "Don't leave all your eggs in one basket" thing. If your analysis shows a longer doomsday period in the cryptocurrency market while other financial instruments like bonds are lucrative, you may consider diversifying away from cryptocurrencies to distribute risk. This approach is yet again a different form of hedging, which I discuss earlier in this chapter. Flip to Chapters 2 and 10 for more on diversification.

Exchange with a Better Crypto

After redoing the IDDA for your crypto assets that are down (see Chapter 9), you may realize that a particular crypto isn't worth holding onto. Unlike the stock market, where you have no choice but to take losses, in the crypto world you may have the option to exchange with a different, better cryptocurrency. For example, say you bought a bunch of a crypto called CrappyCoin at a high price, but its value has been plummeting with no signs of recovery, the founder of the blockchain has gone missing, and their Discord channel is full of bots. At the same time, you hear of a new, cheap cryptocurrency with a bright future, legit community, and a project that will help humankind. Though you may not be able to buy a ton of the new crypto with your devalued CrappyCoin, you still may benefit from cutting your losses on CrappyCoin early and exchanging with the better crypto.

Think about Adding to Your Current Position

Warren Buffett is a famous investor who adds on to his losing position — buys more of a falling stock at a cheaper price — when the markets drop. This is also known as *buying the dip*. But of course, he does so only for assets that have strong fundamentals and are in the midst of a temporary, healthy pullback. He also can handle the risk because, well, he's a gazillionaire (although, at the time of writing, he still hasn't given in to cryptocurrency investing).

The buy the dip strategy has the potential to work for cryptos as well. Before you get too excited, keep in mind that the cryptocurrency market may act differently than the stock market (which is what Warren Buffett invests in) and may continue to be unpredictable and volatile in the coming years. That's why you must make sure you can afford a bigger prospective loss for a period of time until the crypto market gets back on track.

WARNING

Avoid using margin and borrowing money from your broker when adding to your losing position. Those approaches increase your investment risk.

REMEMBER

By adding on to your losing position, you can bring your average holding price lower and therefore profit more when the price eventually goes back up.

Contemplate Cutting Losses

Personally (and famously), I'm not the biggest fan of *stop-losses*, which are market orders you set to cut losses if the price of an asset like a crypto is going against your investment position. In my time working at brokers on Wall Street, I discovered that stop-losses mainly helped the broker make money while you lost. However, sometimes you have no other option for various reasons, including personal risk tolerance and market conditions. In that case, you may want to consider simply getting out of your losing position, calling it quits, and focusing on a different source of profit.

REMEMBER

Short-term traders are more likely to use stop-losses (see Chapter 19). Long-term investors (see Chapter 20) are supposed to have made the risk-management calculation ahead of time, making sure they have enough time to wait things out.

TIP

Taking losses can be very emotionally draining. If you decide to take a loss, remember not to beat yourself up too much. I've had students who had given up investing altogether before joining the Invest Diva Movement, because they had lost money in the markets. There is no success without failure. Your long-term success is only defined by your ability to get back up. Let this be a learning lesson, and move on to other opportunities!

Chapter **26**

Ten Challenges and Opportunities for Crypto Investors

This chapter introduces you to ten opportunities and hurdles you may face during your cryptocurrency investing adventures. I bundle challenges and opportunities together because you can turn an obstacle into profit if you treat it the right way.

New Cryptos on the Block

Bitcoin, the first ever cryptocurrency, turned 14 years old in 2022. But it's hardly the only cryptocurrency that investors are interested in anymore. For better or for worse, new cryptocurrencies keep popping up left and right, and you can expect that number to increase. Most likely, not all the 20,000 cryptocurrencies available in 2022 are going to make it big within five years. On the other hand, a single cryptocurrency that isn't even born yet may explode and replace Bitcoin for good in the future.

REMEMBER

I mark this concept as both an opportunity and a challenge because you must remain open-minded and have a vision for the future in order to screen through the newcomers and pick those with true potential. For more on selecting the best cryptocurrencies, flip to Chapter 9.

Finding Real Economic Data

Avoiding clickbaits and scams is the name of the game! Some of the biggest ups and downs in the cryptocurrency market have been thanks to celebrities and the media creating fear or greed in the market out of thin air, often with no solid financial statement to back it up. To avoid falling into such traps, you may want to consider following more than one crypto news organization and even then take what you read with a grain of salt.

TIP

Here are some financial and crypto news organizations (in alphabetical order) that you can follow for a better understanding of the markets:

» AMBCrypto: ambcrypto.com

» Benzinga: www.benzinga.com/crypto

» Bitcoin Exchange Guide: bitcoinexchangeguide.com

» CCN: www.ccn.com

» CoinDesk: www.coindesk.com

» CoinGape: coingape.com

» CoinGeek: coingeek.com

» Cointelegraph: cointelegraph.com

» Crypto Briefing: cryptobriefing.com

» Crypto Daily: cryptodaily.co.uk

» Crypto News: cryptonews.com

» The Daily HODL: dailyhodl.com

» Forbes: www.forbes.com

» Global Coin Report: globalcoinreport.com

» MarketWatch: www.marketwatch.com

» NewsBTC: www.newsbtc.com

» Next Advisor by TIME: time.com/nextadvisor

I contribute to many of these outlets regularly so say hello if you see me!

Regulations

At the time of writing, cryptocurrency regulations are still in their infancy. Some countries are ahead of others in terms of regulations, creating an opportunity for their residents to take advantage of the crypto industry early. However, don't be disappointed if things take time. Lack of regulation is a big concern in the industry, but it may also give early investors the advantage of investing when the prices are low. As more countries regulate the cryptocurrency market and recognize it as a real financial instrument, the prices of cryptos may go up.

Hackers

You may ask how a hacking incident can be an opportunity. Well, if you're a direct victim of a hacking incident, that's a clear challenge. (Flip to Chapter 7 for methods to protect yourself and your cryptos from getting hacked.) Hacking is a real issue in the industry, and unfortunately, it may not go away in the future. However, hacking incidents normally impact the crypto market price in a negative way only temporarily. That's when it can turn into opportunity for the rest of the market players to buy at lower prices.

WARNING

Taking advantage of a hacking incident doesn't mean you should invest in the company that was compromised. You must always do your research and analyze the circumstances. If a specific cryptocurrency or a crypto exchange is compromised in an irreversible way, you may want to stay away from it. However, the news may impact other cryptos in the market for no fundamental reason other than the fact that they're part of the same industry. When one player goes down, the negative wave impacts all others as well. You may consider focusing on those cryptos instead.

Bubbles

You may think that the latest crypto bubble has already burst and is now on its way to stabilization. But nothing suggests that yet another bubble won't pop up in new cryptocurrencies, or even in existing ones. With research and analysis, you can identify bubbles by rapid price growth that has no fundamental reason behind it — that is, growth based just on market hype. That's the best time to either sell your crypto assets at higher prices or simply stay away from it all until things calm down. The "stay away" part is the true challenge, because you've got to fight your FOMO ("Fear Of Missing Out").

A Down Market

When your crypto portfolio is down, it may take your self-confidence and positive attitude down with it. However, you must remember that a losing position isn't an insult of your intelligence, your family heritage, or anything else personal. It's likely just a natural movement of the market based on the market sentiment, and you shouldn't let it get to you. In fact, you may even be able to use it as an opportunity by expanding your investments and hedging as I discuss in Chapter 25.

REMEMBER

A losing portfolio isn't an indication that you're a bad investor and don't have what it takes to make profit in the market. Similarly, a winning investment doesn't prove that you're Einstein's (or Warren Buffett's) cousin, nor does it indicate that you've mastered the art of investing.

New Currencies and Projects

An undeniable wave of new economic systems is building, and it may or may not end with blockchain-backed cryptocurrencies. (See Chapter 4 for an introduction to blockchain.)

Projects going on at the time of writing include:

>> Avalanche (AVAX): An eco-friendly blockchain with fast transaction times

>> Battle Infinity (IBAT): A decentralized metaverse P2E (play to earn) gaming platform

>> Shiba Inu Coin (SHIB): A community building crypto ecosystem

WARNING

By the time you pick this book up some of the hottest cryptocurrencies I mention here may have already gone bust or exploded as the next best thing since sliced bread! This is what makes the cryptocurrency market exciting — so long as you have sufficient risk tolerance to stomach the ups and downs. Check out Chapter 3 for more on taking a measured risk.

TIP

Once you calculate your risk tolerance (flip to Chapter 3 for more on this) remind yourself to be open to taking a measured risk to maximize profitability. Risk and reward are directly correlated. Once you've done all five points of the Invest Diva Diamond Analysis (IDDA, which you can find out more about in Chapter 9), you may need that extra push to invest with confidence. Before you hit the Buy button, as yourself these two questions to determine your true willingness to take a risk:

>> If I buy now and its price drops by 50 percent tomorrow, will I panic or will I buy more?

>> If I don't buy now and its price doubles tomorrow, will I beat myself up or wait for a pullback to buy more?

Diversification

I talk about diversification in detail in Chapter 10. Though diversification is typically a golden risk-management strategy, too much diversification may be harmful to your portfolio. Why? Because by spreading too much of your investment fund across so many different assets, chances are you'll miss out on investing big in the top performers. And if you invest too little in the real winners, your returns will be little as well.

TIP

If you've done a thorough Invest Diva Diamond Analysis (IDDA; see Chapter 9) on a specific cryptocurrency and you believe it's going to make it big, you can consider allocating a bigger chunk of your portfolio to it rather than buying a ton of cryptocurrencies that you're not sure about. Sometimes only one or two great investments are all you need to get you to your financial goal.

Falling in Love with a Crypto

REMEMBER

Investing requires discipline and tough decisions. Cryptocurrencies may be charming, but getting too emotional over them may harm your investment account in the long run. If it's time to say goodbye to a crypto you considered to be a winner in the past, just do it. Falling in love with what you do is great, but you're in this business to make profit.

WARNING

Don't let emotions drive your investment decisions (too much; you can use a tiny bit of gut feeling when you've done all the logical analysis, though — see Chapter 9). But keep in mind that your cryptocurrencies likely won't love you back in a sentimental way.

Using Invest Diva Diamond Analysis

No matter what type of investor or trader you are, the Invest Diva Diamond Analysis, or IDDA for short, is there to guide you along the way. However, using IDDA (as I discuss in Chapter 9) requires patience and understanding of how the markets work. You can't just wing it. Even if a celebrity you love is promoting a specific cryptocurrency, that doesn't account for fundamental analysis. If you think you discovered a strong trend only on one time frame, you can't call it technical analysis without checking for other indicators. Make sure all elements of the IDDA are pointing in the same direction before making an investment decision.

TIP

When in doubt, you can always come visit me here for help: investdiva.com/masterclass.

Appendixes

Check out the best places if you're an active cryptocurrency trader.

Find help taking control of your financial future and building generational wealth even if you're not a math whiz and are super busy.

IN THIS CHAPTER

» Investigating the top 200
cryptocurrencies by market cap

» Summarizing information services
to help you with cryptocurrency
investing

» Checking out lists of crypto
exchanges, wallets, brokers,
and more

Appendix **A**

Resources for Cryptocurrency Investors

I n this book, I cover a great deal about how to pick a cryptocurrency and how to analyze the markets before investing. In this appendix, I give a little bit more detail for where you can find the things you need.

REMEMBER

Keep in mind that the information is as of the time of writing, and things may change by the time you get this book.

Exploring Top Cryptocurrencies

More than 21,000 cryptocurrencies exist as of 2022, and the number is increasing. One way of exploring cryptocurrencies is to compare them based on their *market capitalization*, which is calculated by multiplying the number of coins out there by their price. People pay attention to this number because the idea is that as investors gain confidence in a specific crypto, its price may go higher, resulting in a larger market cap.

Market capitalization ranking is subject to change every single day. But for your reference, in this section I classify the top 200 cryptocurrencies by market cap as of the time of writing. (See Chapters 8 and 9 for more information on market cap, different types of cryptocurrencies, and identifying top cryptocurrencies for your needs.)

REMEMBER

You shouldn't analyze cryptocurrencies based on their market cap only. This section is just for your reference. Many other underlying factors can impact the future success of digital assets. For more, check out Part 2.

Top 100 cryptos by market cap

The top 100 cryptocurrencies by market capitalization are frequently subject to speculation by investors. The fact that they've made it to the top 100 indicates that the market has trust in them. However, always keep in mind that no cryptocurrency is too big to fail, and you may very well find a gem in lesser known cryptocurrencies.

Here's the list of the top 100 as of the time of writing according to CoinMarketCap (coinmarketcap.com). For more details on a particular crypto on websites such as CoinMarketCap, go to the homepage, find the cryptocurrency you're interested in learning more about, and click on the name of the crypto in the table.

TIP

Each of the following coins has its own website that you can find by looking it up on your search engine. If the name of a coin is too generic (like Ark), consider typing its symbol or the keyword "crypto" next to it to narrow down your search results. Websites like Crypto Briefing (cryptobriefing.com), CoinMarketCap (coinmarketcap.com), and CoinGecko (www.coingecko.com) can provide more information in terms of the most recent rankings, prices, and market capitalization.

» Bitcoin (BTC)

» Ethereum (ETH)

» Tether (USDT)

» BNB (BNB)

» USD Coin (USDC)

» Binance USD (BUSD)

» XRP (XRP)

» Cardano (ADA)

- » Dogecoin (DOGE)
- » Polygon (MATIC)
- » Polkadot (DOT)
- » Solana (SOL)
- » Dai (DAI)
- » Shiba Inu (SHIB)
- » TRON (TRX)
- » Avalanche (AVAX)
- » Uniswap (UNI)
- » Litecoin (LTC)
- » Wrapped Bitcoin (WBTC)
- » UNUS SED LEO (LEO)
- » Chainlink (LINK)
- » Cosmos (ATOM)
- » Ethereum Classic (ETC)
- » Stellar (XLM)
- » Monero (XMR)
- » Cronos (CRO)
- » Algorand (ALGO)
- » Bitcoin Cash (BCH)
- » Near Protocol (NEAR)
- » Toncoin (TON)
- » VeChain (VET)
- » Quant (QNT)
- » Filecoin (FIL)
- » Flow (FLOW)
- » Terra Classic (LUNC)
- » Chiliz (CHZ)
- » OKB (OKB)
- » Hedera (HBAR)

- » Internet Computer (ICP)
- » MultiversX (Elrond)
- » ApeCoin (APE)
- » Tezos (XTZ)
- » Theta Network (THETA)
- » Huobi Token (HT)
- » The Sandbox (SAND)
- » Aave (AAVE)
- » Decentraland (MANA)
- » EOS (EOS)
- » Pax Dollar (USDP)
- » Chain (XCN)
- » Gemini Dollar (GUSD)
- » KuCoin Token (KCS)
- » TrueUSD (TUSD)
- » Maker (MKR)
- » Bitcoin SV (BSV)
- » BitDAO (BIT)
- » Axie Infinity (AXS)
- » BitTorrent-New (BTT)
- » USDD (USDD)
- » Aptos (APT)
- » PancakeSwap (CAKE)
- » IOTA (MIOTA)
- » Neutrino USD (USDN)
- » Synthetix (SNX)
- » eCash (XEC)
- » Zcash (ZEC)
- » PAX Gold (PAXG)
- » Klaytn (KLAY)

- Fantom (FTM)
- Neo (NEO)
- The Graph (GRT)
- Trust Wallet Token (TWT)
- EthereumPow (ETHW)
- Nexo (NEXO)
- Mina (MINA)
- GateToken (GT)
- FTX Token (FTT)
- FEI USD (FEI)
- BinaryX (BNX)
- Basic Attention Token (BAT)
- THORChain (RUNE)
- Dash (DASH)
- Helium (HNT)
- Curve DAO Token (CRV)
- Lido DAO (LDO)
- Enjin Coin (ENJ)
- Loopring (LRC)
- Casper (CSPR)
- Osmosis (OSMO)
- Arweave (AR)
- 1inch Network (1INCH)
- ImmutableX (IMX)
- Zilliqa (ZIL)
- XDC Network (XDC)
- Stacks (STX)
- Decred (DCR)
- NEM (XEM)
- Kava (KAVA)

>> Convex Finance (CVX)

>> Holo (HOT)

REMEMBER

Keep in mind that finding a consistent source for cryptocurrencies is pretty difficult, and the info on Crypto Briefing about the cryptocurrencies' market capitalization may be different from the info from other sources. You shouldn't consider what you find on any website a definitive interpretation of the markets, at least until all websites start using similar metrics for the cryptocurrency market. At the moment, they don't.

Cryptos ranking 101 to 200

This list, ranking cryptos from 101 to 200 at the time of writing on CoinMarketCap, includes many cryptocurrencies that top investors are putting major bets on because they can buy them cheap, and these cryptos have the potential to overtake higher ranking cryptos in the future.

(See the previous section for information on how to find additional details on these cryptos.)

>> Compound (COMP)

>> Ravecoin (RVN)

>> Waves (WAVES)

>> Bitcoin Gold (BTG)

>> Oasis Network (ROSE)

>> SwissBorg (CHSB)

>> Ethereum Name Service (ENS)

>> GMX (GMX)

>> Theta Fuel (TFUEL)

>> IoTeX (IOTX)

>> TerraClassicUSD (USTC)

>> STEPN (GMT)

>> Gnosis (GNO)

>> Balancer (BAL)

>> yearn.finance (YFI)

>> Optimism (OP)

- Qtum (QTUM)
- Celo (CELO)
- Kusana (KSM)
- Terra (LUNA)
- Ankr (ANKR)
- Gala (GALA)
- VIDT DAO (VIDT)
- Kadena (KDA)
- JUST (JST)
- Livepeer (LPT)
- Harmony (ONE)
- Golem (GLM)
- Reserve Rights (RSR)
- Symbol (XYM)
- Polymath (POLY)
- Dogelon Mars (ELON)
- OMG Network (OMG)
- Chia (XCH)
- ABBC Coin (ABBC)
- Moonbeam (GLMR)
- IOST (IOST)
- Amp (AMP)
- Celsius (CEL)
- WOO Network (WOO)
- Render Token (RNDR)
- Ox (ZRX)
- Ontology (ONT)
- SushiSwap (SUSHI)
- Hive (HIVE)
- Audius (AUDIO)

- ICON (ICX)
- Astar (ASTR)
- APENFT (NFT)
- BORA (BORA)
- Threshold (T)
- Braintrust (BTRST)
- Horizen (ZEN)
- Siacoin (SC)
- Storj (STORJ)
- Ribbon Finance (RBN)
- WAX (WAXP)
- Flux (FLUX)
- Injective (INJ)
- Secret (SCRT)
- UMA (UMA)
- MXC (MXC)
- SXP (SXP)
- DigiByte (DGB)
- Smooth Love Potion (SLP)
- SKALE (SKL)
- Energy Web Token (EWT)
- ConstitutionDAO (PEOPLE)
- dYdX (DYDX)
- DAO Maker (DAO)
- Serum (SRM)
- Kyber Network Crystal v2 (KNC)
- Tribe (TRIBE)
- PLayDapp (PLA)
- Lisk (LSK)
- MediBloc (MED)

- » COTI (COTI)
- » Civic (CVC)
- » MetisDAO (METIS)
- » Nervos Network (CKB)
- » Pundi X (New) (PUNDIX)
- » Synapse (SYN)
- » Ren (REN)
- » Mask Network (MASK)
- » WINkLink (WIN)
- » CEEK CR (CEEK)
- » API3 (API3)
- » Persistence (XPRT)
- » Ocean Protocol (OCEAN)
- » Celer Network (CELR)
- » Request (REQ)
- » Frax Share (FXS)
- » Nano (XNO)
- » ssv.network (SSV)
- » Band Protocol (BAND)
- » Vulcan Forged PYR (PYR)
- » MX TOKEN (MX)
- » Syscoin (SYS)
- » Illuvium (ILV)
- » Status (SNT)

Cryptocurrency Information Websites

As cryptocurrencies become more mainstream and investors allocate a higher percentage of their portfolios to digital assets, you can expect traditional financial media to cover crypto-related topics more often. However, there is definitely no shortage of crypto-specific information websites that you can follow. Different websites focus their energy on different topics, such as breaking news, mining information, market information, and so on. In this section, I provide information resources for different aspects of the industry.

Cryptocurrency news

In this section, I list both crypto-specific websites as well as traditional news websites that also cover cryptocurrencies.

Crypto-specific news sites include the following:

>> AMB Crypto: ambcrypto.com

>> Bitcoinist: bitcoinist.com

>> Bitcoin Magazine: bitcoinmagazine.com

>> Blockonomi: blockonomi.com

>> CCN (Crypto Coins News): www.ccn.com

>> CoinDesk: www.coindesk.com

>> CoinGape: coingape.com

>> CoinGeek: coingeek.com

>> CoinJournal: coinjournal.net

>> Cointelegraph: cointelegraph.com

>> Coin Insider: www.coininsider.com

>> Crypto Briefing: cryptobriefing.com

>> Crypto Crimson: cryptocrimson.com

>> Crypto Daily: cryptodaily.co.uk

>> Crypto Recorder: www.cryptorecorder.com

>> Crypto Vibes: www.cryptovibes.com

>> Cryptolithy: cryptolithy.com

>> Ethereum World News: ethereumworldnews.com

>> ETHNews: www.ethnews.com

>> Hacked: hacked.com

>> NewsBTC: www.newsbtc.com

- » Ripple News: `ripplenews.tech`
- » Smartereum: `smartereum.com`
- » The Daily HODL: `dailyhodl.com`

Traditional news sites that offer crypto updates include the following:

- » Bloomberg: `www.bloomberg.com`
- » CNBC: `www.cnbc.com`
- » Forbes: `www.forbes.com/crypto-blockchain/#1c35cd8b2b6e`
- » Market Watch: `www.marketwatch.com`
- » Wall Street Journal: `www.wsj.com`
- » Yahoo! Finance: `finance.yahoo.com`

TIP

If you're looking for news on a specific cryptocurrency, you can simply search its name on your favorite search engine and click on the "News" tab to get the latest coverage.

Cryptocurrency investment analysis

Many of the websites I mention in the previous section also provide investment analysis on the digital assets. Here are some that are more investment focused:

- » FXStreet: `www.fxstreet.com/cryptocurrencies/news`
- » Invest Diva: `investdiva.com/investing-guide/category/cryptocurrencies`
- » Invest In Blockchain: `www.investinblockchain.com`
- » Investing.com: `www.investing.com/crypto`
- » Nasdaq: `www.nasdaq.com/topic/cryptocurrency`
- » NextAdvisor (In Partnership with TIME): `time.com/nextadvisor/investing`

REMEMBER

Always make sure you understand your risk tolerance and investment goals before following investment strategies provided in such websites. Check out Chapter 3 for more on risk, Chapter 19 for more on short-term strategies, and Chapter 20 for more on long-term strategies.

TIP

In Invest Diva's Premium Investing Group (PIG), our award-winning coaches provide investment strategies for cryptocurrencies, stocks, and Index Funds and for diversifying your portfolio among these assets without falling for the market noise and hype, and without having to spend hours researching and creating an investment strategy that suits your current financial situation and goals. You can join free at http://investdivapig.com.

Crypto-related stock news

As I cover in Chapter 15, you can diversify your portfolio by investing indirectly in the blockchain and cryptocurrency markets through stocks with exposure to these industries. Many traditional financial news sources provide such information. Here's a list of some of the most dominant ones:

>> Benzinga: pro.benzinga.com

>> Business Insider: www.businessinsider.com

>> CNBC: www.cnbc.com

>> Financial Times: www.ft.com

>> Fortune: fortune.com

>> New York Times: www.nytimes.com/section/technology

>> Reuters: www.reuters.com

>> Wall Street Journal: www.wsj.com

Cryptocurrency live market data

Many cryptocurrencies' news websites provide market data on a select page. However, some websites put most of their energy on providing live data. Here's a list of such websites:

>> CoinCap: coincap.io

>> CoinCheckup: coincheckup.com

>> CoinCodex: coincodex.com

>> CoinGecko: www.coingecko.com/en

>> Coinlib: coinlib.io

>> CoinLore: www.coinlore.com

» CoinMarketCap: coinmarketcap.com

» Coinratecap: www.coinratecap.com

» CryptoCompare: www.cryptocompare.com/coins/list/USD/1

» Live Coin Watch: www.livecoinwatch.com

» OnChainFX: onchainfx.com

Comparison tools

Some websites are dedicated to delivering comparisons and alternative sources to resources you may already be familiar with. For example, if you're looking to find an alternative to a crypto data source like CoinMarketCap, you can simply search that on these services' sites to find the alternatives. Here's the list of the top comparison service providers:

» AlternativeTo: alternativeto.net

» Finder: www.finder.com/cryptocurrency

» Product Hunt: www.producthunt.com

Cryptocurrency Marketplaces and Wallets

All types of crypto enthusiasts can find an appropriate marketplace, from active traders to investors to those who simply want to buy a digital asset and hide their wallets away under the mattress. The following sections list the places you can conduct these activities.

Crypto exchanges

As I explain in Chapter 6, exchanges are one of the main places where you can buy and sell cryptocurrencies. Here are some of the most popular ones as of the time of writing:

» Binance: www.binance.us

» Bisq: bisq.network

» Bitfinex: www.bitfinex.com

- >> Bittrex: bittrex.com

- >> Binance: investdivabinance.com (note that this is a referral link)

- >> Coinbase: investdivacoinbase.com (note that this is a referral link)

- >> Gemini: investdivagemini.com (note that this is a referral link)

- >> Huobi Global: www.huobi.com

- >> Idex: idex.market/eth/aura

- >> Kraken: www.kraken.com

- >> KuCoin: www.kucoin.com

- >> NEXT.exchange: next.exchange

- >> Poloniex: poloniex.com

REMEMBER

The preceding list includes different types of exchanges, and you should compare them based on security, fees, the number of cryptocurrencies they carry, and so much more. I dive into the methods to choose the best crypto exchanges for you in Chapter 6.

Brokers

Brokers are alternatives to exchanges and operate similarly to traditional stocks and forex brokers as I explain in Chapter 6. Here are some brokers that provide cryptocurrency trading services:

- >> AVATrade: www.avatrade.com/?tag=87597&tag2=~profile_default (note that this is a referral link)

- >> eToro: partners.etoro.com/A75956_TClick.aspx (note that this is a referral link)

- >> Plus500: www.plus500.com

- >> Robinhood: earn.investdiva.com/robinhood (note that this is a referral link)

- >> Voyager: www.investvoyager.com/?campaignId=HOguzEW4egR4AcSwguCgd 1FnPGM&referralCode=hGCBM99&code=ZINGER (note that this is a referral link)

TIP

More brokers may start offering cryptocurrency trading services. You might like to try tracking the best ones in your location here with my referral link: forestparkfx.com/?id=UU1UckhZSVN3OW1WNnNuNHIxaH1qUT09.

Other services

Besides trading and investing, many other services enable you to buy Bitcoin and other famous cryptocurrencies as I explain in Chapter 6. Here's a list (all these links are referral links):

>> CoinTracker: www.cointracker.io/i/eALc60xcyXpD

>> Coinmama: go.coinmama.com/visit/?bta=53881&nci=5360

>> LocalBitcoins: localbitcoins.com/?ch=w7ct

Cryptocurrency wallets

Many of the exchanges I mention earlier in this chapter provide investors with an online wallet. However, as I explain in Chapter 7, saving your cryptocurrencies in more secure hardware wallets is best. Here are the most popular ones as of the time of writing (note that these are referral links):

>> Ledger Nano S: earn.investdiva.com/ledger

>> Trezor: shop.trezor.io?a=investdiva.com

Charting and Tax Resources

To analyze the price action of cryptocurrencies, you need a charting tool to conduct your Invest Diva Diamond Analysis (see Chapter 9) properly. But your job as an investor isn't done when you make or lose money. As cryptocurrencies become a recognized asset, you must make sure that you complete your residence responsibility by paying taxes. For that, you need to keep track of your trading activity.

TIP

Most crypto exchanges and brokers provide trading tools such as charts for technical analysis. However, their charting services may not enable you to use the advanced technical analysis techniques I showcase in Chapter 18. One of my favorite charting tools is TradingView (www.tradingview.com).

In most countries, including the United States, you must pay capital gain taxes on your cryptocurrency activities. Here are some resources (via referral links) that help you with managing your activity for tax purposes (see Chapter 23 for an introduction to taxes and cryptocurrencies):

» CoinTracker (www.cointracker.io/i/eALc60xcyXpD)

» CoinTracking (cointracking.info?ref=I248132)

» CryptoTrader.tax (cryptotrader.tax?fp_ref=behp6)

Appendix B

Resources for Personal Portfolio Management

Portfolio management is an art, and I strongly believe you're the best person to manage your own money!

Even if you decide to hire someone to manage your investment portfolio for you, it's wise to have a basic knowledge of how the markets work so you can understand and supervise the way your manager is handling your money. At the end of the day, no one cares about your money as much as you do!

In this appendix, I introduce additional resources to help you become the master of your money.

Making Your Money Work for You

In the decade I've spent coaching thousands of students to take control of their financial future, I've discovered that, in general, there are two types of people:

» **Type One:** People who believe they have to "work hard" to earn money (and many are very good at it)

>> **Type Two:** People who put their money to work to create even more money

Which type of person do you think ends up with more money? If you said the second type, you are correct! I believe it should be your mission to become a Type Two person as quickly as possible!

Why do the rich keep getting richer? It's because they've discovered the secret to getting their money to work for them instead of working hard for money. I created my *3 Secrets to Making Your Money Work for You Masterclass* to show you the exact strategies I use to generate wealth that you can start implementing right away:

>> **No-sweat investing:** The easiest, low-risk way to start controlling your money

>> **No-math investing:** Why being a math whiz can actually cost you when it comes to investing

>> **No-time investing:** How to make profitable investments in just one hour per week, even if you're super busy

TIP

Start making your money work for you right now! Head to investdiva.com/masterclass to join the next available workshop.

Getting Away from Your Computer Screen While Still Making Money

Time is your most valuable asset in life. The thing I love the most about Invest Diva investment strategy is that I don't have to be online analyzing the markets all the time. I'd rather be sleeping or spending time with my daughter, Jasmine. Plus, constant monitoring has its drawbacks:

>> It's not good for your health, your eyes, or overall happiness.

>> Day trading the markets brings out the worst fear and greed in people, and those emotions may lead you to use poor judgment and make snap investment decisions that hurt your portfolio.

>> You lose time you can be spending with your family and friends.

In the *3 Secrets to Making Your Money Work for You Masterclass*, I walk you through the steps to develop a financial plan, create an investment strategy based on your unique financial situation and risk tolerance, and create a budget so that you can sit back, relax, and let your investment strategy do its job of making you money.

REMEMBER You need to learn about this stuff only once. It's not rocket science (those money managers who make you feel intimidated by throwing out vocabulary you don't understand are trying to prevent you from discovering their secrets).

Creating Your Unique Investing Strategy

Many investing gurus create one-size-fits-all trading signals . . . also known as the fast track to losing your money or missing out on maximizing your investments.

TECHNICAL STUFF In fact, a study by Online Trading Academy in 2016 showed that 86 percent of managed funds underperform market average. In 2022, the S&P Indices versus Active (SPIVA) scorecard, which tracks the performance of actively managed funds against their respective category benchmarks, showed 79 percent of fund managers underperformed the major market indexes like the Dow Jones Industrial Average and the S&P 500 in 2021.

Everyone is different. You're different from the investment guru, and from everybody else in the guru's group. Your money mentality, your financial history, your current financial situation, your risk appetite, your risk tolerance, your financial goals, and your timeline for achieving those goals are all different.

By understanding the fundamentals of financial planning and calculating your own risk tolerance, you can create an investment strategy that is just right for you to realize a greater return than parking your money in a managed fund.

Fund managers may have years of experience. They're probably incredibly good at managing their own money and have created a huge amount of wealth for themselves by setting up strategies that are unique to them. But what worked for them may not work for you and may not help you generate wealth. How many people have you heard of who've become millionaires by parking their money in a managed fund? I haven't heard of any.

TIP Join our Premium Investing Group (PIG) so you can become your own money manager even if you're super busy and don't have time to do research: investdivapig.com.

Building More Wealth

I went from what I call a "Welfare Diva" to a "Millionaire Diva" (my net worth at the time of writing is over $10 million) by using a system I call the Diva Wealth Ecosystem. No, it was not just investing in crypto or other online financial markets that got me to that number. Investing is just one element of my Diva Wealth Ecosystem.

Since I was able to achieve this seemingly impossible goal I have become obsessed with teaching others to do the same:

To build more wealth, break generational trauma, fulfill your purpose on earth, and raise wealth-aware, loving, and peaceful children so you can make the world a better place.

That's why I wrote my seventh book, *Million Dollar Family Secrets* (Transcendent Publishing, 2021) which became an instant *USA Today* and *Wall Street Journal* best-seller: to show you how to build a wealth ecosystem that increases your income and puts your money to work so you can create generational wealth.

If you purchase my bestselling book on the wealthdiva.com website, you will also get over $721 worth of bonuses to help you on your wealth creation journey.

TIP

If you'd like to dive deeper into building more wealth, consider joining the *Build More Wealth 5 Day Challenge*. You can join the challenge here: buildmorewealth.com.

Taking a Look at Textual Investment Resources

In this section, I list a number of supplemental books that deliver information about alternative markets to help you diversify your portfolio. Check your local bookstore, library, or favorite online book seller for these helpful titles.

Stock Investing For Dummies

Stock investing is one of the most popular methods for investment. Many established strategies exist that you can use for your own portfolio. Personally, I allocate at least 50 percent of my portfolio to stocks. (I talk about stocks with exposure to the cryptocurrency market in Chapter 15.)

In his book *Stock Investing For Dummies*, 6th Edition (John Wiley & Sons, Inc., 2020), Paul Mladjenovic lays out the process of selecting, investing, and taking profit from this market. He also points out what to avoid, when to cut losses, and what basics of risk management are necessary to be a successful stock investor. The strategies in this book are suitable for newbies and high-level investors alike.

You can find this book on Paul's website, Raving Capitalist, at www.ravingcapitalist.com/home/stock-investing-for-dummies-5e.

Investment Psychology Explained

I talk a lot about psychological levels and market sentiment throughout the book you're reading right now. If you're interested in discovering more about what drives the markets in order to be able to overcome emotional and psychological impediments that distort decision making, I recommend that you check out *Investment Psychology Explained* by Martin J. Pring (John Wiley & Sons, Inc., 1992). This book goes through the classic trading principles that may apply to the cryptocurrency market as well as when the market becomes more saturated.

Ichimoku Secrets

My book *Ichimoku Secrets* (CreateSpace Independent Publishing Platform, 2016) is a fast and furious guide to using the technical indicator I introduce in Chapter 22, Ichimoku Kinko Hyo. I've aimed to make this complicated topic super easy. You can probably finish the book in a few hours and be ready to create investment strategies unique to your risk tolerance using the combination of Ichimoku and Fibonacci retracement levels.

You can get this book at ichimokusecrets.com.

Million Dollar Family Secrets

My *USA Today* and *Wall Street Journal* best-selling book *Million Dollar Family Secrets* (Transcendent Publishing, 2022) uncovers the myths around money that are putting you and your children in financial danger. It also reveals the hidden truths that could be preventing you from creating generational wealth.

The truth is that money moves from those who don't put it to work to those who do. Most people think that financial literacy is a side effect of wealth, but wealth is a side effect of financial literacy.

You can get this book and free bonuses at milliondollarfamilysecrets.com.

Index

C

call risk, 21
calls, 233
Camuso, Patrick, 308
Camuso CPA, 308
Canadian dollar, 244–245
candlestick charts, 254–255
capital appreciation, 25–29
capital gain assets, 324
capital gain taxes
  long-term, 307
  reducing, 309
  short-term, 308
capital gains and losses, 36
Cardano (ADA), 72, 128–129
cash, buying cryptocurrency with, 103–104
CDN (content delivery network), 215
Celsius exchange, 37
centralized cryptocurrency exchanges (CEX)
  Binance, 89
  Coinbase, 90
  crypto/crypto pairing, 89
  fiat/crypto pairing, 89
  Gemini, 90
  overview, 88–89
CFTC (Commodity Futures Trading Commission), 46
CGminer software, 204
Chainlink (LINK), 130, 133
channels, 259
Charted Market Technician (CMT), 260
charts
  inserting Fibonacci retracement levels into, 302
  short-term trading
    four-hour charts, 273–275
    hourly charts, 273
    overview, 271–272
    30-minute charts, 272
  technical analysis
    bar charts, 254
    bearish reversal patterns, 261
    bullish reversal patterns, 260
    candlestick charts, 254–255
    line charts, 253
    moving averages, 261–263

Chiliz (CHZ), 138
circulating supply (CS), 121, 151–152
clock for blockchain, 73–74
Cloudflare, 215
CMT (Charted Market Technician), 260
Coinbase, 90, 111, 215, 242
CoinDesk, 153
Coinmarketcap, 179
Coinomi wallet, 115
coins
  defined, 120
  metaverse, 177
CoinTracker, 311
CoinTracking, 312
cold storage for majority of funds, 94
cold wallets, 106
commodity currencies, 244–245
Commodity Futures Trading Commission (CFTC), 46
communication industry, 169–170
communities
  BitcoinTalk, 14
  Discord chat room, 14
  Reddit chat room, 14
  Telegram groups, 13
  TradingView chat room, 14
comparison tools, 349
compounding, 37
Consumer Price Index (CPI), 239–240
content delivery network (CDN), 215
country risk, 156
crashes, 26–28. See also bubbles
credit cards, buying cryptocurrency with, 103
CRO (Crypto.com), 137
Cronos Token (CRO), 134
cross-crypto trading, 161
crowd psychology
  long-term investing and, 283
  technical analysis, 252, 255–256
crowdfunding. See initial coin offerings
Crypto Climate Accord, 61
crypto mining. See mining
crypto mining exposure, stocks, 221–222
crypto news, 152–154, 330, 345–347, 348
crypto ownership, 114–115, 117
crypto payment exposure, stocks, 222

D

Danial, Kiana
Ichimoku Secrets, 275, 292, 297, 357
Invest Diva's Guide to Making Money in Forex, 22, 98, 143
Million Dollar Family Secrets, 356, 357
Dash, 52
data, blocks, 55–56
day trading, 266–269
DCEs (digital currency exchanges), 87. *See also* exchanges
DCR (Decred), 135
dead cryptocurrencies, 9
debt ratio, 48
Decentraland (MANA), 139
decentralized blockchain, 2, 8, 76
decentralized cryptocurrency exchange (DEX)
  atomic swaps, 90
  Curve, 91
  DODO, 91–92
  impermanent loss, 92
  liquidity and, 91
  PancakeSwap, 92
  smart contracts and, 90
  Uniswap, 92
Decentralized Finance (DeFi) cryptos
  Avalanche, 130, 132
  Chainlink, 130, 133
  Uniswap, 133
Decred (DCR), 135
default risk, 156
delegated proof-of-stake (DPoS), 72
Deloitte's Smart Identity System, 64
derivatives, 229. *See also* futures; options
desktop wallets, 110–111
DEX. *See* decentralized cryptocurrency exchange
diamond hands, 41
digital assets, 177
digital contracts. *See* smart contracts
digital currency exchanges (DCEs), 87. *See also* exchanges
digital ledgers, 211
Discord chat room, 14
Diva Wealth Ecosystem, 356

diversification, 326, 333
  bonds, 20–21
  foreign exchange, 21–23
  long-term, 158–164
  overview, 155
  precious metals, 23–25
  risk and, 51–52, 156–157
  short-term, 164–165
  stocks, 18–20
  traditional, 156
  wallets, 117
dividends
  exchanges and, 30–31
  HODLing, 30
  proof-of-stake, 30
  traditional, 29–30
DODO exchange, 91–92
Dogecoin, 130
dollar. *See also* U.S dollar
  Australian, 244–245
  Canadian, 244–245
  New Zealand, 244–245
DOT (Polkadot), 72, 151
dot-com bubble, 28–29, 45
double bottom chart pattern, 260, 293–295, 303
double dipping, 224
double top chart pattern, 261
down markets, 332
downtrends, 256, 258–259, 325
DPoS (delegated proof-of-stake), 72
due diligence, when launching ICO, 196

E

EasyMiner software, 204
economic calendars, 247
education sector, 169
EEA (Enterprise Ethereum Alliance), 125
Electrum wallet, 115, 116
emergency fund, building, 47, 49
emergency fund ratio, 48
emotions
  as driver of cryptocurrency market, 26
  market sentiment, 143, 298
  role in decision-making, 284, 292–295, 324, 333–334

market sentiment
    bearish market, 298
    bullish market, 298
    defined, 143
    stocks, 223–224
marketing, 197
MAs. *See* moving averages
MCO (Monaco), 137
Mesh for Microsoft Teams, 181
Meta Platforms (META), 181
MetaMask, 111–112, 115
metaverse
    avatars, 167–168
    business, 170
    communication, 169–170
    education sector, 169
    entertainment industry, 171
    gaming industry, 168–169, 171–172
    metaverse-related stocks, 181
    non-fungible tokens, 174
    overview, 167–168
    payments and financial transactions, 174
    privacy, 174
    real estate, 172–173
    role of blockchain technology in, 173–174
    security, 174
    starting business in, 175–176
    travel, 172
    using cryptocurrency in, 176–181
    Web3 and, 182–183
metaverse cryptos, 139
MFA (multi-factor authentication), 94
Microsoft (MSFT), 181, 222
Microsoft Azure, 73
Microsoft's authenticator app, 64
MicroStrategy Inc. (MSTR), 226
Million Dollar Family Secrets (Danial), 356, 357
minimum viable product (MVP), 189
mining
    cost of, 320–321
    defined, 9
    hardware, 203–204
    mining calculators, 206–207, 321
    mining farms, 201
    mining pools, 204–205

overview, 70–71, 199–201
PoS method, 61
PoW method, 61
profitability, 202–203
proof-of-burn method, 61
setup example, 205–206
software, 204
mining calculators, 206–207, 321
mining pools, 204–205
minting, 215–216
Mladjenovic, Paul, 229–230
mobile wallets, 109–110
Mobius (Stripe), 52
Monaco (MCO), 137
Monero (XMR), 11, 52, 135
money, defined, 8–9
moving average convergence divergence (MACD), 224, 262
moving averages (MAs)
    basic, 262
    overview, 261–262
    sophisticated, 262–263
MSFT (Microsoft), 181, 222
MSTR (MicroStrategy Inc.), 226
Mt. Gox exchange, 43
multicurrency wallets, 115
multi-factor authentication (MFA), 94
MultiSig wallet, 44
Musk, Elon, 130
mutual funds, 101–103
MVP (minimum viable product), 189
Mycelium wallet, 115
MyEtherWallet, 115

N

Nakamoto, Satoshi, 9, 11, 25, 62–63, 122, 200, 254
Namecoin, 120
Nasdaq, 153
National Healthcare Anti-Fraud Association, 64
NBA Top Shot app, 138
neckline chart pattern, 260
NEM platform, 38, 74, 76
NEO (NEO), 136
net worth ratio, 48

R

range trading, 269

RBLX (Roblox), 181

real estate industry, 172–173

Reddit chat room, 14

regulation, 46, 331

reinvestment risk, 157

relative strength index (RSI), 224, 262–263, 275

Renewable EnergyWorld.com, 65

research
  downtrends, 325
  fundamental analysis, 145–148

resistance levels, 292. *See also* Fibonacci retracement
    levels
  position trading, 270
  technical analysis, 257–258

returns
  capital gains/losses, 36
  compounding, 37
  current income, 36–37

reward vs. risk, 38–40

Ripple (XRP), 38, 70, 76, 137, 293–295
  Bitcoin vs., 126–127
  characteristics of, 127–128
  history of, 126
  market volatility, 1
  overview, 125–126

Ripple Labs, 126, 127

risk management
  building emergency fund, 47, 49
  business risk, 156
  capital gains/losses, 36
  compounding, 37
  country risk, 156
  day trading, 268
  default risk, 156
  diversification and, 156–157
  diversifying, 51–52
  event risk, 157
  exchange rate risk, 157
  executive risk, 156
  financial risk, 156–157
  government/regulation risk, 157
  hype risk, 40–41, 294

income, 36–37
  interest rate risk, 157
  liquidity risk, 45
  market risk, 157
  measuring risk tolerance, 49, 318, 324
  options, 233–234
  overview, 35
  patience and, 49–51
  political instability risk, 157
  regulation risk, 46
  reinvestment, 157
  reward vs. risk, 38–40
  risk-return tradeoff, 38
  security risk, 41–44
  short-term trading, 276–277
  systematic risk, 157
  tax risk, 47
  unsystematic risk, 156–157
  vanishing risk, 45–46
  volatility risk, 44

risk-return tradeoff, 38

risk-reward ratio, 277

Robinhood app, 99–100, 224

Roblox (RBLX), 181

Rosetta Stone, 69

RSI (relative strength index), 224, 262–263, 275

rug pull scam, 42

rule of three, 165

S

S&P Indices versus Active (SPIVA) scorecard, 355

safe havens, 243–244

Samourai wallet, 116

The Sandbox (SAND), 139, 180

saucer bottom chart pattern, 260

saucer top chart pattern, 261

scalability, blockchain technology, 60

scalping, 269

Securities and Exchange Commission (SEC), 46, 61,
    100, 190

security
  Bitcoin investing schemes, 42
  blockchain technology vs. other database and
      tracking systems, 58

About the Author

Kiana Danial is an internationally recognized personal investing, entrepreneurship, and wealth creation expert who has featured in *The Wall Street Journal*, *TIME*, *Forbes*, *Kiplinger*, Business Insider, TheStreet, Nasdaq, Fox Business, CNNi, Yahoo! Finance, and Cheddar.

Kiana is a highly sought-after commentator, professional speaker, and executive coach who has reported on the financial markets directly from the floor of NYSE and NASDAQ; using her Diva Wealth Ecosystem, she built a $6 million-plus net worth within three years.

Kiana's books include *WSJ & USA Today* bestseller *Million Dollar Family Secrets*, *Cryptocurrency Investing For Dummies*, and the co-authored best sellers, *Million Dollar Identity* and *Million Dollar Moms*.

Kiana has also won the 2CC and 2CCX Awards from ClickFunnels and has spoken at the same stage as Tony Robbins.

Born and raised in Iran to a Jewish family as a religious minority, Kiana was awarded a scholarship from the Japanese government to study Electrical Engineering in Japan in 2003, where she obtained two degrees in Electrical Engineering and researched on Quantum Physics, being the only female and foreigner in each of her classes. She also became a recurring guest star on the Japanese TV show *Generation Y*. Kiana came to the United States in 2010, securing a job on Wall Street within two weeks of her arrival, and going on to become an Adjunct Professor of Finance at Baruch College in Manhattan, New York.

As the CEO of Invest Diva, Kiana's mission is to empower and educate women to take control of their financial future by investing in the online financial markets. Kiana provides her Invest Diva students with daily personal finance and investing content via social media, and financial education via Invest Diva's free Master-class and the "Make Your Money Work For You" PowerCourse. Kiana has grown a large social media following thanks to her fun and educational TikTok and YouTube videos on investing and personal finance, as well as her show/podcast "The Invest Diva Movement," where she features timely financial advice and has interviewed investors such as Guy Spier, Anthony Scaramucci, Nancy Tengler, James McDonald, and Christina Qi; development coaches such as Brian Tracy, Bob Proctor, and Jack Canfield; and Financial Advisor, Author, and Podcast Host Suze Orman.

Kiana's mission with Invest Diva is to help one million moms take control of their financial future and build generational wealth so they can change the world and build a better future.

Dedication

To all the Invest Diva students who inspire me to continue leading the Invest Diva movement by sharing their wins daily.

Author's Acknowledgments

I'd like to thank numerous people for their help in making this book a reality. I would like to thank my family and my amazing Invest Diva team who kept my household, our company, and our mission afloat while I dedicated my time to completing this book. In particular, Tristan Craige, who wrote two new chapters for this edition of *Cryptocurrency Investing For Dummies*, as well as Jacqui Short and Arleny Lopez-Cordero for their continued support.

I'd like to extend a special thank you to Dan Mersey for shepherding this project to completion. Thank you for your thorough edits, advice, and suggestions. Thank you to Paul Morris for keeping the book accurate. Last but not least, thank you to Tracy Boggier and Rita Rosenkranz for all your help in pushing the project through and backing me to create a great guide.

Publisher's Acknowledgments

Acquisitions Editor: Tracy Boggier
Project Manager: Dan Mersey
Technical Editor: Paul Morris
Proofreader: Debbye Butler

Production Editor: Tamilmani Varadharaj
Cover Image: © Chinnapong/Getty Images

Take dummies with you everywhere you go!

Whether you are excited about e-books, want more from the web, must have your mobile apps, or are swept up in social media, dummies makes everything easier.

Find us online!

dummies.com

dummies
A Wiley Brand

Leverage the power

Dummies is the global leader in the reference category and one of the most trusted and highly regarded brands in the world. No longer just focused on books, customers now have access to the dummies content they need in the format they want. Together we'll craft a solution that engages your customers, stands out from the competition, and helps you meet your goals.

Advertising & Sponsorships

Connect with an engaged audience on a powerful multimedia site, and position your message alongside expert how-to content. Dummies.com is a one-stop shop for free, online information and know-how curated by a team of experts.

- Targeted ads
- Video
- Email Marketing
- Microsites
- Sweepstakes sponsorship

20 MILLION PAGE VIEWS EVERY SINGLE MONTH

15 MILLION UNIQUE VISITORS PER MONTH

43% OF ALL VISITORS ACCESS THE SITE VIA THEIR MOBILE DEVICES

700,000 NEWSLETTER SUBSCRIPTION TO THE INBOXES OF

300,000 UNIQUE INDIVIDUALS EVERY WEEK

# of dummies

Custom Publishing

Reach a global audience in any language by creating a solution that will differentiate you from competitors, amplify your message, and encourage customers to make a buying decision.

- Apps
- Books
- eBooks
- Video
- Audio
- Webinars

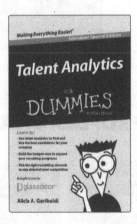

Brand Licensing & Content

Leverage the strength of the world's most popular reference brand to reach new audiences and channels of distribution.

For more information, visit **dummies.com/biz**

A Wiley Brand

PERSONAL ENRICHMENT

Staying Sharp
9781119187790
USA $26.00
CAN $31.99
UK £19.99

Facebook
9781119179030
USA $21.99
CAN $25.99
UK £16.99

Guitar
9781119293354
USA $24.99
CAN $29.99
UK £17.99

Investing
9781119293347
USA $22.99
CAN $27.99
UK £16.99

Beekeeping
9781119310068
USA $22.99
CAN $27.99
UK £16.99

Digital Photography
9781119235606
USA $24.99
CAN $29.99
UK £17.99

Meditation
9781119251163
USA $24.99
CAN $29.99
UK £17.99

Pregnancy
9781119235491
USA $26.99
CAN $31.99
UK £19.99

Samsung Galaxy S7
9781119279952
USA $24.99
CAN $29.99
UK £17.99

iPhone
9781119283133
USA $24.99
CAN $29.99
UK £17.99

Crocheting
9781119287117
USA $24.99
CAN $29.99
UK £16.99

Nutrition
9781119130246
USA $22.99
CAN $27.99
UK £16.99

PROFESSIONAL DEVELOPMENT

Windows 10
9781119311041
USA $24.99
CAN $29.99
UK £17.99

AutoCAD
9781119255796
USA $39.99
CAN $47.99
UK £27.99

Excel 2016
9781119293439
USA $26.99
CAN $31.99
UK £19.99

QuickBooks 2017
9781119281467
USA $26.99
CAN $31.99
UK £19.99

macOS Sierra
9781119280651
USA $29.99
CAN $35.99
UK £21.99

LinkedIn
9781119251132
USA $24.99
CAN $29.99
UK £17.99

Windows 10
9781119310563
USA $34.00
CAN $41.99
UK £24.99

      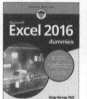

SharePoint 2016
9781119181705
USA $29.99
CAN $35.99
UK £21.99

Fundamental Analysis
9781119263593
USA $26.99
CAN $31.99
UK £19.99

Networking
9781119257769
USA $29.99
CAN $35.99
UK £21.99

Office 2016
9781119293477
USA $26.99
CAN $31.99
UK £19.99

Office 365
9781119265313
USA $24.99
CAN $29.99
UK £17.99

Salesforce.com
9781119239314
USA $29.99
CAN $35.99
UK £21.99

Coding
9781119293323
USA $29.99
CAN $35.99
UK £21.99

dummies.com

dummies
A Wiley Brand

Learning Made Easy

ACADEMIC

9781119293576
USA $19.99
CAN $23.99
UK £15.99

9781119293637
USA $19.99
CAN $23.99
UK £15.99

9781119293491
USA $19.99
CAN $23.99
UK £15.99

9781119293460
USA $19.99
CAN $23.99
UK £15.99

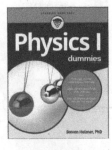

9781119293590
USA $19.99
CAN $23.99
UK £15.99

9781119215844
USA $26.99
CAN $31.99
UK £19.99

9781119293378
USA $22.99
CAN $27.99
UK £16.99

9781119293521
USA $19.99
CAN $23.99
UK £15.99

9781119239178
USA $18.99
CAN $22.99
UK £14.99

9781119263883
USA $26.99
CAN $31.99
UK £19.99

Available Everywhere Books Are Sold

dummies.com

Small books for big imaginations

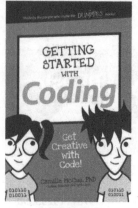

GETTING STARTED WITH Coding
Get Creative with Code!
Camille McCue, PhD

9781119177173
USA $9.99
CAN $9.99
UK £8.99

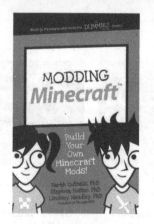

MODDING Minecraft™
Build Your Own Minecraft Mods!
Sarah Guthals, PhD
Stephen Foster, PhD
Lindsey Handley, PhD

9781119177272
USA $9.99
CAN $9.99
UK £8.99

MAKING YouTube® VIDEOS
Star in Your Own Video!
Nick Willoughby

9781119177241
USA $9.99
CAN $9.99
UK £8.99

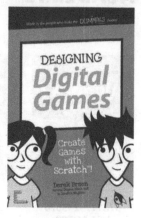

DESIGNING Digital Games
Create Games with Scratch™!
Derek Breen

9781119177210
USA $9.99
CAN $9.99
UK £8.99

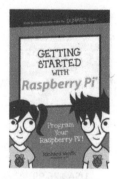

GETTING STARTED WITH Raspberry Pi®
Program Your Raspberry Pi®!
Richard Wentk

9781119262657
USA $9.99
CAN $9.99
UK £6.99

EXPERIMENTING WITH Science
Think, Test, and Learn!

9781119291336
USA $9.99
CAN $9.99
UK £6.99

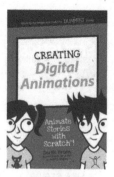

CREATING Digital Animations
Animate Stories with Scratch™!
Derek Breen

9781119233527
USA $9.99
CAN $9.99
UK £6.99

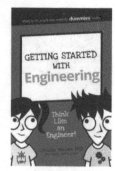

GETTING STARTED WITH Engineering
Think Like an Engineer!

9781119291220
USA $9.99
CAN $9.99
UK £6.99

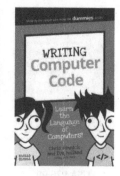

WRITING Computer Code
Learn the Language of Computers!
Chris Minnick and Eva Holland

9781119177302
USA $9.99
CAN $9.99
UK £8.99

Unleash Their Creativity

dummies.com

dummies®
A Wiley Brand